HOW THE GRINGOS STOLE
TEQUILA

The Modern Age of Mexico's Most Traditional Spirit

CHANTAL MARTINEAU

Trinity University Press
San Antonio, Texas

For Richard and Rita,
thanks to whom I'm high on life

Published by Trinity University Press
San Antonio, Texas 78212

Copyright © 2015, 2019 by Chantal Martineau

Paperback edition published by arrangement with Chicago Review Press.

ISBN 978-1-59534-880-7 paper
ISBN 978-1-59534-881-4 ebook

Cover design by Sarah Cooper
Cover: Jacobo Roa, *Catrin*, 2018; mural, Mérida, Yucatán, Mexico. Photograph by Roberto Ayala Pérez, 2019.
Book design by Jonathan Hahn
Photographs by Chantal Martineau

Trinity University Press strives to produce its books using methods and materials in an environmentally sensitive manner. We favor working with manufacturers that practice sustainable management of all natural resources, produce paper using recycled stock, and manage forests with the best possible practices for people, biodiversity, and sustainability. The press is a member of the Green Press Initiative, a nonprofit program dedicated to supporting publishers in their efforts to reduce their impacts on endangered forests, climate change, and forest-dependent communities.

The paper used in this publication meets the minimum requirements of the American National Standard for Information Sciences—Permanence of Paper for Printed Library Materials, ANSI 39.48-1992.

CIP data on file at the Library of Congress

23 22 21 20 19 | 5 4 3 2 1

CONTENTS

In the Beginning, There Were Body Shots

One tequila, two tequila, three tequila, floor.
—GEORGE CARLIN

In a dusty field, under a high, hot sun, a man is working the land. He looks like a cowboy, wearing crisp blue jeans with a big-buckled belt, a clean white shirt, and a wide-brimmed hat curled up at each side. His mustache is epic: thick, black, and curved down around the corners of his mouth, framing it like a photograph. He doesn't smile—or, if he does, the brim of his hat shadows it from sight. Squaring his hips and winding up like a batter, he grips the long rod of his primitive-looking instrument as he plunges its blade down into tough, fibrous flesh.

We're in an agave field in the state of Jalisco in central-western Mexico, surrounded by large spiky plants that look like aloes on steroids, the sun beating down like an audible presence. The instrument in question is called a *coa de jima*, a long-handled hoe designed specifically to harvest agave, the native succulent plant from which tequila is made. The coa, forged by a local blacksmith who specializes in the rustic tool, looks tarnished—antique, even—but it's dangerously effective thanks to regular and careful whetting by its user. The rounded blade lops off several of the plant's long, plump leaves as it sinks into its monstrous pale yellow heart: the pineapple-like core aptly called the *piña*. Each strike produces a satisfying *thwack*. It's tempting to steal a glance at the man's sandaled feet, browned from the sun and grimy from the sandy soil, to count the ten toes he still has (just to be sure) as he winds up for another strike.

It's hot. Inevitably, one's thoughts turn to icy margaritas. But out here, in the agave fields in the heart of tequila country, there is not a frosted cocktail pitcher in sight. The work the man is doing is much harder than he makes it look. He is the latest in a long family line to do this for a living—that is, until his son or nephew gets inducted into the brotherhood of men who harvest agave for tequila production. It's a highly skilled task, a job shrouded in lore, that for hundreds of years has been passed down from generation to generation.

Here is where I wanted the story to begin: amid the blue-green expanse of an agave field, under the unrelenting Mexican sun, sweat beading on the brow of a rugged man immersed in the age-old task that first gave birth to what is now called tequila. But for most of us the story of tequila starts in a much different way. Like, back when we first had the misfortune of being introduced to the hot, harsh liquid a great number of people have come to associate with tequila. To tell the story of tequila properly, one has to recall days probably best left forgotten and, too often, virtually impossible to remember anyway. One's initial encounter with the spirit is rarely a pretty one. In my case, the story starts when I was still a snot-nosed college kid experimenting with freedom and self-destruction, much like you might have done at that age. The tale of my first tequila is not one I like to tell, for fear of glorifying youthful stupidity and the crude way many people think tequila should be taken. Yet, it's important to acknowledge how most of us came to know tequila in order to fully understand how it—and we, as imbibers—have evolved.

The story usually goes something like this: salt, shot, lime wedge worn like an unhappy smile, repeat. In the worst of cases, the ritual ends in a blackout. In fact, that's *exactly* how my story went. The memory is fuzzy, but it involves a dare and multiple shot glasses all lined up in a row, each one filled with a clear liquid you could smell the moment the bottle was uncapped. The shots were accompanied by the customary lick of table salt from the back of the hand to anesthetize the tongue and wedge of lime to take the edge off the sting afterward. The lime doubled as something to bite down on as I shivered and gagged, the painful burn drawing a line down my esophagus. The taste is permanently etched into my brain. Like gasoline cut with rubbing alcohol, then cut again with dirty socks. The ensuing drunkenness that first night came on as it does in a cartoon. I hiccuped. My eyes stopped blinking in unison. The rest is a blur.

Sound familiar?

Tequila is only now beginning to recover from its longtime reputation as the firewater of our youth. A certain breed of drinker has discovered tequila's potential as a complex and sophisticated sipping spirit, but the vast majority of people still associate it with salt, lime, bad decisions, and a nasty hangover. Yet what so many of us recall haplessly knocking back in those bad old days is not even true tequila. Or rather, it isn't pure tequila, distilled from 100 percent agave, those big desert plants often mistaken for cacti. Instead, most of us were introduced to tequila via something like José Cuervo Especial, that sweet golden poison, which is actually a cheaper, less-refined hybrid distillate derived from just 51 percent agave. The popular term used to refer to tequila that is not made from 100 percent agave sugars is *mixto*, and what makes up the other 49 percent of a mixto is usually distilled from less expensive ingredients such as corn or sugarcane. Few of us have the opportunity to taste real tequila until we're past the age of drinking as sheer sport. By then, it's often too late. We equate the spirit with shots, blind drunkenness, and regret. Or we think of it as something foul and insufferable, filing it away in the been-there-done-that department of our brains. Why force ourselves to rediscover something we've already learned is bad for us?

Well, for one thing, tastes change. Your palate has likely matured since you last slammed a shot of tequila, just as you may have discovered a fondness for brussels sprouts or blue cheese as an adult that you didn't have as a child. The sprouts themselves have surely also changed. The fresh and seasonally available vegetables from your local farmer's market are probably nothing like the frozen orbs heated up to go with defrosted fish sticks at your school's cafeteria. So, yes, people change. And tequila has changed, too.

For many years, only industrial-grade tequila was available north of the border. When American demand for the spirit exploded around the 1970s and '80s, traditional production couldn't keep up. Automated, large-volume methods were adopted to help meet the swelling foreign demand, which affected the quality of the final product. Most Americans didn't know good tequila from bad, anyway, and weren't exactly consuming it in the most enlightened way. Tequila in America was taken almost exclusively as a means to get plastered. Pop culture references by figures like Hunter S. Thompson (from *Fear and Loathing in Las Vegas*: "We had two bags of grass, seventy-five pellets of mescaline, five sheets of high-powered blotter acid, a salt shaker half full of cocaine . . . and also a quart of tequila") and later Jimmy Buffett (from his hit song "Margaritaville": "Wastin' away again in Margaritaville . . . But there's booze in the blender/And soon it will render/That frozen concoction that helps me hang on") perpetuated the stereotype.

It didn't help that tequila arrived in the United States saddled with several myths. The spirit was said to act unlike whiskey, gin, or any other form of alcohol. Instead, reminiscent of absinthe's reputation, it was rumored to be a hallucinogen. Another popular myth was that the bottle contained a worm and that this little critter held even more powerful psychotropic properties for any drinker brave enough to swallow it. For Americans, tequila quickly became a way to flirt with hedonism, to pretend to trip. Most people certainly did not sip it for its aromatics or subtle complexities. It was either mixed into sugary frozen cocktails or slammed with lime and salt—a ritual that became so synonymous with the spirit that, for a long time, the majority of Americans believed it to be the correct way to drink tequila. Today, as more and better tequila hits US shelves, the lime-and-salt ritual is no longer necessary. You don't want to anesthetize your tongue from a drink that is delicious. And you don't want to swallow it in one shot either. You want to sip it slowly, to make it last.

So, what is tequila, exactly?

Tequila gets its name from a town in the Mexican state of Jalisco, whose name in turn may have had its origins in an ancient Aztec word for work or task: *tequitl*. Another theory is that it might be a corruption of the name of a local native tribe called the Ticuilas.[1] It may even be a corruption of the word *tetilla*, referring to the breast-shaped volcano near Tequila. Like its predecessor mezcal, tequila is distilled from the agave plant. But by law, the agave for tequila production must be a particular variety grown in a specific part of Mexico. You might say that mezcal is the wider category of agave-based spirits and that tequila is really just mezcal from the area surrounding the town of Tequila. (You might say that, but certain people in the tequila industry certainly wouldn't like it.) The spirit is protected by an appellation of origin status, like cognac and champagne are. We don't necessarily think of it this way, but cognac is really just brandy from the area around Cognac, in France, and champagne sparkling wine from the region of Champagne.

The appellation of origin status recognizes tequila as a distinct product of Mexico, made and sold according to strict rules. For one, tequila has to be made from a specific type of agave: blue Weber or *agave tequilana*. "Good" tequila—and this is a pretty sweeping generalization—is the kind made from 100 percent blue Weber agave. The Distilled Spirits Council of the United States estimates that while sales of the spirit in the United States have nearly doubled in the past ten years, lower-purity mixto hasn't kept up the pace with the most premium tequilas, which are growing at a rate of up to four times that of the tequila category as a whole. The 100 percent agave category now makes up more than half the volume of total tequila exports to the United States. It's clear that more and more Americans are seeking out better tequila. True tequila. To the tune of nearly twenty-five million gallons in 2017 alone out of about forty-five million gallons of all types of tequila brought into the United States the same year, according to Mexico's Tequila Regulatory Council, the Mexican organization that oversees the production and sale of tequila.

People are drinking better, although not necessarily more. As we refine our palates—be it for tequila or stinky cheese or fresh, seasonally available vegetables—we tend to consume more carefully, less greedily. We also tend to care more about where these products come from and how exactly they made it to our table. The journey tequila takes from the agave fields of central Mexico to your glass is a fascinating story, filled with intrigue and history, science and a good dose of magic, more than a little scandal, and a great deal of money.

The main reason tequila's story is so complicated and compelling boils down to the raw material required to make it: a plant. Not just any plant. In Mexico, agave is more than just a perennial succulent whose sap can be transformed into alcohol. It's a precious natural resource whose price per kilo rises and falls like that of gold or oil. Agave has long played a central role in the country's mythology, folklore, culture, and economy, having been used for centuries for everything from nourishment to housing to healing and spiritual enlightenment. One translation of the word Mexico itself from the ancient language of the Aztecs is "from the navel of the maguey"—maguey being another word for agave.[2]

Once the cornerstone of life in many parts of Mexico, agave is now the chief commodity in the country's thriving spirits industry. The fluctuating cost of agave can bring families and companies to the brink of financial ruin. Its widespread cultivation has botanists and other scientists lamenting the dangers of such an intense monoculture to Mexico's rich biodiversity and scrambling to find solutions. And demand for it continues to rise alongside the explosive global demand for tequila. But tequila, a fundamentally Mexican product, is no longer controlled primarily by Mexicans. American and European companies dominate the market, selling luxury tequila brands the average Mexican could never afford.

And it all began with a plant. Granted, agave is a remarkable plant. Blue agave can grow to be ten feet tall and just as wide. Average sizes range from 100 to 200 pounds per piña, with larger ones found in the highlands thanks to cooler temperatures and more rain. The lowlands, with their warmer and drier climate, tend to produce smaller, faster-growing piñas. These are no easy plants to farm or harvest, not only because of their size but also due to their sharp-edged leaves. Each succulent leaf is lined with sharp thorns and grows a razor-sharp needle at the tip. For generations, Mexicans plucked the needles from the ends of the leaves of these elephantine plants to use for sewing their clothes, conducting ritual bloodletting ceremonies, even writing and drawing. The leaves themselves were dried and used to build thatch baskets, floor mats, clothing, and roofs for simple peasant homes. Before it was ever distilled into tequila, agave was fermented into a sour, fruity sort of beer called *pulque*. The brew was drunk during religious ceremonies as a way for holy men to speak with the gods.

The agave plant can be harvested only once it reaches maturity, which can take up to a decade or more. Then it dies. Let that sink in for a moment: grapes are perennial crops, meaning they grow back each year. For wine production, they're harvested annually, as is grain for whiskey production. But it takes six to ten years to grow a single agave plant that can only be used once. It's a miracle the spirit isn't more expensive given the effort expended to raise the sole ingredient required to make it. And because harvesting an agave kills the plant, a new agave must be planted in its place and tended for another six to ten years before it, too, can be used for tequila production. This is just one aspect of tequila's story that illustrates why it's so prized.

Today tourists can follow an officially sanctioned Tequila Trail through the Amatitán-Tequila Valley, a UNESCO World Heritage site, to see how and where the spirit is made. Funded by the Inter-American Development Bank and managed by the Tequila Regulatory Council with the help of the Cuervo Foundation and other distilleries, it's dotted with a growing number of boutique hotels and B&Bs, not unlike the designated routes you find in wine country. [3]

On the trail, tourists get to see the waves of lavender-blue plants from which the spirit is made, as well as the mariachi singers and Mexican cowboys, called *charros,* that the region is also known for. They may also see a man who looks like a cowboy using a coa to harvest agave at one of the big tequila companies that host tours of their facilities. While our man sports his clean blue jeans and crisp white shirt, others like him might be dressed in a folky costume—loose white cotton trousers and shirt, with a red kerchief around the neck and a red sash at the waist, completed by the requisite sombrero. These men are known as *jimadores* (pronounced hee-ma-DOR-ays), proud agriculturalists who grow and harvest agave for tequila production—a craft passed down from father to son for generations. The word *jimar*, for which the jimador is named, comes from the Nahuatl word for shaving wood, stone, or hair: *xima.*[4] (A tequila worker told me that the word may have been born of the grunting sound one makes when toiling: *hunhhh*. But a linguist I consulted balked at the theory. Regardless, you do hear a lot of grunting and sighing during the jimador's workday.) The physical motion of striking the agave plant to slice off its leaves is less like swinging a bat at a ball, actually, and more like planting a flag, again and again, like a colonizer claiming an unknown land.

The scene in the agave field is something of a fantasy. The man who looks like a cowboy is all too familiar. His photograph is recognizable from the cover of guidebooks and magazine articles. Google the word *jimador* and his image comes up almost immediately, usually leaning his weight casually on a coa, looking like a Mexican Marlboro Man. His name is Ismael Gama and he is the face of Cuervo's jimadores. He has appeared in countless photos taken by press and tourists passing through tequila country, his movie-star looks and bushy black mustache all but iconic by now. Ismael plays the sort of role performed by actors hired to dress up as blacksmiths and bakers at the historical villages schoolchildren visit on class trips. According to the company, he still works the fields, grunting and sweating through hot mornings of backbreaking labor. Considered one of the fastest in the land, he is able to harvest and prepare a piña in a few minutes, which is how he became Cuervo's resident superstar jimador. But today, with his too-clean costume and barely damp brow, Ismael is part of the manicured façade big tequila companies expose to visitors passing through. His fellow jimadores certainly don't take time out of their grueling workdays to demonstrate to tourists how to do the job they've known since boyhood. They don't don delightful costumes for their workdays, either. Still, in the moment, watching this man in the field feels real enough.

As each leaf is sliced off, it falls heavily to the dry, dusty ground, eventually leaving behind only the piña, as big as a beach ball. This is the part of the plant that gets cooked and mashed, fermented and distilled, to eventually become tequila. The jimador slices through one agave in minutes, first removing the mammoth leaves, then cleaving the colossal piña in half like he was cutting into nothing more menacing than a big, crunchy apple. A jimador can harvest more than a hundred agaves in a day's work, as the sun beats down like a mallet. He hacks away at the leaves thick like wild, prehistoric arms, each one tipped with its fine needle sharp enough to draw blood with a single prick. And he does this with what looks like a rusted old blade. The job has its hazards, to say the least.

At the other end of tequila's journey from field to glass are the people who pour shots and mix margaritas. Among the sort of serious bartenders who sometimes refer to themselves as mixologists and the growing community of cocktail enthusiasts who revere them, tequila is the darling of the moment. Mezcal, the mother of tequila, is not far behind: still a niche product, but gaining cultish popularity. Tequila and mezcal bars or *tequilerías* and *mezcalerías* are cropping up in cities around the country, while upscale Nuevo Latino restaurants—themselves a hot gastronomical trend nationwide—are putting just as much thought into curating their agave spirits lists as into designing their progressive Latin-influenced menus.

Tequila is now a multibillion-dollar industry expected to reach more than $9 billion in value globally by 2021. It's sold in at least 120 countries, with Spain, Germany, France, and the United States as the biggest international markets. In fact, the United States swallows some 80 percent of global tequila exports—and roughly three times as much tequila as Mexicans themselves drink. But the lion's share of what is available to Americans includes fewer independent or even Mexican-owned brands. Unearthing those small, rogue operations can feel like discovering treasure: troves of liquid silver and gold.

Before getting into the nitty-gritty of tequila's journey from field to glass, here's a primer on what you might find behind the bar. Un-aged tequila is referred to as *blanco* or *plata*, which translates as "white" or "silver." It can be harsh, but it can also be a high-end sipping spirit. It can smell of cooked pumpkin, citrus, fresh herbs, petroleum, pepper, jalapeño, dark chocolate, and even baby powder. It can be complex and aromatic. Or it can bring to mind diesel and dirty socks. *Reposado* or "rested" tequila refers to a spirit that's been aged for at least two months and up to a year in oak barrels. During this short nap, the tequila takes on some of the characteristics normally associated with aged spirits, including caramel, vanilla, and spice notes. But the flavor of cooked agave should still come through. The color can be barely kissed with wood for a straw-like hue or it can be a deep gold. *Añejo* or "aged" tequila has been matured for at least a year in oak barrels, most often used bourbon or American whiskey casks. This tequila will take on an amber shade and smell of dried fruit and nuts, vanilla and caramel, wood and tobacco. It's the tequila you reach for at the end of a meal as a digestif.

"Tequila is aged in the field," people in the business sometimes say. It's a reference to the six to ten years it takes to grow an agave plant. But it also alludes to the view held by certain tequila lovers that aging of the spirit is superfluous, that its purest expression is clear and untainted by wood's influence. Still, many tequila lovers believe the spirit only gets better with age. José Cuervo claims to have introduced the first añejo around the turn of the nineteenth century. The idea was inspired by the fine whiskeys and brandies many wealthy Mexicans enjoyed at the time, and the result is reminiscent of these spirits, both in color and flavor. You might expect that reposado came before añejo, because it comes first in an aged tequila's lifespan, but the first reposado didn't make its appearance until 1974, according to the Herradura brand, which claims to have masterminded the style.

The company says the first reposado was developed in direct response to a product Cuervo had proposed. Cuervo wanted to tap the US market and, in particular, cash in on the love Americans had for brown spirits by adding caramel coloring to its silver tequila. The family that owned Herradura found the idea shameful and instead proposed launching their own dark spirit after resting their silver tequila in barrels. Both Cuervo and Herradura petitioned the tequila industry's governing body with their ideas. After much deliberation, it was decided that Cuervo would be permitted to bring its caramel-infused tequila to market. The style would be called *joven* ("young") or *oro* ("gold") and still exists today. Herradura was also granted the right to make its reposado. The concept was considered doomed to failure given the financial investment necessary to buy barrels and the warehouse space to store them, as well as the extra time required to age tequila. Añejo, at the time, was not popular and most people preferred to drink their tequila un-aged. But it caught on. Today, some 80 percent of tequila consumed in Mexico is reposado.

Aging is a part of just about every major spirit's story. Barrels were originally used to store and transport whiskeys and rums, which is how the practice of aging was born. Essentially, the barrel has a symbiotic relationship with the spirit, alcohol seeping into the wood just as the wood is diffused into the alcohol. Over time, this interaction causes the amount of liquid in the barrel to diminish. The portion that evaporates is known as the angel's share. It's no wonder an aged spirit is usually more expensive than an un-aged one: the producer must first buy expensive barrels, build an aging cellar to store them, then hold off on selling the product while it matures, and must literally watch some of his hard-earned product disappear into thin air.

One of the newest tequila categories is extra añejo. It's aged for at least three years, resulting in an even darker and more barrel-influenced spirit. It can be taken much like a fine whiskey or brandy, sipped after dinner or enjoyed with an expensive cigar. These tequilas are generally not mixed into cocktails, if only for the sheer cost of them. You probably wouldn't use a rare single malt for a whiskey sour, either.

New types of product materialize each year. For example, several tequila makers have started taking aged tequila and filtering it to remove the color so that it ends up looking as crystal clear as a blanco. Tequila now comes in flavors like strawberry, citrus, chocolate, and jalapeño. And there's at least one brand of tequila that's dyed a soft baby pink. Notably, additives are permitted even in unflavored tequilas. Accepted ingredients include caramel coloring to darken the spirit, oak extract to suggest barrel influence, glycerin for a glossier texture, and sugar syrup to sweeten it. A number of brands, both premium and low-end, adjust the color, flavor, and texture of their products. It's difficult to tell which ones do just by glancing at the bottle. Nowadays tequila is often packaged with an eye toward ostentation—in leather, snakeskin, gold, crystal. One brand holds the Guinness World Record for costliest tequila with its diamond-encrusted $3.5 million bottle.

What fancy bottles and pink liquid don't communicate is the powerful connection tequila can have to the place it's made. There is whiskey from Scotland, Ireland, and America, and, yes, each is unique to its country of origin. But the differences between them have less to do with the raw ingredients used—namely, grains, which can grow anywhere—and more to do with how they're manipulated. Specifically, whiskey has almost everything to do with how it's aged. Likewise, there are brandies, rums, and gins made around the world according to local traditions. (And there is vodka from just about everywhere, made from just about everything, that is rarely distinct.) But there is only tequila, made of native agave, from Mexico.

So, maybe this is where the story starts.

The tequila industry has become an intricate organism with many interwoven and conflicting facets and players. The club goer buying a bottle to share with friends behind the velvet rope of the VIP section may not realize he has a connection to a farmer in a Mexican field, but he does. There are the makers of the spirit, some of whom are independent artisans crafting a product that is rather personal to them. Others are day laborers or assembly line workers, dutifully playing their role as a small cog in a much larger machine turning out a mass-market product. There are the corporations that banked on tequila's projected growth decades ago and swooped in to buy up all the promising small brands available. Then there are all the family-owned distilleries struggling to set themselves apart from better-known competitors with slick ad campaigns and celebrity endorsements. Marketers are enlisted to persuade people to buy tequila. Bartenders exist not only to pour the stuff but, increasingly, to be the face of various brands—ambassadors, they're called. Then there is you, the consumer. And me, the media. When you're standing before the liquor store shelf or bellying up to the bar, you're not alone. We're all there with you.

With so many players in the tequila game, the industry has swelled. The growing demand for better tequila and, by extension, record amounts of agave has had a range of repercussions in Mexico. These effects are also part of tequila's story. It's a story spanning many centuries, beginning with a family recipe for a fragrant liquid made from a desert flower that evolved into a mass-market product, then evolved again to become a luxury good.

Researching a book about tequila is fun, make no mistake. But it's not all margarita parties and mariachi bands. I met scientists who study the potentially devastating effects of an ever-growing agave monoculture and others who seek to expose how modernization within the industry has corrupted the tradition of tequila. What's more, this book was written as Mexico's horrific drug wars raged on, which made driving around rural Jalisco frightening at times. (Travel advisories warned of fake roadblocks set up by gangs on otherwise deserted roads that could be pretenses for kidnappings or worse.) Rumors that at least one ex-cartel member was trying to break into the tequila game provided little comfort, if a little morbid entertainment. But there's nothing funny about the fact that certain high-profile tequila producers and their families have become targets for kidnapping and extortion. It was disheartening to learn that a number of them are forced to hide in their own towns, taking different routes and vehicles to work every day to avoid detection. Others have opted to move away altogether and commute to their distilleries, surrounded by an entourage of bodyguards.

For the most part, Mexico is a warm and welcoming place, especially for the solo traveler. When you tell people you're drinking your way around the country to research a book about the local booze, they're even more welcoming. They ask, incredulous, "So, you get *paid*? To *drink*?" Well, yes. But booze writers also get paid to think about what they drink. That being said, I've partaken in the salt-and-lime ritual just like everyone else and, as a bartender in my youth, even witnessed said salt being licked off the taut bellies of young women more adventurous xviiiPREFACE

than I. There have been tequila-fueled hangovers, the worst of which led to a years-long abstinence from the stuff. And, honestly, at least a few more since the research for this book began.

If you're the kind of person who has been known to think about what he drinks and perhaps lately have found yourself drinking and thinking about tequila, then this book was written for you. It was also written for the person who thinks about what she eats and wears and buys in general. In this era of E. coli outbreaks and antibiotic-resistant meat contamination, the desire to demystify the food chain and increase the transparency of consumables has become something of a zeitgeist. The same curiosity that we indulge for our heirloom tomatoes and grass-fed beef can be applied to the life cycle of the wines and spirits we imbibe. Of course, if you're still happily slamming shots with a side of salt and citrus, read on. There may be a tequila purist in you yet.

{1}

Before Tequila Came Pulque

Esta noche corro gallo
hasta no encontrar velorio,
para preguntarle al muerto
si hay pulque en el purgatorio.
—TRADITIONAL MEXICAN DRINKING SONG

In Mexico City, the night air just about crackles with energy. Officially, it's La Ciudad de México, Distrito Federal. DF, as the natives and jet-setters know it, is one of the most vibrant, edgy, colorful, bustling, artsy, chaotic, stylish cities on earth. Springtime here is even more colorful than usual: the city's countless jacaranda trees are in bloom. Like the cherry blossoms of Japan, they are an iconic sight to behold, an endless mauve garland lacing the city and filling the air with its heady perfume. In the spring of 2012, on a lively strip in the trendy neighborhood of Roma Norte, where the beautiful people flock, wisps of black fabric were draped over the branches, setting off their deep lavender-colored flowers and absorbing their sweet aroma. The way the fabric pieces flapped and waved in the breeze gave the impression of dark, looming ghosts. The sheets were a public artwork protesting the senseless mass killings of innocent people in the country's high-profile drug wars.

If you were to look down instead of up at the trees, you'd see the sidewalks around the neighborhood lined with stick figures, like a child's cutout craftwork, representing the more than two hundred thousand cartel-related murders to date. In Mexico City's streets, parks, and galleries,

1

artists install, paint, and graffito-tag their dissent. At art openings, they sip champagne and newly chic mezcal, discussing the country's future and the United States' role in it.

But it's not just the purple-flowered trees, or even the proliferation of artists and activists, that make Mexico City pulsate with life and color. It's the street food and high-end restaurants, the glitzy clubs and old-man saloons, the lively public squares and bustling street markets, the bike paths and parks, the students, the workers, the tourists, the hipsters, the hippies, the wealthy, the poor. It's the city's rich palette: the bright cobalt blue of homes like Frida Kahlo's, which is now a museum of the artist's life and work; the butter yellow and Pepto pink of other buildings, like Casa Luis Barragán, a private museum that was once the modernist architect's private residence; and the wild splashes of Mexico's history painted right on the city's most important institutions, like the Diego Rivera murals adorning the arched walls of the National Palace, where pre-Hispanic earth tones give way to the violent blacks and reds of the Mexican Revolution. How many cities cover the walls of their government buildings with loudly antiestablishment art?

Inside a bar in the Roma neighborhood, sawdust covers the floor. Here the lights are dim, the music so loud it forces people closer. Faces are hard to make out, but the painted image on the wall near the entrance is unmistakable: the Aztec goddess of fertility and agave, Mayahuel. The image is a little racy. She's squeezing a milky liquid out of her left breast into a bowl for a man decked out in regal headdress. Sometimes she's depicted as having four hundred breasts for feeding her four hundred children, the *Centzon Totochtin* or four hundred rabbits, a pack of partying deities said to be the gods of drunkenness. But here she looks like a normal woman, despite the green shade of her skin and hair. A young man looks up at the mural, raising an eyebrow at the image. He's here for the first time. Taking his inaugural sip of the house drink, he squeezes his boyish face into a grimace at the tangy, milky liquid, then smiles. So this is what all his friends have been talking about. He has finally caught up to the crowd and can now be the one who asks the uninitiated, "Have you tried pulque yet?"

The bar is a *pulquería*, a place that specializes in the ancient Aztec beverage called pulque (pronounced *POOL-kay*), a fermented agave nectar. This is the drink that predates tequila and mezcal in the same way that beer predates whiskey: fermentation must come before distillation, after all. Pulquerías have been cropping up all over Mexico City in the last few years, a new phenomenon that, like so many drinking trends today, is inspired by a very old one. There were once hundreds of pulquerías peppered around the Mexican capital, and a few from that era still stand. Modern ones now compete with those antique establishments, opened by young, educated types looking for a link to their past. The older places, once all-male hangouts with peeling paint and sticky floors where the barflies came in both human and insect form, have been forced to evolve with an interior redesign or the addition of a Facebook page. These bars attract artists and scholars, creative types and philosophers, but also the old indigenous men and *mestizos* (those of half native, half European descent) who have long been associated with a penchant for pulque.

Like mezcal, pulque has made a comeback in the Mexican capital. The bar in Roma is relatively new, but La Hermosa Hortensia, a pulquería on Plaza Garibaldi, dates back to 1936. Its sunny pale lime exterior and Facebook page attract tourists, but locals frequent the tiny bar as well. Presided over by the octogenarian Señora Lilia, it serves flavored pulques by the glass or liter as mariachi ensembles play nearby. The square is swarmed by these flamboyantly dressed musicians, who have flocked here for so long that a mariachi statue was erected just outside La Hermosa Hortensia. At an outdoor table one day, a visibly intoxicated couple is being serenaded by a band of guitar-strumming singers. The two roar with laughter at the lyrics the mariachis come up with on the spot to tease them, then break into a sloppy dance in the late-afternoon sun.

The pulquería fad has surely come as a surprise to older folks in Mexico City who have long considered pulque the drink of the lower classes. It's all part of a greater trend of young Mexicans embracing their pre-Hispanic culture and history in rebellion against the European-influenced generations that came before them. Everything ancient is cool nowadays, pulque and mezcal included. Young people raise their quaint little clay cups, called *cantaritos*, or the traditional one-liter *cañones*, in a toast with (and to) an ancient fermented drink.

The stories of pulque and agave are intertwined with that of the goddess Mayahuel, and thus with the mythology of Mexico. The legend of Mayahuel tells the story of a beautiful young deity whose death gave the world agave. The ancient Aztecs believed in an evil goddess named Tzitztimitl, who lived in the sky with the stars and devoured light. In one version of the legend—and there are too many to count—Tzitztimitl watches over her granddaughter Mayahuel, who sleeps through the day and night in a perfect state of well-being. The feathered serpent god Quetzalcoatl, who in Aztec mythology is associated with creation, craft, and knowledge, one day ascends to the heavens to kill Tzitztimitl. Instead, he finds her sleeping granddaughter. Taking the form of the wind god, he gently brushes his breeze against her, awakening her. The two fall in love and he takes her back to earth so that they can be together.

When the evil goddess discovers what has happened, she is furious. She searches the globe for the couple, but they flee and take cover. They hide in different places around the world, their love finally becoming so strong that they transform into a tree with a branch on either side. The evil goddess eventually finds the tree and rends it in half, killing Mayahuel in the process. Tzitztimitl rips her granddaughter's branch from the dead tree and thrusts it upon her demon followers to devour. Quetzalcoatl, devastated and angry, pursues the demon goddess and ends up killing her after all. He takes the remains of his lover and buries them. From these, the maguey plant grows.[1] Its nectar, sweet like honey, is said to be Mayahuel's blood, infused with her spirit. When Quetzalcoatl drinks it, he feels warm and fuzzy and a little loopy: a gift from the gods.

Agave is a perennial succulent plant that can grow in a range of arid and semi-arid climates, from rocky, dry land to thick, brambly forest, from high, cool hillsides to hot, harsh valleys. Known in English as the century plant for its "once in a century bloom," more than two hundred types of agave exist around the world. (It should maybe have been dubbed the quarter-century plant: wild agaves live an average of twenty-five years, not one hundred—although in one documented case of an agave kept indoors in Boston, the plant lived until the ripe old age of fifty.)[2] The vast majority of agave varieties are native to Mexico.

Agaves come in assorted shapes and sizes. The heart of the plant, the piña, also varies from one variety to the next. It might be a colossal orb, or a gargantuan egg, or even long and narrow like a baseball bat. Depending on whom you ask, anywhere between twenty-five and forty species of agave are suitable for human consumption. Other varieties don't have enough sugars or are too fibrous to make for enjoyable eating or drinking, or they contain toxic compounds. Four or five varieties of agave are sought out for pulque production. Blue Weber agave, the type used for tequila, is not one of them.

Once a plant reaches maturity, it pushes out a long stem from its center: its sexual organ, called a *quiote* (pronounced *KEE-oh-tay*). The quiote can grow twenty-five feet tall and sprouts flowers at the top. Once an agave has flowered, it soon dies. Long ago, not only the piñas but also the leaves and flowers were boiled or roasted and eaten. You can still find agave flowers in certain Mexican markets. (It's not only people who consume agave. Cows love the roughage the plant provides—should you ever come upon agave growing in the wilds of the Mexican countryside, you may notice large bite marks in the hefty leaves. Apparently, cows don't mind their sharp thorns.)

Botanically speaking, agave has been reclassified several times over. It was once considered part of the lily family and is now deemed closer in nature to asparagus. It shares its current taxonomical classification with other desert dwellers like the yucca and Joshua tree. Researchers say agave has been consumed by humans for at least eleven thousand years.[3] But the plant itself is said to date as far back as ten million years.[4] For early Mexicans, it was an important source of carbohydrates and other essential nutrients. Remnants of agave found at archaeological sites around the country suggest that it would have mostly been eaten crudely roasted over a fire and sometimes even raw.

Visit just about any tequila factory in Jalisco today and you'll get a vague idea of how agave might have been consumed centuries ago. A distillery tour usually includes a chunk of cooked agave to taste. The sweet pumpkin-like sample isn't for swallowing whole. Instead, you chew it, pulling the soft, honeyed pulp from the rough fibers with your teeth, then spitting out the stringy leftovers. This is especially true of the outer parts of the piña, which get extra caramelized during cooking. The very center of the piña can cook up soft enough to bite into and swallow. But beware this sweet snack: too much and you'll soon feel the digestive effects of such a fiber-rich food. Let's just say that prune juice has nothing on cooked agave.

Pulque is just one of a couple dozen alcoholic beverages made from agave. Tequila is another; there's also raicilla, bacanora, and many, many more regional mezcales. But it's safe to say that pulque was the first of the agave drinks. How the ancient Aztecs and the Maya before them discovered the technique for fermenting the fresh sap of the maguey plant—the *aguamiel* or "honey water"—to turn it into pulque is a mystery. One legend tells of an opossum or *tlacuache* becoming the world's first *borracho* ("drunk") after extracting the agave's sweet nectar with its small, humanlike hands. Pulque is also associated with the Centzon Totochtin, or four hundred rabbits, who are said to represent the four hundred shapes inebriation can take—sleepiness, silliness, violence, lust, discombobulation, and everything in between. Another legend says the gods revealed pulque to humans by striking an agave with a lightning bolt, splitting it open and spilling its intoxicating nectar.

Over time, pre-Columbian Mexicans developed a process for producing pulque that is still used today. It begins with finding a plant that has reached maturity, which happens at ten to twelve years of age, depending on the variety of agave. Agaves that are used for pulque production tend to be much larger than the variety used for tequila, big enough for a man to crawl inside. The magueys have their quiotes cut. Amputating the quiote, also known as castrating the plant, helps preserve energy it would otherwise spend on flowering. It also allows all the nutrients the plant pulls from the earth and the sugars those nutrients help it produce to be concentrated in the base stem or the piña. As in all alcohol production, more sugars make for a better transformation into alcohol.

To collect the plant's nectar, a cavity is carved into its heart. In the past, a long gourd would have been hollowed out and dried to use as a tube through which to suck out the aguamiel, like an oversized straw. Today, a plastic tube fashioned out of an empty soda bottle might be substituted. In certain villages, a tin scoop is used. Once the sap has been collected—up to three liters per day—the extra goo at the heart of the plant is scraped out, encouraging it to keep producing more sap, not unlike picking a scab causes more bleeding.[5] The cavity is then covered with pieces of the plant's large leaves to keep bugs and other unwanted critters out of the aguamiel. A plant will produce sap like this for up to six months, and sometimes longer, before it dies. The sweet liquid is taken back to the pulque maker's home or modest production facility, which might be nothing more than a nearby shack, where it is fermented.

While beer is fermented with yeast, pulque is borne of a bacteria, called *Zymomonas mobilis*, which lives on agave plants in the wild.[6] It's the same bacteria used to make African palm wine. The natural fermentation process can take anywhere from five to twenty days and sometimes longer, depending on weather conditions (yeasts and bacteria come alive in warm temperatures and get sluggish in cooler weather). The result is a viscous, milky, almost slimy liquid with a sour, yeasty taste. Pulque clocks in at anywhere from 4 to 8 percent alcohol by volume. Not strong stuff, but when you consider that pulquerías traditionally serve it by the liter, it's easy to see how the drink can do its share of damage.

Modern pulquerías infuse their house pulques with fruit flavors like pineapple and guava, even celery and beet, a practice that can be traced back as far as the sixteenth century when pulque was first making the transition from sacred beverage to recreational drink. These *curado* (cured) pulques were thought to be more palatable to customers back then, just as they are to today's young, urban drinkers. During the height of the original pulquería craze in Mexico City, certain bar owners might also have flavored their pulques with fruit peels to correct foul flavors from poor fermentation.[7]

Purists, of course, drink their pulque plain—except in Puebla, where it's fermented with the aromatic herb epazote and ancho chilies to make *chiloctli*. In Saltillo, in Mexico's northern state of Coahuila, the funky maguey beer is used to make the local *pan de pulque*, a type of bread. Across Mexico and in certain parts of the United States you can find pulque packaged in cans, like beer. Bigger pulque producers have figured out how to increase the beverage's shelf life for large-scale manufacturing and distribution, but true handmade pulque doesn't last very long. It's made to be drunk fresh.

Pulque as a drinking trend among young Mexicans is an urban phenomenon, concentrated in culinarily progressive cities like Mexico City. Most people in the pueblos still associate it with dive bars and drunk old men. It's a little like mezcal in the United States, which despite its swelling popularity among spirits enthusiasts can still only be found in certain cities, in certain bars. Elsewhere it's still thought of as the firewater with the worm at the bottom of the bottle.

When pulque was first consumed two thousand years ago, however, it was not a drink for the masses. It was sacred. Only high priests and tribal chiefs were permitted to partake of the beery liquid, which they believed allowed them to communicate with the gods. The general population was mostly banned from drinking pulque; exceptions were made for the elderly or those who had taken ill and were in need of pulque's mysterious healing powers. Drunkenness, in those days, was a state deemed divine and not appropriate for just anyone at anytime. Specific religious ceremonies and holy days were special cases, when pulque could be shared by all—occasions like Days of the Dead or the human sacrifices the Aztecs were so fond of. Otherwise, the punishment for public drunkenness was a beating, public shaming, or even death. Interestingly, pregnant women and nursing mothers were encouraged to drink pulque, their state being about as close to sacred as mere mortals can get. Pulque was seen as nutritious for both expectant mothers and babies in utero.

When the Spanish first came to Mexico, they saw that pulque was an important part of the local culture, drunk during sacred rituals, to celebrate births, and to mourn deaths. The original Nahuatl word for the drink was *iztac octli* or white pulque. The word *pulque* is likely a Spanish bastardization of *octli poliuhqui*, which translates loosely as "that which has withered or spoiled"—in other words, fermented. The beverage wasn't all that palatable to the Spaniards, who preferred their wine to be of the grape variety and also liked it distilled into brandy. But they did see an opportunity for some government income to be made off the popularity of pulque. The Spanish crown first began collecting tax on pulque as early as the mid-seventeenth century, although it was difficult to regulate the sale of such a rural product. Many producers brought their pulque into Mexico City illegally to avoid paying taxes on it and sold their product in the streets at far more competitive prices than could be found in pulquerías.[8]

Meanwhile, the Spanish conquest brought with it tools and infrastructure that allowed for commercial manufacturing of the product. Indigenous and mestizo populations continued to be the primary market for pulque. They could not afford and did not take to the European-made spirits being imported at the time. On the production side, however, a good chunk of pulque operations shifted from the natives to the Jesuits, who had been in Mexico nearly two centuries already.[9] These religious men built haciendas—large estates from which they ran mostly agricultural businesses, in this case, pulque production—and staffed them with local people. The haciendas featured not only housing for certain workers, but a church for them to worship in. By the mid-eighteenth century, more than fifty million pounds of pulque came into Mexico City annually to be sold in the capital's pulquerías. Much more was trafficked under the table, brought in by donkey, wagon, or on the backs of human mules in order to avoid taxation.[10] But what was sold legitimately was taxed at a rate that made pulque one of the government's most important sources of revenue.

By the twentieth century the drink had become synonymous with the lower classes—and with a swarm of health risks. Unsanitary conditions in production facilities plus poor handling, storage, and shipment of pulque were rumored to be the cause of widespread poisoning. Competing beer companies circulated stories that pulque's fermentation was kickstarted with bacteria from human feces (these claims have never been confirmed, and producers continue to firmly deny them).[11] Both the drink's production and the bars that served it came under strict regulation. Not that such rules or even the foulest of rumors about its production could fetter the flow of under-the-table pulque. It continued to be sold by street vendors and out of back alleys.

Around the time of the Mexican Revolution that sprang up in 1910 to overthrow longtime leader General Porfirio Díaz, pulque came under attack by reformers and intellectuals. Several presidents over the next two decades would denounce recreational use of alcohol, especially among the country's disenfranchised poor, for whom pulque was a staple. President Emilio Portes Gil in 1929 suggested disseminating the slogan, "Worker: spend in books what you would otherwise spend on alcohol. The books will teach and educate you and alcohol will only make you a brute and kill you."[12]

In particular, the anti-alcohol campaign targeted women, who were said to be the biggest victims of the effects of alcoholism. *Campesinos* (farmers), day laborers, and other lower-class men may have been the ones most prone to drunkenness, but it was the women in their lives who suffered, as the men drank away their hard-earned wages, leaving wives and children to starve. And when they did come home, drunk men could be aggressive and violent. It was not difficult to convince women to join the postrevolutionary anti-alcohol campaign. They were encouraged to give up pulque during pregnancy, still a customary drink for expectant and breastfeeding mothers, and to rid their homes of the beverage.

If the anti-alcohol campaign sounds familiar, it's because a similar story unfolded in the United States around the same time. While the reformers tried to get alcohol banned in Mexico, the United States was conducting a Noble Experiment of its own with Prohibition. The Volstead Act, passed in 1919 and enacted in 1920, made the production, sale, and transportation of alcohol illegal until Prohibition was repealed in 1933. The thirteen-year folly was deemed a complete failure, especially considering how much Americans drank during the time and the high levels of corruption it created. In Mexico, the temperance movement did not quite succeed in banning alcohol altogether. But instead of approaching the issue the way the Americans did—as a puritanical initiative punishable by harsh federal laws that were impossible to enforce—Mexican authorities went the route of making it more of a cultural campaign, using patriotic ideals to influence people to stop drinking. Alcohol was briefly outlawed in certain states, like Sonora, which shares a border with Arizona. But the temperance movement's biggest success in Mexico was helping reshape the image of the drinker as undesirable and unhealthy, bringing to light the many dangers of excessive drinking.

While all alcohol was maligned, pulque in particular was vilified. (Tequila, as a distilled spirit, was seen by upper-class Mexicans as more modern and sanitized. Beer was marketed as a family friendly beverage.[13]) Stigmatized as dirty thanks to production methods that today would be deemed artisanal—and the indigenous and mestizo people who drank it—pulque contradicted the reformers' vision for a clean, sober, and contemporary Mexico. Poor native Mexicans who made and drank pulque weren't in much of a position to defend themselves or the drink. Intellectuals and politicians were telling them that giving up pulque would improve their health as well as save them money, all of which would bring them and their families more dignity.

Conversely, the new pulque drinker is young, independent, and educated. He or she drinks pulque as a point of pride in Mexico's pre-Columbian culture and history. It's as much a celebration of the past as it is a protest against the older generations' cultural admiration of all that is foreign and imported. Consuming pulque is also a way to save an ancient tradition and preserve the places in central Mexico where that tradition continues to be practiced.

This new subversive image of pulque—as anticolonial protest or preservationist activism—has even spread beyond the Mexican border.

Or at least pulque as a hipster trend has. Pulquería, a basement bar and restaurant in New York City's Chinatown, is frequented by the same sort of young, urban professionals as many pulquerías in Mexico City. Aztec symbols and designs are featured prominently in the décor and traditional pre-Hispanic foods show up on the menu. You might find a Mayan pumpkin seed dip called *sikil pak*, a dish with a thousand-year history reinvented as a vegan bar snack. *Huitlacoche*, served on tostadas, is described as "Mexican truffle" as a way to soften the blow to diners: known in English as corn smut, the ancient Aztecs considered this maize a delicacy.

The highlight of Pulquería's menu is the list of pulques, including the plain *clásico* and half a dozen cocktails made with pulque, mezcal, or tequila and fruit juices like coconut, mango, tomatillo, watermelon, and tamarind. Are the cool downtown customers at this establishment aware that they are part of the millennia-long history of agave-based drinks? Perhaps. But most are probably as blissfully oblivious to the fact as anyone bellying up to a tequila bar. They can hardly be blamed. Not even the Aztecs or the Maya before them, who discovered agave's sweet, secret gift of inebriation, could have imagined how consumption of their sacred plant would evolve over the centuries.

The Mysteries of Distillation

Here's to alcohol, the rose colored glasses of life.
—F. Scott Fitzgerald, *The Beautiful and Damned*

Once upon a time, rail transport in Mexico thrived. Today, only a handful of passenger trains still run. There's the metro in Mexico City, the second largest urban rail system in North America after the New York City subway, the metro systems of Guadalajara and Monterrey, and El Chepe, in the North, that connects Chihuahua to the western coast. Then there are the tequila trains. The Tequila Express takes thirsty tourists from Guadalajara to Casa Herradura in Amatitán. José Cuervo has its own train, too. Final destination: Mundo Cuervo ("Cuervo World"), in the town of Tequila, a picturesque pueblo of some twenty-five thousand people located in the valley of a dormant volcano.

Cuervo World is like Graceland for tequila drinkers. Located right off the main plaza in Tequila, it takes up so much of the town center that it feels as though Tequila was built up around it. (It wasn't: the town was founded in 1530 by Franciscan monks, long before the Cuervos took up residence.) Set on some ten acres in an impressive colonial structure, the walls at Mundo Cuervo are painted a mustard yellow patina. The roof is that handsome terra-cotta tile you find on nice homes throughout the country. The site houses La Rojeña, the oldest legal tequila distillery in continuous operation, as well as the company's official visitors' center, event spaces, and a small amphitheater for performances of traditional folk dance. There's also a rodeo for charro (Mexican cowboy) horse-roping demonstrations, a small museum, barrel aging cellars, and a bar.

You can have your wedding at Mundo Cuervo for about a hundred dollars per person, which covers an unlimited open tequila bar and live music. For those coming in on the José Cuervo Express, many of whom are funneled in from nearby Puerto Vallarta for the day, the train ride from Guadalajara is just under forty miles, but you barely notice the time fly by. There are margaritas and mariachi singers to keep you sated and entertained along the way, and waves of blue agave to gaze upon out the windows. Tickets for the ride start at roughly one hundred dollars, which includes a guided tour of the distillery as well as a tasting, live performances, and an open bar on the train. Premium packages include dinner at the estate. Should you opt to venture out on your own for dinner in the tiny town of Tequila, you might come upon Fonda Cholula, a restaurant that, as it turns out, is also owned by Cuervo. Now you can even sleep in Cuervo. The company built a four-story, ninety-three-room boutique hotel, Solar de las Ánimas, in the town center.

José Cuervo's story dates back to 1758 when José Antonio de Cuervo secured a land grant from the king of Spain, which he planned to use to grow agave for tequila production. *Vino de mezcal* or mezcal wine, as it was known at the time, was gaining popularity throughout the region. The Cuervo distillery was prolific and within decades was turning out hundreds of thousands of gallons per year. Soon, however, the king of Spain became concerned that the popularity of mezcal wine was outshining that of Spanish wines and spirits. In 1785, King Carlos III banned all production of agave-based alcohols in Mexico in order to promote the sale of Spanish beverages instead. It didn't quite succeed in getting people to abstain from drinking or making the local liquor. It only meant that for a decade or so mezcal was relegated to the status of moonshine. Carlos III's successor, a far wiser Carlos IV, lifted the ban in 1795 and began taxing vino de mezcal on behalf of the Spanish Crown. The revenues generated were used to help fund several municipal projects, including developing a drinking water system and building the

University of Guadalajara, now one of the most prestigious institutions of higher learning in the country. It also paid for the palace where the state government is still headquartered.

José Antonio's son, José Maria Guadalupe de Cuervo, was granted the first official license to produce what became known as mezcal de Tequila. His distillery, dubbed Taberna de Cuervo, was the first to be registered for legal production. When he died in 1812, he left the distillery to his son and daughter, José Ignacio and Maria Magdalena. The daughter married Vicente Albino Rojas, who accepted the distillery as his wife's dowry then promptly renamed it after himself: La Rojeña. Over the years, the company has mostly remained in the hands of Cuervo family heirs. In 1860, it was taken over by Jesús Flores, who owned two other distilleries at the time. During his forty-year tenure, the company continued to flourish, bottling its tequila in glass for the first time instead of selling it in barrels. After he died, Flores's widow married José Cuervo Labastida, which served to bring back the family name. The tequila brand became known as Cuervo—"crow," in Spanish. The ominous black bird has since figured into the brand's crest.

Today, the company is run by Juan Domingo Beckmann, a tenth-generation member of the Cuervo dynasty. In 2011, Cuervo entered into buyout talks with Diageo, a London-based multinational deemed the largest producer and distributor of spirits worldwide. Diageo already held international distribution rights for Cuervo and was an obvious choice for a possible acquisition of the brand, valued at some $3 billion at the time. But by the end of 2012, the talks had ended and the relationship with Diageo was completely dissolved.[1] José Cuervo remained one of the last and largest Mexican-owned tequila corporations in operation until it went public in 2017. It's the number-one-selling tequila in the world, the company unloading some nine and a half million cases per year all told, about half of which is sold in the United States. In 2017, the industry as a whole produced some seventy million gallons of tequila and exported around fifty-five million of them. Cuervo, by its own estimates, is responsible for roughly one-third of those numbers.

The vast majority of the company's cache is what people refer to as mixto (much to the ire of the Tequila Regulatory Council), or tequila that is derived from 51 percent agave sugars and 49 percent "other sugars." But the company also produces several 100 percent agave tequilas, including 1800, Tradicional, and Reserva de la Familia. The 1800 brand was named for the year tequila was allegedly first aged in oak barrels. Tradicional is Cuervo's oldest brand. Reserva de la Familia was first released in 1995 to celebrate Cuervo's two hundredth anniversary, an extra añejo made from the company's best ten-year-old agaves and aged for at least three years in the family's private cellar in the bowels of Mundo Cuervo, a dimly lit underground storage room carved out of volcanic stone for natural temperature and humidity control. Each year, Cuervo commissions a different Mexican artist to design the packaging for Reserva de la Familia, which retails for approximately one hundred dollars per bottle. Some twenty thousand bottles of the Reserva are released each year.

Visiting Cuervo's old distillery is not quite the same as visiting just about any of the other distilleries in tequila country. This is Graceland, after all. The tour begins when you are handed an icy margarita to sip as you watch a promotional video telling the noble story of tequila and the Cuervo family's legacy. Guests are required to don disposable hairnets as they are marched past the brick ovens, called *hornos*, where the agaves are cooked and the heaps of fresh agave piled before them. There are workers splitting the agaves with their sharp machetes and feeding the piñas into the ovens. Guests are then led past the mechanical shredders and fermentation tanks and on to a series of large copper pot stills, all lined up like fat-bellied kings.

Along the way, visitors get to sample once-distilled agave mash, which doesn't taste quite like tequila just yet and is far lower in proof. Then they get to taste the finished product. If you're a VIP—and for better or worse, a booze writer is almost always considered one—you're taken to the underground cellars to sample the family's reserve tequilas with master distiller Franz Hanal, a compact man with bushy eyebrows and a disciple's love for his company and its products. He recounts with twinkling eyes how the company came across large glass vessels of blanco in the far recesses of the cellar that dated back one hundred years. It was decided that the treasure would be aged for three years to blend with five-to-twenty-year-aged tequilas for Cuervo's 250th anniversary bottling. Just 450 bottles of the Aniversario tequila were released in 2009, each retailing at $2,250.

No matter who you are, the visit includes a show, either folk dancing or a charro demonstration. A personable guide takes you through the whole process while you ask questions, take pictures, and drink more than your share. It's good fun. But in the end, you still haven't seen where the bulk of Cuervo's tequila is made. The facility where Especial Gold and Cuervo's other mixtos are manufactured, in Zapotlanejo, is closed to the public. Still, seeing the process at Mundo Cuervo gives you a good idea of how tequila *can* be made. Production methods differ from brand to brand, with the biggest companies generally employing the most modern, automated technologies. Regardless of volume, the process must go like this: cooking and crushing the agave, fermenting the juices, then distilling at least twice.

William Faulkner has been credited with saying that "civilization begins with distillation." It's a quote booze hounds love to repeat; it certainly has a nice ring to it. Like so many great writers before and after him, Faulkner was a drinker. His tipple of choice was whiskey and he was known to sip it as he wrote late into the night. So, the assumption is that he knew a thing or two about the subject. Sometimes the quote is recited with "distillation" swapped out for "fermentation," which comes first, both historically and chemically. Unfortunately, no one knows for sure what Faulkner said or how he meant it. But it's easy to believe his boozy musings were over the hard stuff. Perhaps Faulkner was trying to communicate that distillation is a higher calling than mere fermentation. To distill something is to reduce it to its very essence, to transform it into a state more acute and refined than can be achieved by simple fermentation—which, as the Nahuatl word for it suggests, amounts to little more than decay. In other words, whiskey is finer than beer; brandy is finer than wine. Or maybe Faulkner was just a little tipsy when he came up with the line and could never have foreseen it becoming such a mantra.

In any case, there is an argument to be made for fermentation being the true start to civilization as we know it. Just as early humans discovered that fire could cook food, making it safer and tastier to eat, they also (probably rather accidentally) found that fruit left fermenting on the ground gave them a funny sort of feeling when they ate it. Eventually they learned to ferment fruits and grains on purpose and this discovery would lead to all sorts of advances and endeavors in industry, medicine, spirituality, gastronomy, and more. In Mexico, the fermentation of agave into pulque was surely stumbled upon in some serendipitous way—whether that involved a crafty opossum or divine bolt of lightning we'll never know. But more than two millennia would pass before Mexicans learned to distill fermented agave into the spirit that would come to be known as tequila.

The accepted theory is that the Spanish brought distillation to Mexico, the same way Europeans are said to have brought the technology to the rest of the New World. They came in search of gold, spices, and other riches. What they were not prepared to find was pulque. While pulque wasn't their cup of tea, it didn't take long for the idea of an agave-based distillate to gain traction. The Spanish had been distilling for several centuries already, having adopted the European craze for the practice as far back as 1100 AD when the Moors brought the technology to Spain.[2] Fermenting and distilling were necessities in Europe, where drinking water was often contaminated. At first, the Spanish would have used local materials to build makeshift stills before eventually bringing copper pot stills from across the Atlantic. The stills would have been used to make vino de mezcal in the area then known as New Galicia: today's state of Jalisco. But could distillation have existed in Mexico before the conquistadors arrived?

Patricia Colunga García Marín, a biologist at the Centro de Investigación Científica de Yucatán, is one of a growing number of scholars who believe that early Mexicans were practicing a primitive form of distillation prior to the Spanish arriving. She and others have presented archaeological evidence that points to pre-Hispanic distillation using rustic tools made of local, native materials. Ancient stills and even older clay artifacts have been found around the Colima volcano that suggest not only that this is where distillation began in Mexico, but also that indigenous peoples here were the first to farm agave for the production of both food and alcohol.

Colunga and her colleagues have spent years combing the foothills of the Volcán de Colima and its two neighboring volcanoes, which straddle the Jalisco-Colima state border about eighty miles south of Guadalajara, to find artifacts that point to early Mexican distillation. The claim that the natives may have discovered the technology without the help of the Spanish has caused quite a bit of debate in both the world of academia and the spirits industry. Most scientists aren't convinced by the evidence presented so far, claiming far more research is required. Even certain distillers say it's wishful thinking to believe the region's indigenous tribes had distillation technology of their own. But wouldn't it be wonderful for the story of mezcal and tequila if they did?

"I think we have several pieces of the puzzle that together indicate that distillation could have begun as early as 1500 BC in Western Mexico," says Colunga, adding that the picture is far from complete. If this theory turns out to be true, it not only turns on its head any previous contention about the origins of distillation, it also makes mezcal, and by extension tequila, even more Mexican, as it were. Just think what it would mean to the local history and culture if agave spirits were actually made first by Mesoamericans instead of by Europeans who taught Mexicans how to do it.

Colunga believes that early Mexicans may have stumbled upon the concept of distillation while cooking beans. Ancient clay pots discovered in southern Jalisco show that beans would have been cooked over a fire in a sort of double boiler that vaguely mimics the early stills found in the region. She also points to handmade figurines found in the area that depict people drinking out of tiny cups, suggesting they're filled with an elixir stronger than pulque. Mezcal, she believes, would have been reserved for the social and religious elite—in other words, those immortalized in sculpture. Colunga entrusted several of these artifacts to a few American scientists for analysis. Time will tell what can be discovered by researchers north of the border about these objects and the people who forged and used them.

One of the researchers studying the Colima artifacts is Pat McGovern, the scientific director of the Biomolecular Archaeology Project for Cuisine, Fermented Beverages, and Health at the University of Pennsylvania Museum in Philadelphia. A professor of anthropology, he helped pioneer the field of biomolecular archaeology, which combines archaeology with chemical analyses like radiocarbon dating to determine the ages and origins of ancient organic materials, including beverages (especially the fermented kind), foods, and textiles. He's bespectacled, sports a Santa-white beard, and has been dubbed the Indiana Jones of ancient ales, wines, and extreme beverages.

"We're hoping to find out what these vessels were used for," he said, referring to ancient clay pots acquired from Colunga on his latest trip to Mexico. "Our main goal is to pick up biomarkers for agave. Then, based on the archaeological and historical information we have and the specific context in which those samples were found, we'll try to figure out if they were fermenting these natural products or distilling them as well."

The analysis could take several years. The researchers will start by using modern replicas of the artifacts to distill agave, then test them for chemical compounds. Afterward, the original vessels will be tested for the same compounds. Any overlapping compounds between the originals and replicas could lend credence to the theory of pre-Hispanic distillation. For now, however, McGovern is not quite convinced of Colunga's theory.

"Oh, I'm still in the skeptical camp because there isn't a whole lot of evidence yet," he admits. "One sample in archaeology is just not a lot to go on. If we can get the chemical evidence, then I'll be much more convinced."

That Mesoamericans invented distillation fifteen hundred years before anyone else discovered it may be difficult to believe. The Greeks are largely credited with discovering distillation in the first century and the Arabs with perfecting it, although certain historians say the Chinese may have come up with their own crude version of the technology around the first century as well.[3] It may be easier to accept that distillation was indeed brought to Mexico by outsiders—only not by the Spanish. Filipinos began traveling to Mexico in the mid-sixteenth century, given that the two countries shared a conqueror, and were known to distill coconut brandy in the Colima region. They fashioned makeshift stills out of hollowed-out tree trunks in the style of early Chinese stills.[4] Colunga points to mezcal producers in the Colima region who continue to use Filipino-style stills to make their mezcal today. If Mexicans did, indeed, learn distillation from the Spaniards instead of the "Chinese Indians," as the Spanish called the Filipinos, they might have evolved their technology along with the Europeans as copper pot stills were brought over from Spain. But they didn't.

Whether local distillation traditions date back four hundred years to the Spanish or to Filipino immigrant communities living in Mexico or much further to ancient times is what researchers like Colunga hope to discover. In the meantime, they continue to gather evidence from archaeological digs and from speaking to local mezcal producers or *mezcaleros*. While these men—they are almost exclusively men—live and work in Jalisco, they are not tequila makers. They produce mezcal from more than a dozen different agave varieties in extremely small batches using simple, handmade tools. Jalisco is second only to the state of Oaxaca when it comes to agave diversity.

Macario Partida Ramos is a local mezcalero whose fields contain about a dozen heirloom varieties of agave. He also hunts in the nearby hills for wild agaves to boost his collection. Some plants, he says, add a sweeter flavor to his mezcal. Others might help his field ward off a pest. Like his forefathers, Macario plants corns, beans, and squash alongside his agave. He believes mezcal—he uses the word for both the spirit and the plant—is as healthful as any of his other crops. His rustic still is made in the Filipino style, from a large hollowed-out tree trunk with a copper pot fitted on top. Like many of the mezcaleros in the region, Macario also refers to his mezcal as *vino*: wine.

"I am an ethnobotanist and since 1976 my interest as a biologist has been in the relationship between humans and plants—past, present, and future," says Colunga, who has spent a great deal of time getting to know mezcaleros like Macario. "Especially the consequences of this relationship on the evolution and diversity of plants."

Cheerful and cherub-faced, with a bob of stiff black curls and a propensity for colorful Mexican folk fabrics, Colunga has for years studied the origin and evolution of the Mesoamerican diet. Her research dates back to the Archaic period, from 7000 to 2400 BC, long before the invention of ceramics and the domestication of plants, including the farming of agave. She has been able to follow the evolution of this diet, with a particular focus on agave, through to modern-day consumption by spending time in the parts of southern Jalisco that haven't changed as much as Guadalajara and the town of Tequila. In addition to early consumption, including distillation, of agave, Colunga is interested in the conservation of traditional varieties, especially those belonging to the same genetic pool as tequila plants or *Agave tequilana*. Blue agave is just one of the varieties that evolved from the *Agave angustifolia* species, which is still found growing wild in the valleys of the Colima volcanoes today. Another descendant of *Agave angustifolia* is *Agave fourcroydes*, commonly known as henequén or sisal.

"When I went to live and work in Yucatán in 1982, it was inevitable to get involved with henequén. It's a plant that was domesticated by the Maya people and it became emblematic for Yucatán for its economic and cultural importance," says Colunga. "After researching henequén for more than ten years, I moved forward to the other very important species that originated from *Agave angustifolia: tequilana*."

The stories of the two plants share a common theme: the effects of industry on the region and its people. Henequén was widely planted in Yucatán around the early twentieth century. Tapped by the DuPont Chemical Company as a raw material for manufacturing textiles, the agave variety at the time was dubbed the state's "green gold." In the 1930s the corporation invented its own synthetic fabric—nylon—and soon outgrew its need for henequén. Both the plant and the farmers who cultivated it were cast aside. Entire plantations were abandoned. Colunga fears blue agave could suffer its own consequences of being nothing more than a raw material for a booming industry.

"There are a lot of uninformed consumers, a greedy spirits industry, and a Mexican government not committed to poor peasants and our biocultural heritage," Colunga says. She adds that tequila was once distilled from multiple agaves, just as mezcal like Macario Partida's still is. She believes this avoided placing undue strain on any one variety the way the tequila industry now strains blue agave. "Consumers buy lots of tequila without knowing that it is a beverage that comes from a clone cultivated as a monoculture—and that means the loss of agave diversity. Soon the biological diversity of plants and the cultural diversity of human processes will be lost. And our culture will be impoverished." She hopes her research on early distillation will shed light on just how rich that culture is and inspire people to cherish it.

So, how is agave distilled into tequila or mezcal? If you remember the basic concept of distillation you learned in high school chemistry class, then you have a pretty good idea of how those spirits are made. Maybe you conducted an experiment that involved desalinating salted water. Some schools use Cherry Coke for the exercise, requiring students to separate the syrupy cola flavorings from carbon dioxide and distilled water. The idea is to demonstrate how distillation is used to separate components of a mixture. Distillation for the purpose of making alcohol follows much the same concept. Just like in your high school chem lab, you need a heat source, a vessel for the original mixture, a condenser to cool the alcohol vapors, and a second vessel to collect the alcohol. These are the basic components of your average alembic pot still. Pot stills are commonly made out of copper or stainless steel, copper being the most desirable material because it naturally leeches impurities from the distillate.

The first step to distilling a spirit is to ferment the juice or mash of the base ingredient. In the case of tequila, the mash consists of cooked agave juices. The stems or piñas of the agave are roasted in the large brick hornos, then crushed to extract their juice. Nowadays this is most often done with a mechanical shredder, a machine not unlike a wood chipper borrowed from the rum industry, where it's used to mill sugarcane. Traditionally tequila producers would have mashed their agave using a stone mill, called a *tahona*, still used by only a handful of producers today. The tahona consists of a large, round pit built into the ground. A two-ton wheel carved from volcanic stone is affixed to an axle radiating from the center of the pit. The wheel rolls over the cooked agave until the flesh of the piñas is mashed to a pulp and all the juices have been squeezed out. In the past, a beast of burden—a horse, donkey, or mule—would have been used to pull this heavy stone around and around the pit. Among the few tequila makers who still use the tahona, nearly all of them now have a mechanized tractor for the pulling. Once the crush is complete, the juices are collected for fermentation, a process that, like baking bread, involves yeast.

Yeasts are found just about everywhere in nature and are brought into the distillery on the flesh of the agaves themselves. Modern fermentation of the agave mash is often enacted when yeast is introduced to it manually. The yeast might be bred in a distillery's lab or purchased from an outside supplier the way you buy baker's yeast from the supermarket. Traditionally, in addition to yeasts coming in on the skins of the piñas, they would also have floated around ambient in the distillery and spontaneously started to feed on the sugars in the agave juice, fueling them to multiply. It's quite common for tequila brands to claim to use natural yeasts for fermentation; few admit to using synthetic yeasts.

As yeasts eat sugars, they convert them to alcohol and carbon dioxide. The carbon dioxide escapes into the air, while the alcohol remains in the mixture. Once the fermentation has begun, the temperature of the liquid starts to climb. When the yeasts are active, happily devouring the sugars in the agave juice, the mixture froths up. Walk into a distillery during fermentation and the air is thick and close, the sweet-sour overripe smell of the bubbling mash filling the room. When the yeasts are done consuming all the sugars, only alcohol and congeners remain. The froth dies down, and the mixture begins to cool. Congeners are made up of chemicals that impart many of the flavors found in a given alcoholic beverage, but they're also said to exacerbate those nasty hangover symptoms. They include fusel alcohols, acetone, methanol, esters, tannins, and aldehydes.

After the agave juice is fermented, it's fed into the still. Small, artisanal producers are most often associated with the use of small-batch copper pot stills. Large companies might use column or continuous stills, which tend to go hand-in-hand with lower-grade products and mass-market alcohol production. For instance, single malt scotch is distilled in a copper pot still, while blended scotch can be made in a continuous still. The main difference between the two is that the pot still behaves more like the makeshift contraption you used in high school experiments, while the column still, invented in the early nineteenth century, works like a series of pot stills.

In a pot still, the liquid—in this case, fermented agave juice—is brought to a boil. Because alcohol boils at a lower temperature than water, it turns to steam first, the vapors rising until they reach the condenser. The condenser cools the vapors, turning them into condensation. The alcohol is then delivered via catheter to another receptacle. To reach a higher proof, the process must be carried out a second time. The column still, on the other hand, is split into a series of chambers, each one behaving like a mini pot still. It sends the alcohol steam up through the columns, undergoing continuous distillation at each stage and climbing higher and higher in proof.[5] It's a far cheaper and more efficient way to distill a spirit, but is not as widely used within the tequila industry as pot stills. The Tequila Regulatory Council requires tequila to be distilled twice, and it's trickier to prove with a column still that a second distillation took place. So, distillers who use a column still often end up using a pot still for one of the distillations anyway.

You sometimes hear of premium vodkas being touted for their purity thanks to three, four, five, or more distillations. Such claims tend to be rather meaningless given that vodka is almost always column distilled. But yes, each time a spirit is distilled it does indeed become purer in that it has fewer congeners. But each distillation also robs the spirit of flavor and character. So, while it might be all right for a vodka to be pure—by legal definition, it should be neutral, devoid of all color, flavor, and odor—that's not quite what you want from tequila. Yet several tequila brands now tout their triple-distilled product. These may be smoother and lighter, but one is left to wonder what has been lost in the flavor profile. I've even been sent a press release for a tequila distilled an astonishing five times. I didn't taste it, but what essence of the original ingredient—agave—could possibly be left over, I cannot imagine.

One of the reasons copper pot stills are less efficient than column stills is that they lack the automation of the latter, requiring a distiller to know precisely when to "make the cuts." This refers to cutting what are called the "heads and tails" and keeping the heart of the spirit. The first part of the distillate, the heads, can be rather toxic. High in methanol, which consumed in the right quantities can blind and even kill you, they also contain volatile compounds like acetone (what gives nail polish remover its smell) and esters, which can impart sweet, fruity flavors to a spirit. Next come the hearts, the best and most balanced part of the distillate containing ethanol and congeners. This is the part that is distilled a second time in tequila. The tails are the last to come off the still, made up of fusel alcohols and other compounds that boil at a higher temperature than ethanol. Making the cuts incorrectly can result in a harsh or even poisonous spirit. It's said that poorly distilled tequila is what gave birth to the lime-and-salt ritual: combined, citrus and salt would cover up the taste of bad hooch.

The equipment used to make alcohol has evolved since the early days of distillation. The biggest distillers have adapted the basic recipe for tequila to allow for the enormous volume they manufacture each year. Automated equipment and additives are now commonplace—not only for efficiency's sake, but also to achieve consistency. For the biggest brands, each bottle must taste the same as the last. Small and medium-sized tequila companies, for their part, experiment with varying levels of automation and tradition to come up with a product they can sustain while fulfilling a certain entrepreneurial vision or maintaining a carefully crafted image.

In other words, no commercially available tequila today is still made like the mezcales of the Colima region. But several brands draw inspiration from those early distillates, favoring low-tech production methods and simple ingredients. They bill themselves as artisans of tequila. These are the brands that resist many of the modern technologies ubiquitous in tequila production today.

Take the autoclave. Originally designed to sterilize scientific equipment, the technology has been used in medicine, tattoo and piercing parlors, dentistry, and prosthetics manufacturing. In the tequila industry, it works as a pressure cooker, using steam to clean and cook agave in at least half the time it takes to cook it in a kiln. Proponents of this method say it cooks not only faster but also more evenly than steaming in a brick oven. They also claim it brings out more delicate citrus and floral aromatics in the tequila. Traditionalists, however, believe it can't provide the complexity and richness of flavor that slow cooking in an oven can.

A growing number of tequila companies are now using an even more modern device that bypasses the cooking of agave altogether: the diffuser. These monstrous, tubular machines loom as large as locomotives. They take uncooked piñas, feed them through industrial shredders, and use hydrolysis—a process involving steam, enzymes, and chemicals—to break down the fibers' complex carbohydrates and extract their sugars.[6] The sugars are then diluted in water and the mixture is cooked using an inline heater. In other words, diffusers don't so much cook agave as dehydrate it to make a sort of agave tea. Not exactly the time-honored artisanal product tequila marketers aim to portray. Yet if you've done a shot of cheap tequila (and I think we've established by now that we all have), you've likely drunk tequila made with a diffuser. Manufacturing the huge volumes of tequila the market now demands at the prices most consumers expect to pay would be impossible without these mammoth machines.

Marko Karakasevic, a thirteenth-generation winemaker and distiller, wanted to make tequila the traditional way. Tall and burly, he's the heir to the Charbay Distillery & Winery in Napa, which makes him an unlikely tequila producer. Unlike so many Americans who start their own brands, he had the opportunity to make his tequila himself, from start to finish, instead of paying someone else to do it. Marko has distilled just about every kind of spirit under the sun. He grew up around the pumps and tanks of his parents' winery. His father, Miles, made wine just like his own father did back in Yugoslavia before the family immigrated to America. The Karakasevics now make a range of vodkas, whiskeys, rums, brandies, liqueurs, wines, and ports. When they were offered the chance to produce their own tequila, they jumped at it. And they would soon discover just how different from any other spirit tequila is.

Marko met Carlos Camarena, whose family has been making tequila for generations, at a tequila bar in Aspen in the early aughts. The two of them talked shop until the wee hours of the morning, discussing all aspects of their shared passion, in time stumbling onto the topic of chemistry. Carlos was trying to explain how tequila distillation worked. Marko, with so much distilling experience under his belt, was skeptical about what he was hearing, which was essentially that tequila distilled backward compared to other spirits. The two decided he had to see it to believe it. Marko and his father made the trip to the highlands of Jalisco to visit Carlos's seventy-five-year-old distillery. Here they saw how tequila has been made, more or less, for generations: the cooking in kilns, the crushing by tahona, the fermenting in small wooden tanks, and distilling in copper pot stills. Then, they turned to modern instruments to make their discovery.

"When you're distilling tequila, most of the time you're doing a double distillation," explains Marko. "You cut the heads and tails from the first distillation, take the best part of the hearts, and then you distill that again." Using a gas chromatograph to measure the chemical makeup of the distillate, they found that the ethanol came out first and the methanol, usually found in the heads of other distillates, came out last, in the tails.

"There's not really a scientifically explained reason why this is happening," says Marko. "To a trained master distiller who is used to dealing with methanol in the heads versus the tails, it blows me away. It's pretty bizarre because it's physically not supposed to happen, but it does. Technically, methanol is a smaller molecule so it should boil at a lower temperature, which is in the beginning, or the heads, of a run of distillation. But in the world of agave, that methanol is being collected at the end with the highest boiling point of the run. It's completely backward from anything else we distill. It's totally bizarre."

I asked him how he believed this affected the tequila, or perhaps those who drink it, but he had no answer. So, not only is the cause of the phenomenon unknown, so are the effects. Other tequila and mezcal distillers I spoke to confirmed the strange chemical behavior of agave spirits. None could explain it. And those I consulted who work with other spirits didn't believe it.

One theory that gets whispered over shots of tequila late into the night is that agave spirits affect us differently than do other spirits. Could it be that their funny chemical behavior is the reason? The evidence is completely anecdotal, of course, and there is not an ounce of hard science to back it up. But those who regularly drink 100 percent agave tequila and, especially, mezcal have reported experiencing a different inebriation than when they drink whiskey, rum, or gin. Not to play into the myths about tequila and mezcal's psychotropic effects, but something about agave spirits does seem to influence certain people more like an upper than a downer.

At least, I've felt it. And many tequila and mezcal lovers I know have admitted to similar experiences. One bartender I spoke to spent his thirty-sixth birthday in Oaxaca, where he had thirty-six *copitas*—little cups—of mezcal over the course of the day. He kept track by drawing tally marks on his bare arm so as not to lose count. The next morning, he awoke without a trace of a hangover. Whether this was the result of a tremendous constitution or mezcal's mysterious properties, we'll never know. He attributes the feat to the mezcal itself, made from a plant that takes a decade or more to grow, making it more "alive" than other spirits. And so, he felt alive the next day, too.

Now, no one is advising you to go out and drink half a bottle of tequila expecting to feel anything but wasted. However, you might find that the sensible sipping of 100 percent agave spirits leaves you feeling rather perky, if still tipsy. The anecdotal evidence I've collected paints a picture that suggests there is a certain magic to agave spirits. But could it be simple chemistry? Is it possible that the backward chemical behavior of agave spirits has a rather backward effect on those of us who drink them, imparting a high rather than a low? The US Department of Human Health and Services would say, categorically, no: all alcohol is classified as a depressant. Scientists agree: tequila, like other alcohols, is made up primarily of ethanol and water. The former gets you drunk. No research has yet to prove that any of the other compounds in alcohol impart psychoactive effects on the drinker. (However, several researchers have observed that certain social situations—from quiet afternoon drinking sessions to wild late-night parties—can affect people's behavior while intoxicated more than the alcohol itself.)[7]

Lovers of tequila and mezcal would beg to differ. The high, if it does exist, is most often reported by those who drink small-batch 100 percent agave spirits. The simpler the process, the fewer the additives and modern tinkering, the more traditional the agave spirit, the perkier many drinkers profess to feel—the more, if you dare to believe it, alive.

{3}

The Long, Hard Life of Agave

The agave beside the stone bench,
where I have sat heavily all day,
reaches out in all directions,
its meaty, grizzled leaves each
the length of a man, each edged
with back-turned venomous thorns
thumbnail billhooks in ranks down
from the empurpled spike at its tip.

—J. D. McCLATCHY, "THE AGAVE" IN *HAZMAT*

David Aguilar Hernández, an inspector for the Tequila Regulatory Council, makes the hour-long drive from Guadalajara to Amatitán every workday for a month before he gets to rotate assignments to a different part of tequila country. His job involves looking in on agave farmers to make sure the harvest is being conducted according to the rules implemented by the council, then reporting his findings. He lets me tag along one day to observe an agave field being harvested. We leave the city early, at the crack of a hazy dawn. The temperature will reach a scorching ninety degrees, but for now a jacket is required. It's that stony cold of early mornings in the desert that keeps chins tucked into turned-up collars and chitchat to a minimum. In the car, we talk about his daughter (the apple of his eye, naturally), drug cartel–related violence (he assures me we are safe on the road), and illegal immigration (which he believes the American government should prosecute to the full extent of US law). Eventually, the conversation turns to tequila. He enjoys it, he says, and has a preference for a smallish, traditional, Mexican-owned brand that also happens to be a favorite of mine. Yet he recalls a time when the spirit most of the world associates with Mexico was not so respectable for Mexicans to drink. When he was young, his parents would never have served tequila to their guests at a party. A generation ago, the spirit would have been considered unsophisticated. When they wished to impress guests, urbane Mexicans served scotch or some other imported product.

The sky is still a pre-sunrise smoke color when we arrive where the field workers—the jimadores—are piling into a flatbed truck. The men brace themselves for the bumpy ride ahead. The truck kicks up clouds of dirt as it rolls along its rocky path. As it picks up speed, the wind blows harder and colder. The only seats in the truck bed are the upside-down plastic buckets a few of the men have brought from home. Most of them stand, expertly wedging themselves against the walls of the vehicle as the rough road does its best to throw them off balance. There is much huddling and stamping of feet to keep the early morning cold at bay. The half-hour ride into the countryside, to the plot of land the men will be working, is made even more precarious by the pile of sharp tools strewn on the floor of the truck. Fall on the wrong end of a hoe and you could be out for the day—or worse. The men ride along mostly in silence. Sips of the sweet, nutty *café de olla*, the cinnamon-spiced coffee that is common to central Mexico, perhaps dosed with something stronger, and tokes of small, hand-rolled cigarettes that smell of my college days warm the men and ready them to face the day.

Upon our arrival at the day's plot of land, the sun has just appeared over the horizon. It's fat and yolky, the sky around it streaked pink. Agaves as far as the eye can see, bluish-green in hue, look like they might poke the low, lazy sun with their spiny leaves. There is not a soul for miles, it seems, unless you believe in the souls of the few large, bony cows ambling around the rocky field. They leave neat, fibrous pats in their wake. The cows serve a useful purpose: they graze the grass and weeds that grow between the agave rows and compete for the soil's nutrients, as well as fertilize the earth with their manure. Should they munch the precious plants themselves, they won't damage the agave's most important part, which is hidden in the ground. The men file out of the back of the truck. A couple of them find a tree behind which to relieve themselves before the shift officially starts. The rest unsheathe and sharpen their tools, blow hot breath into their cupped hands, and get to work.

The legend of what these men do for a living and how it's connected to tequila is part of the industry's—and the country's—folklore. Pay a visit to any of the major tequila companies and they will have a man demonstrate how agave is harvested using a coa de jima, like our Mexican Marlboro Man at Cuervo. The man is usually decked out in some folky costume that resembles nothing actual jimadores wear. But to see one piña prepped for show is nothing compared to watching a band of men, including baby-faced teenagers and weatherbeaten grandfathers, dig up and slice through hundreds of them on a cold morning in the dusty countryside.

The jimadores wear comfortable clothes, sturdy work boots, and long sleeves—more to guard against sharp agave thorns than the risk of cold or sunburn. In tequila lore, they are depicted as singing throughout their shift. There isn't much singing among the crew I've joined, but they have set up a little pink-and-purple radio that looks like it was borrowed from one of their daughters. It emits a tinny sound. A couple of guys wearing earphones slowly bob their heads. One man is indeed singing over the music blaring in his ears, but thanks to the expanse around us vast enough to swallow sound, his off-key trilling doesn't carry past his own personal space. The rest only emit grunts and exhausted sighs.

The cold has been replaced, almost like a switch being flipped, by a dry and scorching heat. The jimadores take turns stopping to rest on the long handles of their coas, wiping the sweat from their brows with the back of their hands. Many of the dozen or so men are related: uncles, nephews, brothers, fathers, sons. In a way, it very much is like the legend of the jimador embraced by big tequila brands: a near-sacred job passed down from generation to generation. These men are skilled farmers and therefore paid more than other day laborers, but few if any will ever own their own land. And, unlike the jimadores from generations past who specialized in the crop, these men might be harvesting agave today, but tomorrow they're just as likely to board a truck that takes them to work a peach orchard or a corn field.

The parameters for the *jima* or harvest are established by the tequila maker, who dictates what the piñas should look like when they're ready to be cooked. Tequila is truly a farm-to-table product: how the agave is harvested in the field has significant effect on the flavor of the final product. Certain distillers prefer a jima that is very close to the grain— *rasurada* or shaved, it's called, because so much of the green leaves or *pencas* are shaved off that only the white flesh of the big, round heart of the plant remains. Other distillers like a bit of green on their piñas. This type of jima is called *normal*. A generous amount of green left on the piña is called *larga*. The fibrous pencas can impart bitterness but also complexity to the end result.

There are producers who prefer to harvest when the plant has just barely reached maturity (although this is often an economic decision, made when agave is scarce and expensive, and buyers are willing to settle for immature plants). Others insist on waiting as long as possible before harvesting, until the agave is practically overripe. At this point, the pencas start to dry and wilt, and the piñas themselves begin leaking a dark red sap that looks like blood. One distiller I met likes to tell his jimadores, "I want to see the piñas bleed!" That dark bloody sap oozing out of the plant, should you be brave enough to dip a finger into it, is sticky and sharply bitter, but turns to sweet caramel when cooked.

Smaller distillers who own their own agave fields are often the pickiest about the jima. Just as winemakers might tout their estate-grown grapes, tequila producers who own their own fields tend to pride themselves on how meticulously their agave is farmed. Arguably, such attention to the crop tends to produce a better tequila, but it's not a given. There are plenty of bad estate-grown wines, and a number of fine tequilas made by producers who don't own their own crops. One such tequila maker, who buys only top-notch organic agave from farmers he knows and trusts, told me that he felt the quality of the jima had fallen in recent years. He lamented the decline in accuracy of the jimadores' work on the piñas, claiming that they no longer delivered on the specifications he gave.

The crew of jimadores I've joined for the morning would take umbrage at the suggestion that their jima was not accurate. They are what you might consider old school. When they aren't grunting and sighing with effort, they're pausing to carefully sharpen their coas, filing the blades as painstakingly as a woman doing her nails. For these men, the morning in the field is a long and hard one, but not a misery. They are paid a rate per kilo for the day's haul and will divide their total earnings among them. Today, they expect to bring in between four and five tons of agave heads at a price they did not disclose. The price per kilo at this time is roughly four pesos.

Come 11:00 AM, after four hours of labor, it's time for *la merienda*. It's a sort of brunch, potluck style, shared by the workers to fuel them for the afternoon's shift. One of the men builds a fire in the shade of some trees nearby. The jimadores make their way over as the fire starts to roar. They stamp out the flames trying to escape the makeshift pit, then throw a piece of sheet metal over top to use as a grill. Soon, tortillas materialize—there are always tortillas, rice, and beans—and the men produce whatever tortas (sandwiches) and leftovers from the previous night's dinner they've brought from home to share.

The food is warmed in steel pots over the fire, the tortillas flung on to the makeshift grill in the careless yet precise way only gruff, handy men can pull off. I try to look busy, taking notes and photographs. But the men encourage me to rest as well, offering to share their meal. I try to decline tactfully: they need all the nourishment they can get. But they insist. In Mexico, food is always shared. They ply me with queso fresco and tomato tortas on the salty-sweet *birote* bread Jalisco is known for. It's the same bread used in Guadalajara's beloved and messy *torta ahogada* or drowned sandwich. There are also tortillas filled with a spicy carne one of the men's wives made the night before and lukewarm bottles of Coca-Cola. Soon, they forget all about their guest and her camera.

They lounge in the shade, smoking and discussing the recent death of Hugo Chávez. The fire slowly dies as the last of the food is scraped from the pans, folded into warm tortillas and devoured. The meal—thrown together by rough, dirty hands in a remote, rocky field as cows looked on—was delicious.

For the men, it's time to get back to work. At the end of their workday, they'll get delivered back to the spot at the edge of town where the flatbed truck picked them up. The agaves they spent the day harvesting will be sent to the distillery that will cook and crush, ferment and distill them into tequila.

Unlike the country's many mezcales, tequila can only be made from one type of agave. *Agave tequilana* or blue Weber agave is named for its bluish hue, especially visible when glimpsed under the white-hot Mexican sun, and for the botanist Frédéric Albert Constantin Weber who first documented it. Weber, who hailed from the German-influenced region of Alsace in France, chronicled the variety in 1902, the year before he died, and promptly had the breed of agave named after himself, as scientific explorers are wont to do. In addition to being farmed, blue Weber and other agave species can propagate themselves naturally through sexual reproduction. The plant's flowers are pollinated much like the flowers in your garden. But unlike many plants you grow at home, agave is pollinated not just by bees, but also by colonies of long-nosed bats.

The agave's flowers at the top of its long stem or quiote open at dusk, giving off a strong, musky scent that attracts pollinators. The first wave might be clouds of hummingbirds. Later, in the dark of night, bats and moths follow.[1] The bats drink the flowers' nectar and the wind does its part to spread the seeds. The other way an agave can reproduce is through its rhizomes, which are offshoots of the mother plant. In Mexico, they are called *hijuelos* (pronounced *e-WAY-los*) or little ones. Once a plant reaches three to six years of age, the root stem begins to spawn hijuelos, which grow up in their mother's shadow and feed off the same nutrients. Blue agave is cultivated by digging up those baby hijuelos and replanting them in groves laid out like huge, craggy vineyards. These agave clones almost always have their quiote cut to preserve energy otherwise spent on sexual reproduction and to ensure that all the nutrients absorbed and sugars produced get concentrated in the piña.

These days, natural pollination of agave plants in tequila country is rare. In turn, the long-nosed bat no longer has much of a job to do in Jalisco. The zoologists Hector Arita and Don Wilson have posited that "the interdependence between bats and agaves is so strong that one might not be able to survive without the other."[2] This may very well be true: as wild agave populations dwindled, the Mexican long-nosed bat found its way onto the endangered species list in both the United States and Mexico. (Thanks to the efforts of conservationists, it was recently removed.) While it's impossible to blame the tequila industry's widespread agave plantations for the bat's misfortune—multiple factors are at play—Arita and Wilson contended that the bats' loss of an important food source contributed.

The agave monoculture has become a problem not only for local bat populations, but for the tequila industry itself. Over time, the farming of a single species in a confined area propagated solely through cloning can weaken a plant's genetic robustness, making it more vulnerable to pests and disease. In the natural world, biodiversity helps plants defend themselves against attackers. A monoculture, however, is at greater risk because all its members share the same genetic weaknesses. Survival of the fittest only works when certain organisms in an ecosystem are more fit to survive than others. In the case of blue Weber agave, the plants' homogeneity makes them less likely to develop genetic variants that help them fight off attackers. It's all too easy for a serious infection or infestation to rip through an entire crop in a flash. The tequila industry has been dealing with this problem for generations.

In the second half of the nineteenth century, a plague hit Jalisco's agave population. José Antonio Gómez Cuervo, the state's governor at the time (and, yes, a member of *that* Cuervo family), offered a hefty reward to anyone who could come up with a cure. At the time, the offending pest was the "worm" found at the bottom of gimmicky mezcal bottles: a moth larva that eats away at the plant from the inside (and sometimes gets picked out and fried up with garlic and onions as a delicacy; *gusanos de maguey* are especially tasty stuffed into soft tortillas).

That first plague came after the deforestation of the area surrounding the town of Tequila, which had made the expansion of vast agave fields that much easier to carry out. The oldest, most influential tequila families, including the Sauzas and Cuervos, encouraged thousands of local farmers to focus on planting blue agave in lieu of other varieties and crops. Big distilleries further contributed to deforestation through their need for vast amounts of firewood to fuel their hornos.[3] Since then, many more bugs and diseases have attacked the region's agaves, and there are surely more to come. Countless pesos and man hours have been spent trying to find a solution to the various illnesses the agave monoculture can suffer.

"We are sad," says the ethnobotanist Ana Valenzuela over coffee, speaking on behalf of her colleagues and the small community of agave spirits enthusiasts to which she belongs. "It's not interesting to us anymore."

She is talking about tequila, which comes as a shock from the self-proclaimed "queen of agave" and the author of a book called *Tequila!*. Much of Valenzuela's research is focused on alcohol and her specialties include tequila and mezcal. Agave spirits are not just a field of study for her: she loves drinking them as well. She has a particular fondness for mezcal. Best known for her well-chronicled criticism of the modern tequila industry, she has spoken out against the intense monoculture of the agave plant and the way tequila companies have dealt with the various pests and diseases a lack of biodiversity enables. The growing popularity of 100 percent agave tequila represents a shift in people's perception of the spirit—a positive shift, most would agree, away from the excess of tequila shots as party fuel. But greater demand for 100 percent agave tequila means a greater demand for agave, which translates into a vast expansion of cultivation beyond traditional farming to large-scale agribusiness. This has put a biological strain on the agave plant, scientists like Valenzuela believe.

In her book, Valenzuela and her coauthor, Gary Paul Nabhan, describe the last big plague to hit the agave population. In the 1990s, growers began to notice their plants dying, putrefying before their eyes.

No one was quite certain why. There were several culprits, it appeared, ranging from fungal pathogens to bacterial infections. They caused the plant's leaves to shrivel and the stems to rot. The disease spread to some forty million plants in 1998 alone.[4] The locals referred to the epidemic as *tristeza y muerte de agave*: "wilting and death of agave." It began, Valenzuela and Nabhan write, "not long after a large quantity of vegetative offshoots were planted in monocultural stands on extensive acreages, in response to meteoric rises in tequila demand." The problem wasn't just the monoculture of blue Weber agave, they explain, but the way the fields were planted: two-thirds of the plants in the region were roughly the same age. If a monoculture is at risk because the entire population shares the same genetic weaknesses, the risk can only be compounded when the entire population also shares the same demographic. Fields of clones of the same age are even less biologically diverse, individual plants less likely to develop the genetic variations needed to help them fight disease. With this type of farming, the authors explain, "all the eggs had indeed been put in one basket."

Small of stature with an open, heart-shaped face, full lips, and big, white teeth that she exposes just about to the gums when she laughs, Valenzuela visibly brightens when she talks about agave spirits. Her pale eyes positively twinkle. She has studied and written extensively on agave and the alcoholic beverages that can be made from the plant. The community she represents (the "we" she speaks as) includes fellow scholars across a variety of fields, from biologists to anthropologists, who study agave and Mexican spirits, as well as bartenders, mezcaleros, a few traditional tequila producers, and a certain breed of drinker. She refers to the group as a whole, a combination of academic and lay experts and enthusiasts, as a movement, and in many ways it is.

Like pulque drinkers, the members of this agave movement see their choice of tipple as a form of activism. They prefer mezcal to tequila, particularly the most traditional of them, made in remote villages around the country without the modern technologies the tequila industry has adopted. Made up of educated, artistic, and predominantly urban people, the movement has just as much of an interest in reforming regulations that govern the production and sale of tequila and mezcal as it does in hosting tastings and promoting small, independent producers.

Valenzuela relocated from her native Mexico to Belgium, a world away from the subtropical heat of her native land, but when she returns home to visit with family, friends, and colleagues, she spends many a long evening sipping agave spirits over esoteric conversations with like-minded individuals. When they're not drinking mezcal, she and her associates are known to meet at the Fondo de Cultura Económica bookstore on Avenida Chapultepec, a wide tree-lined promenade filled with students and skateboarders in central Guadalajara. The bookstore is a modern, airy space that gets flooded with light on sunny days. Patrons take advantage of the free WiFi in the café area, nibbling sweet corn cake with their coffee as they read, surf the Internet, or just gaze out the window at the parade of people going by. This is where she suggests I meet her on a sun-splashed weekday morning.

"With mezcal, it's more of a cultural product," Valenzuela explains, describing the exploration of the spirit as an intellectual pursuit. "With tequila, there is too much fluff. When Americans see all the beautiful bottles, I wonder what they think. It has nothing to do with us. It's a lot of marketing."

Valenzuela laments not only the biological state of agave but the overall state of the tequila industry. The two do not exist independently, she says. The explosive growth of the tequila category is directly linked to a change in the landscape in tequila country. It's not just a question of monoculture, she adds. Agave was cultivated for centuries without any major epidemics. It wasn't until the scale of plantations swelled that problems arose. The shift from traditional farming for small-batch production to vast agribusiness and industrial-scale production reflects how the plant is now treated: as a commodity, and a global one at that. Non-Mexican companies have seized upon tequila as a trend without considering how to sustain its growing production. Valenzuela is among those sounding the alarm: should the tequila industry continue to boom, blue Weber agave is at risk of becoming genetically depleted. Tequila may be a victim of its own success.

Like other global commodities, agave is at the mercy of the elements—a predicament more farmers are likely to face in this era of climate change. In 1997, it snowed in the highlands, killing large swaths of young agave plants. The weather, coupled with an epidemic of disease infecting nearly a quarter of all blue agave in tequila country that year, was disastrous. By 2000, it led to a nearly 1500 percent jump in the average price of piñas per kilo.[5] Large-scale growers deal with fluctuations in the agave market by planting more than they need, taking into account that a portion will be lost to pests and disease each year. But the compounded disasters at the turn of this century left growers and distillers scrambling. Many went out of business. Rumors began to spread of agave farmers from the tequila region sneaking off to Oaxaca, a state at the southern end of Mexico decidedly outside the parameters of tequila country, to load up their trucks with local agaves to smuggle back into Jalisco and pass off as blue Weber. The agave species in question was espadín, native to the state of Oaxaca and widely used in the production of mezcal. Espadín happens to be the genetic ancestor of blue agave, so it's entirely plausible as a stand-in for tequila production. Talk to a mezcalero in Oaxaca long enough and he's sure to tell you he's seen the trucks from tequila country making off with the local espadín.

"This is a problem that goes back to 1991," says Blanca Esther Salvador Martínez, a lawyer in Oaxaca who specializes in foreign trade and human rights law. At the time of researching this book, she was trying to figure out what sort of legal action might be taken to protect Oaxaca's maguey growers. "When the tequila makers are lacking in blue agave, they come to Oaxaca to buy espadín. When they started doing this, mezcal was not as popular as it is now. So, there wasn't a problem in terms of supply. Today, it's different because mezcal sales are up both in Mexico and abroad."

The black market sale of espadín to tequila companies leaves fewer plants for the growing mezcal industry in Oaxaca, says Salvador. And while espadín is the main variety sought, wild agave varieties are at even greater risk.[6] Some fifteen varieties native to the state may be in danger of extinction thanks to overharvesting.[7] Salvador and others hold tequila companies at least partly responsible. Oaxaca is one of the poorest states in the country; agave farmers there cannot always be picky about whom they sell their plants to, especially when tequila companies are willing to pay top peso (by Oaxacan standards, which can be lower than the going rate in tequila country). But certain mezcaleros fear the toll that letting tequila companies in on their crops could take on the land and the local espadín. No one wants to see espadín suffer the way blue Weber agave has. There is also a threat to the local culture: most espadín farmers are mezcaleros, too. In Oaxaca, the old model of farmer-producer is still the norm. Mezcaleros who sell their agave might not have any left to produce their own mezcal—in many cases, the mezcal their family has made for generations. Never mind that it's illegal for tequila companies to use Oaxacan agave for their product.

Some of the biggest tequila companies have been accused of buying Oaxacan espadín, but few people are willing to go on record specifically calling them out. And no company admits to it. So far, the only verifiable witnesses are the growers themselves who sell their agave to out-of-staters. The rest is hearsay. The trucks piled high with piñas are said to travel under cover of night. According to Salvador, the growers and mezcal makers of Oaxaca must first mobilize and decide for themselves how they would like to pursue the matter. The vast majority of them are campesinos operating small family farms. While some have joined public protests against the sale of agave to out-of-state companies, many aren't even aware of the legal implications of tequila makers buying Oaxacan agave.

For now, the Mexican government has turned a blind eye to the situation, which Salvador says comes as no surprise given that Oaxaca is so often neglected. And there are few lawyers within the state who practice the sort of law required to understand the intricacies of such a case. Oaxaca's agave growers are left to depend on their accountants to advise them on business decisions. Salvador consults them on her own time.

But can agave growers in tequila country really be blamed? Planting blue Weber agave in Jalisco is tantamount to gambling. The blue agave market is extremely volatile, oscillating between stark shortages and massive gluts. Given the time it takes for a plant to reach maturity, a farmer raising blue agave never can know for sure if a favorable agave market will coincide with the moment his plants ripen. The industry is filled with stories of farmers who lost it all or made a killing, depending on their timing. It's a cycle that seems impossible to break.

One tequila producer described the problem this way: a few campesinos start to notice their fellow farmers striking it rich by selling agave to tequila companies, so they plant agave fields of their own. Only by the time their agave reaches maturity, seven years later, everyone else who has also bet on the crop is already flooding the market with agave, forcing the price per kilo of the plant to drop dramatically. When this happens, farmers can be stuck with no way of unloading the crop they've spent years tending. These farmers end up losing their shirts, taking what can amount to irrecoverable losses. And those who do might vow to never grow agave again. So then, in another seven years or so, when only a few farmers have stuck it out with agave and supply is short once more, tequila companies are willing to pay dearly for mature piñas. The remaining agave farmers now come out on top. Their fellow campesinos see the potential of agave farming and the whole cycle begins again. Factor in the waning genetic health of the plant, record rates of pests and disease, and climate change, and the situation is made even worse. And it's been going on for generations, according to those studying the tequila industry. For some reason, no one has figured out how to crack the cycle's code and put a stop to it. The only agave growers that can sustain such volatility are big farming companies.

Among tequila producers, you often hear of how a distillery was started because a grower got stuck with a surplus of agave. A farmer with no one to buy his ripe crop has little choice other than to spend even more money to invest in a production facility so he can process his own plants and try to carve out his minute sliver of the ever-growing tequila pie. At the time of researching this book, the price of blue agave in Jalisco was high, but nowhere near its highest. In the mid-1990s, market fluctuations led to a glut and the price of agave plummeted to 0.75 pesos per kilo. By 1999, a shortage had spurred the price of agave to soar to a staggering 14 pesos per kilo.[8] (Using today's exchange rate, this would be like the price leaping from $50 a ton to nearly $1,000 a ton in just a few years.) In 2013, the average price of agave was roughly 4.5 pesos per kilo (about $275 per metric ton). Reported sightings of tequila trucks in Oaxaca piled high with espadín to run back to Jalisco were rampant. In 2014, the price reached 6 pesos per kilo. In 2018, it hit an unprecedented 23 pesos per kilo. Experts predict that the shortage will ease by 2021.

Yet, back in Jalisco, there is still plenty of agave being farmed. By the end of 2012, more than 260 million agave plants were growing in the tequila-producing region. It takes about fifteen pounds of agave to make a liter of tequila, so the numbers translate into quite a bit of juice per plant. The exact number of plants growing at any given time can be precisely tracked using microchip-embedded cards issued to each farmer by the Tequila Regulatory Council, the body that regulates tequila production in Mexico. (In Spanish, it's el Consejo Regulador del Tequila, known in the industry as the CRT or, to the natives, simply as "el Consejo.") Each time a grower registers new plants with the council, a CRT inspector is dispatched to check that the information reported is accurate and that the field is well within the boundaries of tequila country. From then on, the card need only be scanned to pull up all the information one might wish to know about how many plants a grower has and when they will reach maturity. The technology is even able to report on the health of the plants.

The CRT regulates every aspect of tequila production, from the cultivation and harvest of agave to the labeling of tequila bottles, and makes the data it collects on the industry public via its website. As a sort of bipartisan consortium made up of private corporations and government agency representatives, the CRT's staff is extremely proud of how regulated tequila is. It's the most regulated spirit in the world, they like to say. And they may very well be right. Inspectors from the CRT are sent out daily to monitor the farming and production of tequila. It's a job that requires a lot of driving in a state where roads aren't always the safest to travel. Thankfully, the CRT's inspectors have so far managed to avoid being targeted in their white cars and pickup trucks with the agave insignia emblazoned on the side. They know which roads to avoid and follow a company policy of not taking any undue risks. Besides, I've been told half-jokingly, even drug lords don't want anyone to mess with their tequila.

Inspectors rotate throughout agave-growing regions so they each get to know every part of the territory, which includes 181 municipalities in five states. Jalisco is the main one. The other states are Michoacán, Guanajuato, and Nayarit, all of which border Jalisco, as well as Tamaulipas, in the northeastern corner of the country. An inspector might have to drive from Guadalajara, the capital of Jalisco, to the nearby towns of Tequila or Amatitán. Or they might have to travel out to Arandas, or some other municipality in the highlands. An inspector might even have to drive to another state. Once he or she arrives at the assigned destination, he is tasked with overseeing a particular part of the process. The CRT employs two types of inspector: agronomists, who oversee the farming of agave, and chemical engineers, who verify production. Inspectors report their findings, which are compiled by the CRT. Sometimes they are required to make surprise visits, just to keep everyone honest.

The goal of tracking tequila's production so closely is not only to control its quality, but also to measure its growth and streamline the process of making it. The CRT's mandate is to "protect" tequila. As in, to ensure that it's made according to strict government standards. But the council is also supposed to be a resource for both agave growers and tequila distillers and must often act as a mediator between the two parties. The microchip-embedded cards for farmers were introduced as a way to eventually—hopefully—break the cycle of agave gluts and shortages by tracking when each field's plants will ripen. The CRT is banking on the technology easing some of the tensions between agave growers and distillers. Knowing how many agave plants will reach maturity at any given time should make it easier to predict the market's behavior. The cards also act as a way to combat fraud, a huge part of the CRT's mission, by forcing growers to report correctly the number of agaves they have. Certain farmers have been known to skew the recorded size of their crop to try to influence agave prices in their favor.

The CRT finds itself fighting fraud from field to glass, as it were. It sends agents into liquor stores, on both sides of the border, to pose as customers as a way of ferreting out fraudulently packaged spirits. Unfortunately, some of what finds its way onto store shelves is made from unidentified ingredients or hails from beyond the legally defined geography of tequila country. When products packaged as tequila don't meet the legal labeling requirements, they are destroyed and the culprits prosecuted.

In order to protect tequila, of course, the CRT must also protect agave. The council conducts its own research into the health of the plant, but budget constraints preclude it from pursuing some of the more progressive approaches touted by scientists and agriculturalists. Martín Muñoz Sánchez, who heads up the CRT research lab, oversees studies on plantation soils, water sources, and how to improve agave's chances against pests and disease. He has a kind, tanned face, compact build, and the shy air of a substitute teacher on the first day at a new school. His black-rimmed glasses match his glossy, jet-black hair.

Muñoz has heard what people like Ana Valenzuela have to say on the subject of agave health. When asked whether or not he believes biodiversity could improve blue agave's genetic robustness, he smiles. "It could," he allows, peering at the hands folded neatly in his lap. "But this is not the line of research that the CRT has chosen. We don't have a lot of information about agave. We need to invest money. At this moment, we are trying to work with the government in Mexico. We need their support. The thought is to combine natural selection and crossbreeding, to combine these two strategies to improve the genetic health of the plant."

As our conversation unfolds, it becomes obvious that the CRT holds official positions on especially touchy matters, forcing its staff to remain tight lipped in the face of certain questions. The health of tequila's sole raw material is, indeed, a touchy subject. So is criticism of the tequila industry. Valenzuela and her colleagues have suggested a number of approaches to increase biodiversity in the agave fields that don't involve expensive experimentation. Plantations that make use of cover crops, like green beans and peanuts planted between the rows of agave, almost always have lower rates of disease. As a more extreme measure, a change could be made to the rules that govern tequila production to allow for other varieties to be included in the distillate. It's not such a crazy idea. Before blue Weber was declared the only variety to be used for tequila, other types of agave were distilled alongside it.

Remember, before tequila became a booming industry, it was just another mezcal. The region's mezcaleros were known to use any of up to a dozen local species of agave in their spirit. Blue agave only became the preferred variety in the late nineteenth century, and there were still four others regularly in use as late as the 1980s. So why is blue agave the only one permitted today? The giants of the industry will readily say it was selected because it's "the best." Better than sigüín, bermejo, moraleño, pie de mula, and any of the other varieties still found growing wild in Jalisco. Valenzuela has an alternate explanation. Blue agave came to be selected not for its genetic superiority, she says, but because it was the most cost-effective and prolific to farm on a vast scale. Blue agave is the quickest to mature, contains the highest amount of sugar, and produces more hijuelos than other varieties.[9]

There are people in the industry who recall when tequila was made with multiple heirloom varieties. One producer I spoke to reminisced about how his family's tequila included four types of agave back when his father was still alive and ran the distillery. I asked him if it tasted different from what he makes today. He said it did, but preferred not to dwell on it.

It's unlikely that the tequila industry will ever allow other varieties to be used again. Now that the super-premium tequila category has become inextricably tied to 100 percent blue agave, adding other varieties to the distillate could confuse consumers. Even mixto tequilas can't be made with other agave varieties. It's difficult to understand how the rules can allow the use of corn or sugarcane that might not even be grown in Mexico, but not ancient agave varieties that are a part of the spirit's heritage. From a marketing perspective, though, it's clear: 100 percent blue agave has become a brand in its own right. Besides, after years of telling consumers it's the best, how could big brands suddenly change their tune?

Tequila Sauza, the second-largest tequila brand in the world after Cuervo, has its own approach to preserving blue agave. José Ignacio del Real Laborde, director of agro-industry at Casa Sauza, deals with scientific research and development for the brand. He is in the agave fields nearly every day, he says. An agronomical engineer and agronomist by trade, he came to work for Sauza in 1999 and has seen firsthand how agave farming practices have evolved over time. He is aware of the concerns and theories about the dangers facing blue Weber agave voiced by Valenzuela and her colleagues, but does not agree that the plant—or the tequila industry—is doomed.

"We have developed and implemented modern agricultural practices for [everything from] the management of agave pests and diseases to the mechanization of agave production practices," says del Real Laborde. "Our focus has always been minimal impact on agriculture and environmentally responsible management."

The company grows twice as many agaves as it did a decade ago on half as much land, he claims, all thanks to more efficient and effective farming methods, including the reduction of chemical herbicides and pesticides, translating into a smaller environmental footprint. Sauza's contemporary crop management approach promotes the use of techniques such as sexual confusion, a tactic that involves setting pheromone-baited traps to thwart pests like the pervasive agave snout weevil. The company also teamed up with Jalisco's Center for Research and Support in Technology and Design for a program that uses controlled pollination with the aims of protecting agave's genetic integrity and breeding more robust plants.

"As scientists, we're very interested in sustaining and maintaining as many species of natural flora in Mexico as possible," he explains. "I've seen the tequila industry focus on one variety of agave and seen it cause ecological concern. So, we've been supporting the research into free pollination in order to keep the species healthy.

"Bear in mind, from the 200 or so species of agave, 90 percent are native to our country. We think it's part of our social and ethical responsibility to keep those species intact. Within about eight or nine years of work, we were able to achieve natural pollination within our plantations. In a natural environment, most of the seeds get lost. But we have been able to track the seeds. We now believe, with what we've collected out in the field, that we have enough genetic diversity within the same variety to be able to sustain the crop."

After the agave crisis of 1999, when companies lost hundreds of thousands of agave plants in just a couple of weeks, Sauza and Herradura convinced the Mexican government to sponsor research into micropropagation and agreed to share the results with the industry at large. The process involved selecting the strongest of the surviving agaves after the crisis and using their plant cells to engineer new agaves. These were grown in sterile laboratory conditions, then once the new agaves were big enough, they were planted in fields. A whole new generation of agaves today are descendants of those grown using this process more than a decade ago.

Ana Valenzuela and many of her colleagues remain unconvinced that the biotechnological initiatives of a few big tequila brands will do much to preserve the genetic integrity of blue agave. For now, the rest of the industry is mostly responding to threats to the plant by developing weapons to fight each individual pest or infection separately rather than attempting a more holistic approach. It's the same strategy the industry has taken since the first plague hit the crop generations ago.

Whether blue agave is doomed may be a matter of perspective. But it may indeed be doomed to repeat its cycle of shortage and glut. During a shortage, tequila makers are forced to tighten their belts and maybe lower their standards. But in years of glut, they must find other uses for all the agave that sits ripening in the fields. One of these uses is agave syrup, an alternative sweetener lauded for its low glycemic index. The health food industry has latched onto the benefits of blue agave syrup, a product that looks and pours like honey. One study the media seized upon reported that agavins, sugars derived from the agave plant, were found to trigger insulin production and lower blood sugar in mice. The study also showed that agavins could help obese mice lose weight.[10]

Other research suggests the opposite. While agave syrup does have a low glycemic index, suggesting that it's a diabetic-friendly sugar, it contains as much as 90 percent fructose, the type of sugar said to be the root of so many of today's health problems, including obesity. Table sugar is made up of sucrose, which breaks down as 50 percent fructose and 50 percent glucose. Much maligned high-fructose corn syrup is 55/45 fructose to glucose. Fructose, found naturally and in relatively small amounts in fruit (you'd have to eat five bananas or nine cups of strawberries to get the amount of fructose in, say, a twenty-ounce can of soda), has been shown to pose certain health risks when consumed in large amounts. These include increased fat production in the liver, insulin resistance, elevated levels of LDL cholesterol (the bad kind), and higher levels of triglycerides, which can increase the risk of heart disease. It's also been said that consuming fructose doesn't trigger feelings of fullness the way consuming glucose does, which only lends credence to the link between high-fructose corn syrup and obesity.[11] Of course, just because agave syrup might not be an outright health-improving sweetener doesn't mean it's not a tasty product and a fun ingredient to play with. For one, it makes the ultimate margarita with fresh-squeezed lime and a good reposado: the syrup brings out the cooked agave flavors in the spirit.

Another use for the surplus of agave: the plant has been identified as a viable biofuel. Its yields are greater than those of other biofuels, like corn and soy, and at least one study has shown agave-based ethanol to produce fewer greenhouse gases than corn-based, which some say can be worse than gasoline.[12] Researchers have also learned how to turn it into diamonds. You won't be getting down on one knee with a tequila rock anytime soon, but there may be a market for diamonds made from agave-based alcohol in various industrial applications, from cutting tools to high-power semiconductors to electrical insulators.[13]

The CRT is eager to find even more uses for agave, which seems counterintuitive to dealing with the many problems that have arisen out of its widespread monoculture. Bling and biofuel are probably not the paths to biodiversity in the agave fields. But more money could, in the best of scenarios, lead to better research into the plant's genetic health. Otherwise, the fate of the ancient succulent could very well be in peril.

{4}

Putting Tequila on the Map

What's in a name?
That which we call a rose by any other name would smell as sweet.
—WILLIAM SHAKESPEARE, *ROMEO AND JULIET*

Over the distillery door at Tequila Fortaleza in the town of Tequila hangs a sign that reads, DONDE SE HACE EL TEQUILA COMO LO HIZO MI TATARABUELO. Translation: "Where the tequila is made like my great-great-grandfather did it." Owner Guillermo Erickson Sauza is not what you expect a Mexican to be. For one, he's a gringo, who looks and sounds more like a cowboy than an Indian with his straw farmer's hat, snowy handlebar mustache, and southern California drawl. His eyes, usually hidden behind black wraparound shades, shine a clear Windex blue. His yellow dog, Sandy, is almost always at his side and he babies her like only an American can. He's a vocal critic of the Democratic Party, likes to target shoot in his spare time, and surely no one who knows him would dispute that he has an easy, charming way with the ladies.

Guillermo grew up in San Diego, but he recalls summers spent at his grandfather's house in Tequila, running around the distillery his family has owned for generations. Yes, he's from *that* Sauza dynasty. Visit the town of Tequila and you'll see the very embodiment of the rivalry that exists between Sauza and Cuervo: the companies' grand estates sit back-to-back, the town's centerpieces. Cuervo is bigger: it's Graceland, recall. But Sauza's presence is impossible to miss.

Cenobio Sauza—Guillermo's great-great-grandfather or *tatarabuelo*, as he calls him—was just a teenager when he landed in the town of Tequila. He knew how to read and write, rare skills for a young man of his standing at the time, which helped to secure him a position working for the governor managing a hacienda that produced tequila. The governor was the illustrious José Antonio Gómez Cuervo. Here Cenobio learned the tequila trade. In the 1870s, he struck out on his own, starting La Perseverancia distillery, where he made Tequila Sauza. By the time of the Mexican Revolution in the early twentieth century, he had amassed thousands of acres of land. The former employee would become Cuervo's biggest competitor.

Cenobio ran his company until he died in 1909. His son, Eladio Sauza, Guillermo's *bisabuelo* or great-grandfather, took over the business until he passed away in 1946. Then it was Guillermo's abuelo's turn. Francisco Javier was in charge of Tequila Sauza for thirty years, until he sold the company to Pedro Domecq, a Spanish corporation, in 1976. In that time, he grew Sauza into a global brand, selling more than a million cases per year. Guillermo says he's made peace with his grandfather's decision to sell the brand, although it still upsets him that he's lost the right to use his family name commercially. He's not even allowed to use his abuelos' images because the old men's portraits are part of the trademarked label on the Tres Generaciones bottle, a premium tequila owned by Sauza.

"I got to work in the distillery, learn the business," recalls Guillermo of his childhood visits to his grandfather's home. Sitting on the back end of his pickup truck under a cloudless night sky, he allows himself to get nostalgic. We're parked on the main plaza in Tequila, our legs dangling off the edge of the flatbed, watching the town's teenagers cruise by with music blaring out of their open car windows. It's a cool spring night, the stars bright above. We've already put away several copitas of tequila.

"When my grandfather sold out, in 1976, he was getting old," he reminisces. "I was too young, only twenty. I don't think he saw me as somebody who could take over the company. He was getting Alzheimer's. I grew up thinking that one day I would run that company. It sold when I was in college. I had an Afro and blue jeans. I was a total partier."

Francisco Javier sold the brand but kept his land. He continued to sell agave to Tequila Sauza until, one day, the Spaniards he'd been dealing with at the company stopped buying it. The Sauza family was stuck with tens of thousands of tons of rotting agave and no one to sell it to. That was the year Guillermo decided he would start making his own tequila. The old distillery on his family's hacienda in the town of Tequila was restored, the antique stone mill used to crush cooked agave kept intact. Guillermo's original plan had been to produce two brands, one made with 100 percent stone-crushed agave and another made with agave that was milled with a mechanical shredder. But after tasting the tequila made using the old stone mill, he changed his mind. He would make only one tequila, a traditional one, the "best damn tequila" he could muster.

"The stone-crushed is literally out of this world. It's something that people haven't tasted in 150 years," says Guillermo. "Everyone has taken the stones out of their distilleries and gone to machine crushing because it's so much more efficient. We crush in a day what a machine will crush in five minutes. So, we're basically drinking a fossil."

To anyone who has ever tasted tequila made from agaves processed the traditional way next to one made with mechanically shredded agave, the difference is astounding. The stone mill, the tahona, is used by only a handful of producers today. The appeal of this primitive tool isn't just romantic nostalgia. The gentle pressing of agave by tahona produces a rounder, smoother tequila than milling with a machine, which shreds the agave instead of crushing it, releasing bitter compounds from the fibers. It's no wonder Guillermo fell so hard for it. He left his computer consulting business to focus on his new tequila venture and started selling his product in Mexico in 2005 under the name Los Abuelos. This unveiled tribute to his ancestors would lead to another unfortunate intellectual property hurdle, this time with a rum company in Panama with a similar name. Guillermo was forced to rename the brand for the American market. Tequila Fortaleza, which translates as "fortitude," made it to US shelves in 2006.

"Oh, I always wanted to make tequila," says Guillermo, ever wistful. "Since I was a boy, I always thought I would run Tequila Sauza. Then, that bubble burst. But now, I make the best tequila in the world. We'll never be the biggest tequila company. That's not our goal. Our goal has always been to make the best tequila. We won't be found everywhere. We don't want to be. We'll be in places that care about what they serve."

Tequila Fortaleza is made in a small factory a short drive from the town square. The little revived distillery is part of an eighty-acre estate that overlooks rolling hills of blue agave. Much of the agave used in Tequila Fortaleza is grown right on the estate, which means the piñas can be trucked in to the distillery as fresh as possible. The rest are purchased from small farmers in the region who avoid the use of pesticides and other chemicals. Guillermo says he offers them a good price for their best plants. The agave heads are slow-cooked in hornos. The large brick ovens, like small rooms, are loaded up with a couple hundred heads of agave. Feeding the ovens alone takes a full eight hours. Then they're heated to 180 degrees Fahrenheit. The ovens act like huge steamers, slow-cooking the agave over thirty-six hours. When the cooking is complete, the agave is transferred to the tahona for pressing.

Once the juices and pulp are collected, they are transferred to open tanks. Today, fermentation tanks are most often made of stainless steel. At Fortaleza, they're still made of wood, as they used to be across the region. Guillermo says wood makes for a better fermentation and richer flavor. The Tequila Regulatory Council discourages wooden tanks, citing sanitation reasons. Stainless steel tanks are, indeed, much easier to clean. But traditionalists argue that wood not only lends flavor and texture to the final product, it's also more conducive to a natural fermentation thanks to the porous, breathable quality of its surface. Besides, it's how Guillermo's great-great-grandfather made his tequila and he tries to stick to that recipe as much as possible.

Guillermo keeps photos of Sauza bottles from Cenobio's time, back when it was labeled "Mexican whiskey" for sale in the US. Both Sauza and Cuervo claim to have brought the first barrels of tequila to the United States in the 1870s. Once they had a taste of it, Americans took to this Mexican whiskey and, thanks to a flourishing network of railroads, it was distributed across the country. In 1893, Cenobio Sauza showcased his spirit at the World's Columbian Exposition, a monumental fair held in Chicago marking the four hundredth anniversary of Christopher Columbus landing on American soil. Sauza's product was well received and honored with an award. The prize would help change how the spirit was perceived, both in the United States and back home in Mexico. The notoriety it won that day set mezcal de Tequila apart from other Mexican spirits, so much so that it soon became known to connoisseurs simply as tequila.[1]

Cenobio Sauza's vision was to make tequila world famous and he knew that gaining popularity in the United States would be crucial to achieving this goal. He was right: Americans today drink roughly twice as much tequila as Mexicans do. Then again, many major brands, Sauza included, are now owned by American corporations. (Pedro Domecq, which bought Sauza from Francisco Javier Sauza in 1976, was absorbed by a British company. Eventually, Sauza was sold to an American corporation, which became known as Beam, Inc. Beam owns Jim Beam, Maker's Mark, Knob Creek, several other premium bourbons, Laphroaig Single Malt, Cognac Courvoisier, Cruzan Rum, and Starbucks liqueurs, among other brands. In 2014, it was acquired by Suntory of Japan.)

"A lot of spirits talk about being 'small batch,'" says Guillermo. "But you go to the distillery and find out it's enormous. The tequila is made with machines. There are no machines in our backyard. We're not cheap: you have to pay for craftsmanship and our distillery probably has more employees per liter produced than anyone. But if you paid more for your tequila than [you'd pay for] ours, you're getting ripped off."

A bottle of Tequila Fortaleza retails for about $45. The company produces some twelve thousand cases annually. It has no advertising budget to speak of, relying on word of mouth and industry endorsements. It spends what few marketing dollars it has on inviting bartenders and press to Mexico to visit the distillery. Big brands do this, too. I have been put up in luxury digs sponsored by tequila companies and, over the course of my solo travels in Mexico, I repeatedly ran into groups of American bartenders and bloggers being wined and dined by big brands. But many of these trips are more about lapping up VIP treatment than learning about a slice of Mexican life. Guillermo makes a point of inviting bartenders who are interested in where the products they use come from. They must pay for their own flights, but once they touch down in Guadalajara, they're ferried by Guillermo and his team to the town of Tequila and put up in a budget hotel. They're taken to a couple distilleries to see how tequila is made, but most of their time is spent learning about Fortaleza.

It's not all educational. The trip involves a lot of drinking, including an all-night party at the distillery. Guillermo stations himself behind the bar in the darkened tasting room carved out of an actual bat cave on the property. He spends much of his time serving his guests, bartenders who get to play the role of customer for a change. Together, they talk the usual bar talk of women, fights, drunken feats, and maybe a little playful trash talking about Fortaleza's competitors. As the night progresses, Guillermo also ends up sharing many of his gripes about how the industry and the very town of Tequila have changed over time. Of course, the company that would have been his birthright has driven much of the change, a fact that is not lost on anyone.

The experience often turns young bartenders into unofficial brand ambassadors. They return to their bars equipped with firsthand information about tequila's origins, preaching the gospel of Fortaleza to their customers. It's also an opportunity to show a group of Americans the "real Mexico." They get to see that there's more to the country than the simple images of Mexico as a beach destination, Mexico as a hotbed of drug trafficking, or Mexico as a dirty, salacious border-town escapade. These bartenders get to see a place where art thrives, gastronomy is lauded, and people are remarkably hospitable. For Day of the Dead, Guillermo invites his guests to toast his abuelos at their graves in the Panteón de Mezquitán cemetery in Guadalajara. Many find themselves transported, even changed, by the experience.

Bartenders and restaurant-industry folk are notorious for partying hard. The group that has joined Guillermo during my visit with him in Mexico is made up of some forty men and women from around the United States. They are young and middle-aged, from all racial backgrounds and sexual orientations, and it's not an exaggeration to say that they are all pretty much thrilled to be here. They look at me strangely when I request a spittoon for an early morning tasting and stranger still when I scribble down notes in my Moleskine after expectorating. They swallow. All day, they swallow. One night, while out on the (albeit small) town, one young man wanders away from the group and is picked up by the *federales* on the road out of Tequila, lost and positively plastered. They drop him off at Fortaleza's distillery door in the wee hours of the morning. Most of the participants are rather reverential about the experience, saying it will allow them to speak more authoritatively about tequila when they get back behind the stick. The four-day visit is a lively one without much time for rest. For Guillermo, who hosts several of these long weekends per year, the experience can be exhausting.

Before the night gets away from us, I ask him to elaborate on the issue of change. There is the change in production method, from brick oven to autoclave, from stone crushing to mechanical shredding. But there's more to it than that, Guillermo explains. A palpable shift in the culture of the tequila industry has taken place in recent years. The most obvious sign of this is the shift in brand ownership. Few big brands are still Mexican-owned, and many small distillers are only able to get into the American market by letting a US company rebrand their product. Yet, for all his criticism of the industry, he finds himself, ever the capitalist, defending the sale of one's tequila brand to the highest bidder—even if that bidder happens to be non-Mexican. He fields proposals constantly from US firms wanting to buy Fortaleza, but claims he's in no hurry to sell.

In addition to the distillery where Tequila Fortaleza is made, Guillermo was able to hang on to the house where his grandfather was born, on the main plaza in Tequila. It now operates as a museum, housing an old tahona, historical memorabilia, and a gift shop selling everything from Day of the Dead figurines carved by local artisans to handmade jewelry made from obsidian, the black, glassy rock found throughout the surrounding volcanic region. The museum in Tequila is not for sale either. Cuervo bought up all the real estate surrounding the old colonial structure to erect its boutique hotel, creating an imposing horseshoe shape around it. The corporation has repeatedly approached Guillermo to broker a deal for his little patch of land. But he's adamant: it and the distillery are the last of what's left of his abuelos' legacy.

"I don't think it's bad, the selling out. This is one of the toughest industries because you have to be involved with your raw materials for seven to eight years before processing them. Then, you have the marketing of your brand. We run it from womb to tomb," says Guillermo, who is proud of his company for being Mexican owned. "I'm Mexican. My heart is here. I'm a Mexican citizen. I'll die here. For Día de los Muertos, I take the bartenders to the cemetery to visit with my bisabuelo and tatarabuelo and have shots there. The tomb is all decorated. Someday I'll be in there, too. A hundred years from now, people will say that we made great tequila and we helped build the category."

Fortaleza's positioning within the category is not quite in the superpremium stratum of luxury brands. It doesn't sit on the shelves next to $200 crystal decanters. Instead, it's part of a subset of tequila brands billed as artisanal. Geographic indicators like tequila's appellation of origin are, in many ways, a protection of artisanal goods. By law, champagne must be made in the *méthode traditionelle*, as must so many of the edible and drinkable products protected by appellation of origin, including single malt scotch, the Basque cheese idiazabal, and Modena's balsamic vinegar. Tequila, however, is unique: by the time its appellation of origin was achieved, the process for making it was already rather modernized. The most traditional ways of producing the spirit are not protected or even encouraged by any sort of legal construct.

According to researchers, geographic indicators have become a main focus of international agricultural policy.[2] Mexico has fourteen products protected by appellation of origin. The appellation of origin status is one of several geographic indicators used globally to protect everything from wines and spirits to cheeses, meats, and other local products. In

French, it's an *appellation d'origine contrôlée*. In Italy, the status is referred to as *denominazione di origine controllata*. In Spain, it's *denominación de origen*. Mexico's protected products include tequila, mezcal, bacanora (an agave spirit from Sonora), charanda (a sugarcane spirit from Michoacán), sotol (a cousin of mezcal made from the evergreen shrub known in English as desert spoon in the states of Chihuahua, Durango, and Coahuila), coffee from both Chiapas and Veracruz, vanilla from Papantla, habanero chilies from the Yucatán peninsula, rice from Morelos, and the sweet mango *Ataulfo del Soconusco* from Chiapas. A group of enthusiasts tried unsuccessfully to secure appellation of origin status for birote bread, the sweet-salty roll used for Guadalajara's signature torta ahogada. Stories of failed attempts to secure the status abound in Europe, too. Genoa, for example, never achieved it for pesto, which originated there, but did manage to get a main ingredient in pesto, Genovese basil, protected.

Geographic indicators aren't used solely to protect food items. Chiapas amber, wood handicrafts from Olinalá, and pottery from Talavera are also appellation of origin products. Securing a geographic indicator not only helps thwart counterfeiting, but also serves to promote products globally, which in turn can boost their value. Cotija cheese, while not protected by appellation of origin, was assigned a "collective mark." Since earning it, the price of the cheese, named for a town in Michoacán, has doubled from some 30 pesos per kilo, and certain producers have been known to charge up to 200 pesos per kilo.[3] A reported 250,000 families in twenty-one states across Mexico rely on protected products for their livelihood.[4] Some seventy thousand of them depend on the booming tequila industry.

Nowadays, we think of tequilas that are made using brick ovens and a tahona as artisanal. But long ago, before people called it tequila, the process was even more archaic. The agaves were not cooked in kilns, but instead roasted in underground pits, much like mezcal, the mother of tequila, still is today. The result was a headier, smokier elixir. In the late-nineteenth century, in response to growing demand from beyond the region, tequila producers started making the switch to brick ovens.

By the early twentieth century, kilns were the norm in commercial distilleries. And just a few decades later, autoclaves began replacing hornos. Industrial diffusers soon followed. Fermentation and distillation methods also underwent modernization before or shortly after the appellation of origin was achieved. Stainless steel tanks replaced wood, commercial yeasts replaced natural, and alembic stills went from small to enormous, some even giving way to more efficient column stills. Today, traditional methods for cooking, fermenting, and distilling tequila are not required by law.

The equipment for making tequila isn't the only part of the process that had already deviated from the traditional by the time the appellation of origin was secured. The first official Mexican standards for making tequila were drawn up in 1949. They stated that the spirit had to be made from 100 percent blue Weber agave grown in Jalisco. As the cycle of agave shortages and gluts plagued producers over the years, the amount of agave required to make tequila was reduced. By the mid-1960s, it fell to 70 percent.[5]

In 1970, just four years before the appellation of origin went into effect, the rules for making tequila were changed once again. The minimum amount of blue agave required for production was set at 51 percent. The rest could be distilled from "other sugars," namely those derived from sugarcane or corn, both of which are grown in Mexico. (Although, in many cases, the sugarcane, corn, or other grains used in today's tequilas are not. There is no law stating that the ingredients must be.) Mixtos were born out of a shortage of healthy agave. These tequilas can be softer, sweeter, and less complex than 100 percent blue agave tequila, although you might experience them as being much harsher than the good stuff. It's just one side effect of high-volume distillation, generic ingredients, and additives: even if the spirit has a lower proof than a well-crafted 100 percent tequila or mezcal, it can come across as more astringent.

By the time tequila's appellation of origin was approved, yet another important change had already come to the industry. Geography is one of the very foundations of any appellation of origin: they are geographic indicators, after all. The defined borders of the tequila region became a point of contention early on. Agave for commercial tequila production was first planted in the state of Jalisco, particularly in the Amatitán-Tequila Valley. The official tequila region was first expanded to include parts of the bordering states of Guanajuato, Michoacán, and Nayarit, where the landscape, soil, and climate are not unlike those of Jalisco. But when a fifth state was proposed for inclusion in the delimited region, certain people within the industry were outraged. The state of Tamaulipas is nowhere near Jalisco; it's clear across the country on the eastern coast. Yet agave has been grown there since the 1960s.

Agrarian reformer Guillermo González Díaz Lombardo, who hailed from the state, lobbied to have it added to the appellation of origin and succeeded when the regulations were modified in 1977. Several large tequila companies eager to meet the growing demand for their product had supported him. One big brand in particular is said to have promised to buy agave from the farmers who were encouraged to plant their crops in the eastern state. But when it came time for the mature piñas to be harvested, the company tried to undercut the farmers with an odiously low price. They were left with tons of agave and no one to pay fairly for it. González decided he would build a distillery in the region and use the local agave himself. He named it La Gonzaleña, after himself, and produced a tequila called Chinaco that quickly became lauded among connoisseurs and, in the 1980s, was the first truly premium tequila sold in the United States.[6]

Unfortunately, not everyone was pleased with his actions. Critics complained that Tamaulipas is not only geographically removed from the tequila industry's main hub, but its biophysical conditions don't match those of the rest of the appellation—Tamaulipas doesn't share the same "terroir." A taste of Chinaco blanco, savory and herbaceous like a mouthful of desert, may convince you this is true. It's robust and delicious, but very distinct from highland and valley tequilas. By expanding tequila's appellation to include a place so far from its home, the spirit's terroir—a French wine term that has made its way into tequila lingo referring to the soil, climate, and cultural traditions associated with a product—was said to be compromised.

European products like cognac, camembert cheese, and prosciutto di Parma are among those safeguarded by appellations of origin, which state specifically how and where each product should be made. Manufacturers located outside a defined geographical area are prohibited from peddling their products under registered names, and expanding a protected product's set geographical region is extremely rare. Tequila's appellation of origin was granted in 1974 and recognized by the World Intellectual Property Organization in 1978. The new status would come to be regulated by Mexico's own Norma Oficial Mexicana standards, and enforced by the CRT.

The Tequila Regulatory Council is housed within a modern concrete block of a building in central Guadalajara. Or rather, that's what the building looks like from the front. Were you to walk around to view the building at an angle or somehow get an aerial view of it, you'd see that it's really not a block at all. It fishtails out at the back so that, from above, it looks like the capital letter Y. The white cement façade is branded with the CRT's insignia and green agave logo. An A-line shape of mirrored glass is carved down the center of the building's hard surface: A for agave. The same mirrored glass is used on the sides of the building, their glinting surfaces reflecting the cloudless blue sky. The inside is cool and clean. It houses labs, conference rooms, office cubicles, and a subterranean garage where the CRT's fleet of scrubbed white pickup trucks is parked.

On my first visit to the office, I'm taken on a tour by Paola Alejandra García Butrón, who works in the council's communications and public relations department. She's tall and willowy, with long dark hair and an oval face. She has the air of a dancer and, as it turns out, she does practice dance in her free time. Her light yet deliberate step, feet shod in ballerina flats, betrays it. She speaks a seductively lilting English (and serviceable German) and gives the impression of suffering no fools. As she leads me from a sleek, modern boardroom to a sterile, spartan laboratory, she explains the functions and mission of the CRT.

Unlike the National Chamber for the Tequila Industry, whose sole function is to promote the sale of the spirit while defending the interests of those who make and sell it, the CRT is charged with quality control for tequila. Founded in 1994, the council has its roots in an organization of tequila industry professionals who first banded together decades earlier. Based in Guadalajara, it also operates an office in Washington, DC, that deals with the American market. At the time of researching this book, the CRT was working toward becoming an organic certifier, like the USDA.

The CRT doesn't just answer to tequila companies, but also to agave farmers, marketers and bottlers of tequila, the government's health and agriculture departments, and the national body protecting intellectual property. Paola is careful when responding to my questions, doling out well-crafted answers that sound officially sanctioned. It isn't until we reach the storage room that holds just a fraction of the thousands of products the CRT tests and regulates each year that she breaks her purposeful stride and rehearsed patter. She has stopped, mid-spiel, to correct me.

We've just poked our heads into the holding cell containing the hundred or so bottles awaiting their turn in the lab. To my host's dismay, I've referred to some of them as mixtos. Nearly imperceptibly, Paola flinches.

"You keep calling it mixto," she says.

"Yes. That is what it's called, isn't it?"

"The CRT prefers not to use this term," Paola tells me, diplomatic yet emphatic. "We prefer to call it tequila. We differentiate between the two by calling the other one 100 percent agave tequila."

"I see. But people do say mixto, don't they?"

"Yes, they do," she allows. "But the CRT uses the terms 'tequila' and '100 percent agave tequila.' So it's best if you do too."

It might sound like an awkward exchange, but it isn't really. Paola is just doing her job. So I promptly agree to watch my language. No need to annoy my host over semantics. The staff at the CRT was open and welcoming when I contacted them to let them know I'd be in Mexico researching the tequila industry. Paola and her fellow CRT employees were gracious and forthcoming with me, answering my questions and setting up hard-to-get meetings with producers and jimadores. But the stern dressing down in the storage room reminds me of how strictly regulated tequila is.

It wasn't always this way. Back when tequila was still called mezcal, it was mostly a rural product. (The word mezcal is said to derive from the Nahuatl *mexcalli*, likely a combination of *metl*, the Aztec word for maguey, and *ixca*, which translates as "to cook.") Small family farms would grow agave alongside other crops and distill just enough for personal consumption or to share with neighbors. Recipes for making mezcal were passed on from father to son, neighbor to neighbor. Word of the spirit spread from one pueblo to the next. From the earliest days, consumption evolved. At first, people drank mezcal for medicinal purposes.[7] By the eighteenth century, commercial production and recreational use were underway. But much of what was made and consumed for generations to follow would remain small-batch—moonshine, really, especially during the spirit's decade-long ban in the late eighteenth century when production moved underground. It wasn't until years later that the process to make tequila became strictly regulated and, eventually, industrialized.

In the meantime, big brands like Cuervo and Sauza expanded their empires. They did so by buying up land for agave plantings and acquiring or leasing smaller family-owned operations. Large-scale producers were even known to move into villages and forcibly appropriate plots of land from the people, a practice condoned by President Porfirio Díaz.[8] The wealthiest hacienda owners who made the most recognizable brands exerted political influence, their ambitions often trumping the rights of the peasant population. The taxes collected on tequila were an important source of revenue to the region.

By the nineteenth century, mezcal de Tequila had become popular among everyone from the miners who worked the prosperous silver mines of Bolaños north of Tequila, to the soldiers on both sides of the Mexican War of Independence. (Consumption of the spirit dipped over the course of the war thanks to so many agave plantations being destroyed.)[9] With independence from the Spanish won in 1821, products from Spain became harder to procure in Mexico. It opened the door for mezcal de Tequila to spread even further. And there were plenty more wars to come in Mexico, each with their share of parched soldiers to supply. The network of railroads that evolved gradually in Mexico helped the spirit spread throughout the country. However, the construction of railways was double-edged: it helped carry tequila to the country's far reaches but also distributed European wines and spirits, which were terribly chic at the time. Under the dictatorship of General Porfirio Díaz, which lasted (only slightly interrupted) from the late 1870s through 1911, when he was overthrown, a wave of Francophilia swept Mexico that would not fade until well after the Mexican Revolution that deposed him.[10]

Tequila's popularity eventually waned, especially among the upper classes in Mexico. At the same time, it spread beyond the Mexican border. During American Prohibition, it was smuggled across state lines, just as Canadian whiskey was brought in from the north, to slake the thirst of a populace no longer legally allowed to make or purchase alcohol. The Second World War was another boon for the spirit. As imported spirits from Europe, like cognac and scotch, stopped flowing, Americans—especially those in the southern states—drank more and more tequila.[11] With the spirit gaining recognition abroad, tequila producers and the Mexican government finally began talking about protecting the name and authenticity of their product legally.

In the 1940s, the modern Norma Oficial Mexicana (NOM) system, which regulates the standards of Mexican products, was not yet in place. The Mexican government used industrial property law to decree that tequila could only be made in the state of Jalisco. But these regulations would prove to be powerless outside of Mexico, where counterfeiting tequila became rampant. By the 1960s, Japan and Spain, in particular, were hotbeds of fake tequila. In 1958, the Lisbon Agreement for the Protection of Appellations of Origin had established a special status for traditional products associated with a specific geographical area. The international recognition of such items was intended to promote them in a global economy while protecting those who make them from being undercut by fraudsters. Mexico soon went after this status for tequila.

The first time intellectual property was addressed on a far-reaching scale was with the Paris Convention of 1883, which sought to legally protect patents of inventions, trademarks, and industrial designs and was initially signed by eleven participating nations across Europe and Latin America. The Lisbon Agreement built on the idea, an international treaty that would recognize qualifying products as special and prohibit them from being copied or counterfeited. Out of more than ten thousand products protected by geographic indicators worldwide today, only about fourteen hundred are from developing nations. And the vast majority are wines or spirits.[12] However, more than fifty years after it was drafted, the Lisbon Agreement only has twenty-seven member countries. Recognition of one's product by the Congo, Burkina Faso, and the Republic of Moldova—as well as France, Italy, Spain, and more—may be a significant victory for artisanal producers of culturally significant products, but it certainly doesn't protect them from fraud globally. Still, it's a status regional governments around the world long for.

The United States, for one, does not recognize geographic indicators as such. Instead, it uses registered trademarks to protect many specialty products, like Florida oranges, Washington apples, and Idaho potatoes. For Idaho potatoes, for example, the rules are defined and enforced by a trade commission that licenses potato growers to use the "Grown in Idaho" label. However, in a growing number of American wine regions, American Viticultural Areas (AVAs) are gaining popularity. These are a type of geographic indicator for American wine dating back to 1980 that mimics the European system. AVAs, governed by the Alcohol and Tobacco Tax and Trade Bureau (TTB), are based on the idea that an area can have a specific terroir, though the term is not actually used in the legal language that governs AVAs. Instead, the focus of an AVA is on geography and the biophysical conditions found within a given area that set it apart. No rules outlining production methods or specific grape varieties are given. It's a staunchly American system in that regard: producers are free to make whatever wine they choose. Unlike most European appellations of origin, AVAs require that only 85 percent of grapes used in a given wine be grown in the defined geographical area.

Long before AVAs became de rigueur, bourbon was protected by appellation of origin–style regulations enforced by the TTB. Unlike the rules for vodka or rum, which focus on the parameters of the final product, bourbon regulations strictly define how the spirit should be made and, in certain cases, where. Kentucky Straight Bourbon, for example, must be distilled from at least 51 percent corn to a proof not exceeding 160 and aged in new white oak barrels in Kentucky. (Other types of bourbon can be made elsewhere in America.) The way the TTB enforces these rules once the whiskey leaves American soil is via trade agreements with individual nations, which is also how other countries enforce how their products are sold in the United States. For example, tequila is no longer sold as "Mexican whiskey" because of a reciprocal agreement signed in 1974 that states the United States recognizes tequila as a distinct product from Mexico and restricts the sale of products sold as tequila to those made in Mexico only. In return, Mexico gives the same protection to bourbon, ensuring that only American-made bourbon can be labeled and sold as such in Mexico.[13]

The champagne industry took a similar approach. For years, California winemakers sold products labeled as champagne. The French Champagne board, backed by the French government, initiated a big push to discourage the practice, inciting grassroots protests against producers who used the term. In 2006, the United States and the European Union signed an agreement that would put an end to the use of what it called semi-generic labeling, such as champagne on wines that did not originate in Champagne, France.[14] American wine with labels approved before 2006 could qualify for a grandfather provision that allowed the use of the word on the label if the true place of origin was also included. But the practice of American winemakers labeling their bubbly as champagne has since fallen out of favor and is now seen as rather gauche. If California winemakers want their products respected abroad, they must respect the products of others. Napa Valley Vintners, a trade association, spends millions on efforts to protect Napa Valley wines around the world by securing trademarks or geographic indicators in individual countries. It's an ongoing effort that most AVAs can't afford to emulate.

Tequila can. The industry has taken a two-pronged approach to protecting its products internationally. Appellation of origin protects it in the countries that recognize the status. In other nations, the CRT aims to draw up agreements like the one it has with the United States. The two different approaches to protecting intellectual property—America's capitalism-driven trademark laws versus Europe's terroir- and culture-protecting geographic indicators—each have their benefits. Which one actually protects specialty products and their makers better remains to be seen.

While counterfeiters surely take a huge chunk out of tequila profits, the legitimate tequila industry might be its own worst enemy. The spirit may very well be the most regulated in the world. But tequila enthusiasts and academics alike worry that those regulations are misguided. Moreover, they're far too easily subject to change driven by the biggest companies and the natural forces of capitalism. Sarah Bowen, an assistant professor of sociology at North Carolina State University who has studied appellations of origin around the world, believes the tequila industry is suffering the repercussions of the way its appellation of origin was initially constructed. In her dissertation, she compared tequila to an appellation of origin product in France to see how geographic indicators function in different places. The product she chose to examine alongside tequila was Comté cheese, made in eastern France.[15]

Bowen finds that certain appellations of origin are more successful than others at protecting a product and the people who make it. In Comté, for example, the rules regulating the production of the region's world-famous semi-hard raw cheese identify precisely how it must be made, from how and where the cows are to be raised to the specific and decidedly traditional cheesemaking techniques that must be adhered to. Only the Montbéliarde and French Simmental breeds can be used to make Comté cheese and each cow must be granted a whole hectare of pasture to graze. Grass and plants are the only approved feed for the cows and GMOs are strictly prohibited, as are additives and dyes. Notably, the language of the appellation of origin rules expresses a direct correlation between the region's terroir and the quality of the product. As Bowen explains, this not only promotes traditional farming and production methods, but also raises the status of the farmer and cheese maker, for they are the precious link between the terroir, the animals, and the delicious end product.

In tequila country, the end product is meticulously tested. Maximum methanol and aldehyde levels are strictly monitored and limits enforced, only sanctioned additives are permitted. But how the agaves are cooked and mashed, fermented and distilled, is rather open. Whereas other geographic indicators are designed to uphold cultural traditions associated with a particular region, in tequila production, modern technology is embraced. By allowing modernization to take over, the process for making tequila has become increasingly industrialized and artisanal producers are being squeezed out. Traditional ways are no longer a mysterious secret guarded by skilled craftsmen, but rather an easy recipe to replicate using state-of-the-art technology.

In addition, the status of the jimador has dropped. Agave's volatile market is constantly forcing people in and out of the business at the expense of the vast wealth of knowledge once transmitted from one generation of jimadores to the next. Workers in tequila nowadays are not necessarily trained by their fathers, uncles, brothers, and cousins as they once would have been. And many of them can only survive by being jacks of all trades, also harvesting peaches or corn or even doing construction or paving roads. Fewer and fewer family agave farms exist. It's become the domain of large agribusinesses that hire cost-effective day laborers to work the fields.

Another problem with tequila's appellation, writes Bowen, is the geography itself. Tequila's defined territory is now spread across more than 25 million acres in five states, some 7.5 million of which are planted with agave. By comparison, the Comté region has only ever narrowed its territory over the years to an area of just 570,000 acres of farms. The sheer size of tequila's appellation not only dilutes the value of its terroir and product, but makes it difficult for the smallest producers to mobilize.[16] Comté continues being produced as it has been for a thousand years thanks in large part to the ongoing efforts of local cheese makers to preserve their ways and the land. In tequila country, rural landscapes are being transformed into oceans of blue agave planted and managed by big agricultural corporations. This reduces biodiversity, as we saw in the last chapter, and makes it nearly impossible for small farmers to compete. They no longer get to be the guardians of terroir, like the cow farmers of Comté.

Yet another aspect of tequila's appellation of origin that differs from Comté's is reflected in the wages and quality of life of producers. The special status of Comté cheese has markedly improved the lives of the region's inhabitants, creating jobs and bolstering small family farms. In tequila country, on the other hand, while the success of tequila has contributed to the overall welfare of people living in Jalisco, the effects of the tequila boom haven't specifically impacted the wages of tequila workers. Independent agave farmers are disappearing and the smallest producers struggle to stay afloat in a sea of big brands. Much of the wealth the industry creates finds its way into the pockets of company shareholders, many of whom are not Mexican.

Jennifer Barnette, a law student at Berkeley specializing in environmental law, also conducted research on the tequila industry. Her findings mirror Bowen's and those of other academics across various disciplines. By comparing the tequila appellation to Colombian coffee, Barnette aimed to determine how geographic indicators can be used as a tool to promote sustainability. Her research suggests that, while both tequila and Colombian coffee have found commercial success internationally, Colombian coffee's appellation of origin status has been far more beneficial to the region's small producers than tequila's.[17]

Like Bowen, Barnette notes that the size of the appellation is a key factor in preserving local traditions and keeping wealth within the region. Colombian coffee's appellation has managed to remain contained within two million acres. (Beans are grown on some seventeen million acres across the country, but the appellation is concentrated on the Central Coffee Belt, where the best beans have traditionally been cultivated.) The limited territory prevents competing farmers from outside the region from reaping the benefits of the coffee's popularity and large foreign corporations from invading it. The appellation's smaller size has also helped the region avoid some of the other dangers of over-expansion, including industrial farming methods, which can cost farmers their jobs and take their toll on the environment. In tequila country, Barnette writes, pesticide and herbicide use is rampant and industrialized farming has far outpaced small traditional agave growers.

Barnette too finds that the way the appellation of origin was originally designed has helped small café de Colombia farmers fare better than those in tequila country. The geographic indicator, in this case, is owned and managed by the local Federación Nacional de Cafeteros de Colombia, a nonprofit group founded in 1927 by an assembly of coffee growers that now represents some 563,000 coffee-growing families. The FNC created the National Coffee Fund, whereby each producer contributes a few cents per pound of beans sold. In return, the fund offers farmers a price guarantee on their crop should they want it. In other words, when coffee prices are high, farmers can choose to sell to the highest bidder. But when they're low, they can sell to the FNC for a guaranteed price. Farmers are never left holding tons of coffee beans in a bad year.

The FNC also runs initiatives that promote biodiversity and sustainability. It has funded more than six thousand schools and 180 hospitals in coffee-growing areas, and provided better drinking water, utilities, and sanitation to its members. While certain tequila brands pride themselves on acts of corporate giving, agave growers are largely at the mercy of the forces of capitalism. Barnette believes that tequila's appellation is subject to far too much influence from some of the biggest companies, whose executives sit on the CRT's board.

Barnette isn't the first to argue that the sway large companies have over tequila's governing body has the potential to undermine the spirit's heritage and integrity. In 2006, regulations were changed to include the production of flavored tequilas, angering traditionalists. There is little doubt that these new mango-, strawberry-, and jalapeño-flavored bottlings are designed to compete directly with the world's flavored vodkas. Extra añejos were added as an official category the same year, arguably to compete with aged whiskeys, rums, and cognacs. Both new categories, one on the lower end and the other on the very high end, move tequila a little further away from its historical and cultural roots.

Another recent change to CRT regulations requires that additives—sugar, caramel, glycerin, and oak extract—be listed on the bottle's label. It's a win for those who demand more transparency in labeling. Of course, one additive is always present in tequila that does not have to be listed: water. Like scotch, most rums, and nearly all vodkas, water is almost always added to bring tequila down to the desired bottle proof. There is no law that specifically states what proof a tequila must be bottled at, but for the American market the unofficially agreed-upon standard is 80 proof, or 40 percent alcohol by volume. Why this particular proof was chosen is unclear, but it was surely driven more by corporate bottom lines than by flavor profiles. Watering down tequila to proof allows distillers to stretch their product, charge more for less. But it affects the taste, making for a vaguer, tamer spirit. It certainly is not how mezcal de Tequila was originally enjoyed. Early distillers preferred to drink their spirit at a higher proof, and traditional mezcal producers still do. A trend in overproof spirits across nearly all liquor categories, inspired by vintage bottlings and encouraged by many of today's bartenders and mixologists, has finally trickled over into the tequila sector. Several producers are bucking the 80-proof norm and offering higher proof tequilas, up to 55 percent ABV. These are great for mixing into cocktails, which get diluted by juice and ice. But overproof tequila is also great for sipping neat: alcohol, like fat, is a natural vehicle for flavor.

Perhaps the most insidious and perplexing bylaw within tequila's appellation of origin regulations that is attributed to corporate influence is the one that allows mixto tequila to be sold in bulk and bottled outside Mexico. In 2010, more than half of all tequila exports were sold in bulk. Once it leaves Mexico's borders, the CRT has much less control over how the spirit is handled, packaged, and sold. Critics of this bylaw argue that allowing tequila to be shipped outside Mexico in bulk hurts the spirit's authenticity and can only serve to profit the largest producers. It directly affects people working in tequila country by reducing the total number of jobs within the appellation.[18] It also prevents the CRT from being able to properly control quality. Worst of all, it makes tequila just that much less Mexican, a product whose final stamp of approval can be bestowed by Texans, Spaniards, the Chinese, just about anyone.

If small farmers and producers were in charge of the original design and current management of the appellation of origin, things might be different. It might not be legal for nearly 50 percent of most tequila to contain ingredients that could come from anywhere in the world. It might not be so easy for foreign entities to buy up so much of the industry. And there might be a stronger focus on the traditional farming and production methods that are quickly disappearing. But it's also quite possible that the industry wouldn't be as vast as it is. So many geographic indicators are tethered to the past. Tequila's seems shaped by the visions its biggest players have for the future.

{5}

The Terroir of Tequila

The soil is the great connector of lives, the source and destination of all.
—Wendell Berry, *The Unsettling of America*

People from Rio de Janeiro are called Cariocas. New Zealanders are Kiwis. Those who hail from Guadalajara are known as Tapatíos. Go figure. The term is said to be a Spanish adulteration of the old Nahuatl word *tapatiotl*, referring to an ancient currency used in pre-Columbian markets by the indigenous people of the Valley of Atemajac, located in what is now the greater metropolitan area of Guadalajara. It supposedly consisted of tiny bags filled with cocoa beans. Three of these were equal to one tapatiotl.[1] The currency eventually became obsolete, but the inhabitants of the region adopted the term to describe themselves: three times better than the rest. Today, only people born and raised in Guadalajara can lay claim to the term, and they do so proudly. Those born elsewhere who move to the city later in life don't even try to call themselves Tapatío. They demur, accepting their inferior status with good humor.

Felipe Camarena was a proud Tapatío who decided to claim the term for his tequila brand back in 1937. His grandfather had grown and distilled agave, which at the time was not unlike making moonshine. The spirit he produced had no name, no printed labels. It was just something he made for himself and his neighbors. The distillery, made of adobe, was out in the middle of nowhere, a rough two-day ride on horseback from the nearest town. It was abandoned and destroyed during the throes of the Mexican Revolution, or maybe during the Cristero War that soon followed. In any case, when the family was forced to stop distilling, they kept growing agave to sell to other established distilleries. The Sauza family bought the Camarenas' agave during times of shortage. But in times of glut, it didn't, despite having a contract with the family. One day, Felipe decided he would no longer be a victim of the fickle agave market. He would make his own tequila like his grandfather had done and set out to build a new distillery on the outskirts of Arandas, a town that today has some forty-five thousand inhabitants.

Felipe and his brother, Augustine, built their distillery in an agave field in 1937. They named it La Alteña, which translates as "she from the highlands." Business was so good that they built a second one closer to town the following year. Their tequila was made exactly the same way from exactly the same agaves in both locations and sold out of Felipe's home in the town center. But soon, customers began asking specifically for tequila from La Alteña. But why, thought Felipe, when both spirits underwent the exact same process, made from agaves from the exact same fields? It turns out that there was one important difference between the two: the distillery closer to town used water from a nearby well, while the one in the fields used natural spring water. Different minerals in the water gave each spirit its own flavor profile and the Camarenas' regular customers could tell. This falls into the realm of what one might refer to as terroir.

Eventually, Felipe and Augustine decided to go their separate ways. Augustine went on to produce his own successful brand that still exists today. His brother continued to produce tequila at La Alteña. He eventually passed the company on to his son, also named Felipe, who passed it on to his son, Carlos, and two daughters, Lilianna and Gabriela.

"I have a lot of family in this area producing tequila," says Carlos Camarena, sitting behind the large desk in his grandfather's old home in Arandas, which doubles as his office and a tiny bottling operation. There are circular stains on the old stone floors where barrels were stacked a generation ago. "It's in our genes, I guess."

La Alteña's house brand is Tapatio, which the company has made for more than eighty years, although the process to make it has modernized. Namely, it's no longer made with stone-crushed agave since the company installed a roller mill. But that doesn't mean the company's old tahona is no longer in use. Carlos's father launched a brand for the export market that became a treasure to tequila lovers north of the border. Fittingly, it was called El Tesoro, a tequila made using 100 percent blue agave and ancient methods, including the tahona to press the agave. It was named in honor of the first Felipe, as in "El Tesoro de Don Felipe," and made in the same facility as Tapatio. The rest of the process for the company's two tequila brands is largely the same: baking the agaves in brick ovens for at least thirty-six hours at a temperature of less than 150 degrees Fahrenheit and fermenting naturally in open wooden tanks for three to five days. El Tesoro is distilled to proof so that no extra water need be added before bottling.

Carlos, with his lean, wiry frame and twitchy mustache, has the nervous, self-effacing air of a well-meaning used car dealer keen to point out the next piece of equipment or cool feature as we walk around the distillery. Or maybe it's just that I've caught him when he's trying to cut back on a decades-long smoking habit and it has him a little jumpy. Over heavily sugared coffee, he explains how the company has had to modernize to keep up with volume as it grows. In 2013, he introduced Tapatio to the US market. The greater demand forced the company out of his grandfather's home, which has acted as its headquarters for three generations. It's a nice problem to have, as Carlos believes his father would have said. He's had to buy a bottling machine. For years, bottling and labeling were done by hand in a room behind Carlos's office; the company in the last decade switched to self-adhesive labels from its own house-made glue mixed from flour and water. Electricity was installed at the distillery only in the last two decades, mostly to run lights. Carlos will not sell his grandfather's house, but he has moved the bulk of operations out to a new building next to La Alteña. The house will remain intact and may even be transformed into a sort of museum like Guillermo Sauza's property in Tequila.

With growth comes the opportunity to try new things. Several years ago Carlos teamed up with international tequila ambassador Tomas

Estes, one of the most influential people in the industry, to create a new brand based on a rather Old World idea. (The National Chamber for the Tequila Industry named two official tequila ambassadors, one to the United States and one to Europe. They each had to complete comprehensive training in how to make and taste tequila and are charged with promoting the spirit in their respective territories.) Together they created Tequila Ocho to showcase the terroir of highland tequila, treating the spirit like a fine European wine instead of a party drink. The idea was to create a line of single-estate tequilas, eight (ocho) in total, each one expressing the distinct characteristics of the individual field where its agaves were grown.

There's the 2009 bottling from Rancho Las Pomez in Jesús María county, not far from La Alteña, which is bright and fruity with a hint of spice on the finish. The hilly field sits at an altitude of more than sixty-seven hundred feet above sea level, where the iron-rich soil is a deep, rusty red. This tequila is distinct from the Rancho Los Mangos, made from agaves grown close to the Michoacán border along the Río Lerma where the altitude is just over five thousand feet above sea level and the soil is ashy brown. The climate at Los Mangos is hot and dry, causing the piñas to come in super sweet, with a sugar content up to 4 percent higher than the industry average. The tequila tends to be spicy and herbaceous. But the different soils and altitudes aren't the only aspects of terroir that affect the flavors in the final product. Each bottle of Ocho is also marked with a vintage, just like wine is: a first for tequila. From year to year, and batch to batch, the tequila from a single estate can change ever so subtly.

"People have talked about terroir in tequila before, but we are really showing it," beams Carlos.

Terroir is a concept considered legitimate enough to be studied and quantified by academics across various fields. Yet even in the world of wine, where it originated, it's a touchy subject. In the world of spirits, it's even more controversial.

For serious wine folk, there is usually a sip that changes everything. Wine lovers like to talk about their moment, the wine that made them wine people. In that one instant, they are transformed from casual drinker into something more precise: a wine lover. An oenophile. For me, the moment occurred some years ago in Burgundy, that most revered of French wine-making regions. In a class at the Burgundy Wine School, students sit in a small theater, as if for a university lecture. Only here the desk has a sink for spitting and the classwork consists of a dozen glasses of wine to taste through. The course material, presented on slides projected onto the wall at the front of the class, amounted to little more than a geology lesson. Tectonic plates rubbing up against each other millions of years ago. Displaced rock. Minerals. Soil. How all this affects what grows in the soil. This was wine. And that's when I knew: this was for me.

I had a similar moment for tequila. Not the stumbling-drunk moment from my first experience with tequila shots, but my true tequila moment. By then I already knew there was good and bad tequila, but had never considered that it—or any spirit, really—could express terroir. During a professional tasting, I sampled several highland and valley tequilas side by side. Those from the same region shared characteristics suggesting that, yes, tequila could taste of its place.

In the Amatitán-Tequila Valley—often referred to as the lowlands, a term promulgated by marketers of highland tequilas that not only suggests the valley is inferior, but also fails to communicate its impressive altitude of some forty-five hundred feet above sea level—the soil is volcanic, the color of smoke. It's here that tequila was most likely first produced on a commercial basis. Agave has been farmed in these soils for centuries. The land is now stressed, according to industry experts, referring to the depletion of the soil's nutrients from overuse. But the valley can still make beautiful tequila. Valley tequilas are said to be more herbal, express more minerality, a result of the volcanic soils and a hotter, drier climate than you find in the highlands. The heat encourages agaves to mature faster, meaning they don't have time to get quite as plump as highland piñas.

The highlands—Los Altos, in Spanish—are known for their red, iron-streaked soils. After a rain the iron oxide is visible to the naked eye, black tiger-striped into brick-colored earth. You can hold a magnet over the dirt and suck the shavings of iron deposits right out of the ground. Agave was first planted in the highlands more than a century after it was cultivated in the Amatitán Valley. The region is said to produce tequilas that are richer and fruitier than those from the valley. The agaves here grow larger and sweeter thanks to a cooler climate that allows the piñas to mature slowly.

Terroir comes up a lot in reference to geographic indicators. It's said to refer to a "sense of place," but what exactly does that mean? In the place where the term originated, ask a hundred different winemakers what terroir means to them and you're likely to get a hundred different answers. But the underlying theme is always the same: terroir is truth. It's an unspoken language that communicates the very essence of a physical location and the traditions that have long been practiced there. It's the earth speaking through plants and the people who tend them. The term was coined by the French as early as the fourteenth century to characterize the elusive quality that results when a specific combination of soil, climate, topography, sun exposure, vegetation, and human intervention comes together. Specifically, it's what links an agricultural product's taste to its biophysical environment.

Assessing terroir is tricky. The oenophilic geologist James E. Wilson, who examined the subject intimately in his book *Terroir: The Role of Geology, Climate, and Culture in the Making of French Wines*, took up many pages waxing poetic on the term. It's about more than simple ecology, he writes:

"Terroir has become a buzz word in English language wine literature. This lighthearted use disregards reverence for the land which is a critical, invisible element of the term. The true concept is not easily grasped but includes physical elements of the vineyard habitat—the vine, subsoil, siting, drainage and microclimate. Beyond the measurable ecosystem, there is an additional dimension—the spiritual aspect that recognizes the joys, the heartbreaks, the pride, the sweat, and the frustrations of its history."[2]

Clearly, terroir is not hard science. Despite the pervasive use of the term when discussing wine and other appellation of origin–protected products, describing it can involve tapping into one's more lyrical sensibilities. So, perhaps it should come as no surprise that in recent years, as wine-making becomes increasingly scientific, the very notion of terroir has come under attack. Malcolm Gluck, the longtime wine critic at the British newspaper the *Guardian*, famously proclaimed, "Terroir is rubbish," earning at once praise and contempt from people at different ends of the terroir-appreciation spectrum. A number of studies conducted in recent years aim to debunk the concept of terroir. Yet professional tasters around the world swear that it's slate they detect in that German riesling, limestone in that Chablis; that the relationship between grapes and rocks, as Wilson puts it, exists.

As for the relationship between rocks and agave, that's a whole other issue. Other spirits producers have dabbled with the idea of terroir. Bourbon makers, for example, will testify that the pure, limestone-rich waters of Kentucky are the key to the local whiskey's flavor. But they rarely make much mention of the grains used being particular to the region. In Scotland, distillers sing the praises of their peat, harvested from lovingly preserved bogs. But even the few scotch companies that own their own barley fields refrain from placing too much emphasis on what the un-malted grain brings to the flavor profile of the final product. The base ingredients in any whiskey—wheat, rye, barley, corn—are hearty staples that can grow just about anywhere. Their flavor doesn't tend to change much whether they're grown in Kentucky or Tennessee or upstate New York or even Ireland, Scotland, Russia, or China. In other words, grain is not a good transmitter of terroir. Sure, there are niche distillers who insist on organic or locally grown grain, but the raw materials aren't necessarily what gives a whiskey its unique flavor. It's the recipe—the ratio of corn to rye and wheat, say, and how the spirit is aged that makes each whiskey distinct.

Herein lies the reason tequila and mezcal are arguably the most terroir-driven spirits out there: they're made from an indigenous raw material that is native and unique to Mexico. The local climate, soil, topography, and human tradition have a significant effect on how the tequila or mezcal ends up tasting. And the final product can be bottled as is, as opposed to being modified by a foreign-made barrel (most barrels are made in the United States or Europe). Once we start talking about mezcal, which can be made from a number of different agave species, each reflecting its own unique biophysical growing conditions, the concept of terroir becomes an even bigger part of the story.

Carlos, who in addition to heading up the company acts as the master distiller at La Alteña, takes me out to the fields just outside the distillery. My feet, foolishly shod in white Birkenstocks, gather dust from the rust-colored earth, which stains my toes and the sandals' leather. Carlos points out a sad, wilted plant, announcing, "Today, we will harvest this one!" It must be ten years old. Few tequila distillers wait this long to harvest their agave. The dried, bowed leaves of the plant belie the fat, ripe piña beneath them. Carlos spends as much time as possible in the fields, which isn't quite as common as you'd expect among tequila company executives. The bigger the company, the further from the fields the CEO tends to spend his time. But Carlos is obsessed with his agaves and the way the different micro-terroirs of his fields affect the piñas.

"I used to say that making tequila is very simple. It only consists of a four-step process: cooking, squeezing, fermenting, and distilling," Carlos says. His thin, tan face is full of expression, his hands always working and gesticulating as he talks and smokes. "However, this considers only the production process inside the distillery. From our particular point of view, it all starts with selecting the raw materials we want to process to make sure they have the desired quality, then not doing anything to compromise that."

And what about the human part of terroir? At La Alteña, it comes in the form of the jimadores who harvest the agaves, many of whom are related and whose families have been working for the Camarenas since the first Felipe's time. Guillermo, who is fifty-two, has harvested agave since he was thirteen. I meet him in the field as he digs up a ripe, bleeding plant, lopping off the long, pointy leaves with the agility of a much younger man. He points out several members of his family working the field alongside him. Carlos knows them all by name, from the strapping young men listening to iPods to the rugged old timers who have done the job for decades. This is another rarity among the CEOs of bigger tequila companies, whose jimadores might change from season to season—even day to day.

The human part of terroir is also present in the distillery workers who cook, mash, and ferment the agaves, and the four brothers who perform distillation. Before the brothers, their father and uncles did the job. Perhaps a young daughter spotted playing outside will one day take over. Even the security guard, if that's what he can be called (he's a slow-moving senior who does little more than grunt at visitors passing through), has spent most of his life at the distillery. He retired years ago, but kept coming to work. Carlos never had the heart to turn him away. He believes all these people help make his tequila taste of its place.

Tequila Ocho, with its focus on terroir and vintage, is a pet project for Carlos. Tapatio is his family's legacy. El Tesoro, a product his father created to export to the United States, is not as easy to characterize. Carlos's father had originally designed the brand in collaboration with the tequila importers Robert Denton and Marilyn Smith, who held on to the brand's distribution rights over the years. The pair were rare in the tequila business. True tequila geeks, they were known for importing well-made, terroir-driven brands like El Tesoro and Chinaco to the United States before most Americans even knew such products existed. They did a lot to educate Americans about good tequila, and many of the Americans who paid heed happened to be winemakers in California. Their understanding of grapes helped them appreciate the nature of agave and tequila. The partners ended up selling their stake in El Tesoro to an American company called Fortune Brands in 1999. This meant that Carlos's family became partners with the firm.

A little more than a decade later, Fortune Brands divested itself of its non-spirits endeavors and reconstituted itself as Beam, Inc. Because it already had such a tequila giant—Sauza—in its portfolio, El Tesoro was overshadowed. The brand became neglected, even though Beam held a 50 percent stake. Sales stagnated while Sauza's sales skyrocketed. Eventually, Carlos, along with his mother and sisters, were faced with the decision to buy back the brand completely (at an outrageous price) or sell it whole. They opted to sell. The tequila would still be made at La Alteña, Carlos the contracted producer, but the brand would be owned entirely by Beam. Sales of El Tesoro dipped even further. And so, Carlos decided to branch out with Ocho and refocus his efforts on Tapatío. Unfortunately, he is prohibited from making another tequila using 100 percent tahona-crushed agave as long as he's still contracted to make El Tesoro. In early 2014, Beam was acquired by Suntory, a Japanese whiskey and beer maker. At the time, it was unclear what the new owners would want to do with El Tesoro. Carlos suspected it might be absorbed by Sauza. Or it might die. Either way, the first thing he plans to do when his contract to make El Tesoro is up is to roll out a new tahona-crushed tequila brand.

After visiting the fields, we return to the distillery, where he pours me a *cuernito* of Tapatío. (A *cuerno*, or the diminutive cuernito, is a hollowed-out horn from a cow or bull used as a tiny cup from which to drink tequila. Consider it the original shot glass.) The tequila is richly flavored, creamy, and full of spice. You might say that the cuernito is also part of the local terroir. The tequila tastes different drunk from this vessel of animal bone than in, say, a Riedel glass, which is probably the most fashionable glass to sip tequila from nowadays.

Oenophiles know Riedel as the Austrian glassware company that specializes in crystal and glassware. For example, it sells a glass specifically designed for crisp, aromatic sauvignon blanc that is tall and slender with an elongated bowl. The company's chardonnay glass is short and fat with a bowl so round it's practically a halved sphere. There is even a glass designed explicitly for scotch that looks like a stretched, narrow, handle-less teacup. Each glass design is created to accentuate the aromas and flavors typically found in a particular type of wine or spirit. When you tip the glass back for a sip, the shape of it ensures that the liquid hits a precise part of the palate to provide the most complete and pleasurable experience.

The company offers "glassware tastings" for those who remain skeptical. I attended one in Riedel's Manhattan headquarters some years back. Its showroom is so filled with breakables that one's instinct is to tiptoe. The tasting was led by Maximilian J. Riedel, the CEO and eleventh generation to head the glassware dynasty. He is slim with fine features and always well put together in a European-cut suit. It's nearly impossible to remain unconvinced by his spiel, delivered in a singsongy accent and designed to appeal to both the scientific and sensual-minded. The real clincher comes once you taste a tightly wound, sharp Pinot Noir in a regular glass, then take a sip of the exact same wine from a Riedel glass. The second sip is inevitably better. The glass is shaped to aerate the wine and when it reaches your tongue, it's full of whatever notes and aromas experienced tasters are meant to pick up: cherry, violet, pencil shavings, perhaps. In a way, you can say that Riedel's glasses are designed to help people taste better. As the flavors bloom in the glass, they become easier to identify.

Riedel's tequila glass, introduced in 2002, was created when the CRT decided Mexico's illustrious spirit deserved a vessel of its own. There already existed glasses for every wine variety under the sun, including fortified wines like port, as well as luxury liquors like cognac and scotch. What better way to reinforce the global status tequila had achieved as a sipping spirit than to invent a glass designed specifically for sipping it? The experts at Riedel joined forces with several tequila makers and tasters to create a delicate flute, not unlike a champagne glass, only slightly shorter. The basic design, which has since been copied by other companies, features a fine stem and elongated, narrow bowl that acts as a sort of traffic channel for aromas. The aromas in a glass of tequila want to emerge from the glass rather boisterously, like kids pouring out of school the minute the bell rings, all grappling for attention. It can be overwhelming. The shape of Riedel's tequila glass forces them to get in line and march out quietly and in order, so that the imbiber can isolate and process them accordingly. It's a far cry from a shot glass.

Equipped with a French wine term and Austrian-designed tasting glass, tequila certainly has evolved. It's now a global spirit and a luxury one, at that. But has its evolution distanced tequila from its sense of place? Modernists will say no; traditionalists will say yes. In my humble opinion, it's well worth it to taste a well-made tequila out of a Riedel glass. And it's just as worthwhile to sip it from a cuernito, should you ever get the chance. One will show you just how refined fine tequila can be. The other will take you back to the spirit's roots.

{6}

La Ruta del Mezcal

Para todo mal, mezcal
y para todo bien, también.
—Oaxaqueño saying

Abel Nolasco Velasco leans in close to a wooden tank that isn't quite as tall as he is. It's filled with gurgling maguey juice and fibers happily undergoing fermentation. Abel cups a thick, rough hand to his ear. He has a bearish build, grizzly black beard, prominent brow, and sweet smile. The sounds emanating from the tank are not unlike the snap-crackle-and-pop of morning cereal. "You can hear the fermentation," he says. "Listen." He leans his head against the tank and listens a while longer, allowing his eyes to flutter closed and a grin to spread across his lips.

We are in Oaxaca, high in the hills of the Sierra Madre del Sur, at Abel's *palenque*, the name given to the ramshackle distilleries where mezcal is made. There is no sign on the door; there is no door. The facility is little more than an open-air shelter with a thatched roof. There is no electricity, none needed. The agave roasts in a conical underground pit for four or five days over red-hot stones. The piñas are covered with a layer of spent agave fibers. The stone mill used for crushing the agave—mostly referred to as maguey around these parts—is pulled by a horse. The fermentation takes place naturally in open wooden tanks. The stills are heated using firewood. The first distillation might take ten hours;

the result is called *ordinario* and clocks in around 12 to 18 percent ABV. The second distillation brings the proof up to anywhere from 55 to 70 percent. Abel is one of sixty mezcal producers—*maestro mezcaleros,* they're called reverentially—who distill under the Yuu Baal brand. It's one of the few producer-owned mezcal brands available for purchase in the United States.

The southwestern state of Oaxaca (pronounced wa-HA-kah) is known as the "land of the seven moles," a culinary capital of Mexico. Really, as one chef shared with me, there are far more than seven of the rich sauces. There are as many as there are resourceful grandmothers who have tossed together peppers, nuts, seeds, and spices in a fragrant puree to serve over chicken and rice. In addition to the cuisine, Oaxaca is also a mecca for mezcal.

Mezcal is the mother of tequila and, for many tequila enthusiasts, the inevitable destination on the path to seeking out the truest expressions of the spirit. It's made in nearly all of Mexico's thirty-one states, but only officially recognized in nine of them. In Oaxaca, it's a way of life. As one brand owner defines it, the mezcal here is "pre-organic." It's often made from wild agaves as opposed to cloned, farmed plants. In many cases, the agave is harvested by the same hand that will ferment and distill it. The spirits made here are truly small-batch, as artisanal as it gets. For generations, mezcaleros in the wilds of the Mexican countryside made their potent spirit just for their families and neighbors. It was rarely peddled beyond the local community. Certain mezcales from Oaxaca, however, are finding their way across the border to the United States.

When I first landed in the city of Oaxaca, I'd hoped to visit the makers of several of the mezcales I'd tasted back home. But the happiest surprise is the many mezcales that are not available outside the region. I arrived on a sun-drenched Sunday. But it could just as easily have been a Tuesday. The blue-skied days are known to bleed together here in a dreamy smear of good vibes. You feel it as soon as you deplane: police officers in the airport and around town are bare faced. They need not hide behind masks like in other parts of the country where being a cop makes you a cartel target.

The city is beautiful. Bright yellows, blues, and pinks make up its palette. It's easy to see why so many artists end up here, often more permanently than they'd planned. It's not only colorful in the literal sense of the word, Oaxaca is also the most multicultural state in Mexico, known as the country's cradle of diversity. The number of ethnolinguistic groups here is officially sixteen, but researchers have counted thousands of subcultures, each maintaining its own customs and folklore. The two largest indigenous groups are the Zapotecs and Mixtecs, who among them speak dozens of different dialects. On street corners in Oaxaca, elderly ladies dressed in colorful woven fabrics sell fresh mango sprinkled with lime, salt, and chili powder. Others sell the festively painted Oaxacan folk art pieces that have enchanted visitors for ages.

My suitcase soon fills up with these intricately hand-carved and painted wooden animal figurines: a gum-ball-sized porcupine with bright fuchsia and mauve spikes, a fire-engine-red cat with devil wings painted in yellow flames, a rainbow-colored armadillo with big cartoon eyes. Pieces that are big enough are signed by the artist on the foot or belly. Often, the artist will include the name of his or her town. It's not uncommon for artists and craftsmen in Oaxaca to work communally rather than individually, selling their wares on behalf of their village. It's the same with the local chocolate makers, who grind cocoa beans by hand to be used in chili-laced chocolate bars or in the region's rich moles. The local potters and weavers are also known to work together as a village to peddle their ceramics and textiles.

Abel and his fellow Yuu Baal mezcaleros work much the same way. Instead of each selling his product individually, they have banded together so that everyone benefits. With such small-batch production, ongoing consumer demand would be difficult for a single mezcalero to meet. Indeed, this is one of the main obstacles for mezcal producers looking to gain access to the export market. Other obstacles include the legal paperwork involved in being certified by the Consejo Mexicano Regulador de la Calidad del Mezcal or CRM, a body similar to tequila's CRT that regulates mezcal production and manages its appellation of origin. Then there are the logistics of getting one's product into a foreign market: distribution, marketing, customer relations, and especially meeting the regulatory standards of the importing country. For people who live and work in remote mountain villages where Spanish is a second language, selling their product abroad is often inconceivable. Yet the export market is an attractive one for mezcaleros: US tariffs on alcohol are far lower than domestic ones.

By working cooperatively, Yuu Baal's members can produce enough mezcal to export the product to the United States on an ongoing basis. Mezcaleros in the group are also free to sell their product via other channels individually in addition to contributing to Yuu Baal if they so desire. By pooling resources, they are able to hire the appropriate agents to represent their mezcal on either side of the border. Of course, don't expect every bottle of Yuu Baal to taste like the last. The flavor profile can change from batch to batch and producer to producer.

The woman who was scheduled to pick me up to take me to visit Abel's palenque is late. I'm not bothered: this is often the way in Oaxaca. Schedules are loosely adhered to, if at all. People here go with the flow. It didn't take me long to let this tide take me. Just days after my arrival, I had already fallen out of the habit of constantly checking my phone for important e-mails or missed calls. When the woman finally arrives, we embrace like old friends. This is also the way here. Flor de Maria Velázquez Mijangos is married to one of the mezcaleros in the Yuu Baal cooperative, Jorge Alberto Ramirez Marquez. He is the leader of the group. In her poky hatchback, we make our way to the tiny Zapotec village of San Luis del Río.

Flor is responsible for Yuu Baal's international sales and marketing. She is a big-boned woman with a broad, round face and a rather foul mouth. Her sense of humor suggests she might have fit in well with my college crowd. Over the long drive, we become fast friends. As we make our way to the palenque, she recounts how Yuu Baal got started. Her husband, Jorge, once belonged to a group of some 170 mezcaleros that traded under the name Lash Doob. In the mid-1990s, around the time the spirit earned its appellation of origin, the demand for good, unadulterated mezcal began to rise.

Like tequila's appellation of origin, mezcal's was to be regulated under the country's Norma Oficial Mexicana standards. Jorge decided to get his mezcal certified under these new regulations. It was a controversial decision. While many mezcaleros supported the idea of an appellation of origin and NOM rules, others did not. They feared the high costs and bureaucratic hoops they would be forced to jump through under the appellation's strict regulations. Certain producers simply worried about no longer being able to doctor their spirit with cheaper distillates and flavorings.

Several mezcaleros who did not support the new regulations threatened Jorge when they caught wind of his plans for certification. According to Flor, they even tried to kill him. They spread rumors about the high costs and regulatory restrictions associated with certification. Under this pressure, Jorge's group of mezcaleros disbanded. A splinter group eventually formed. In 1995, led by Jorge, its members became some of the first to be officially certified under the new NOM rules to produce, sell, and export their mezcal. The group decided it needed a brand name and settled on the Zapotec words Yuu Baal, which translate as "earth and fire." The name represents the duality of mezcal: the spirit hails from the earth, but must be made using fire; maguey and mezcal are seen as female, but the mezcalero is usually male. You can even perceive—if you look very closely at the label—a penis and vagina in the logo, which was designed by a friend of Flor's from Universidad Tecnológica de la Mixteca in Oaxaca.

In Flor's hatchback, it takes a couple of hours for us to leave the zigzag of the paved road. We turn off onto a rocky path that affords us incredible views of the imposing Sierra Madre. Less than thirty minutes from our destination, a large object falls from the sky and almost strikes the car. It is a piña that has rolled down the steep hill above us, forcing us to come to an abrupt, dust-scattering stop. We step out of the vehicle and look up to where the piña came from. A lone figure stands on the hill with a large machete in hand. He is harvesting agave on a slope so steep that we must crane our necks to talk to him. We ask if he would mind us coming up to watch him work. He grunts his consent. Without proper hiking boots, we struggle up the incline to where the man is working and anchor ourselves at an awkward angle so as not to slip back down. He agrees to being photographed with a shrug, but doesn't pose or smile. He keeps his back to us and answers our questions shortly and gruffly.

In tequila country, an agave field is harvested by a team of men. It's surprising to see a man doing this grueling work alone and on such a perilously sharp bluff. Any misstep might cause him to roll down the hill after one of his piñas, although the chances of him landing in the path of a speeding car are slim: the dirt road is deserted. After a brief, laconic exchange, we pick our way back down the hill toward the hatchback. On the way, Flor plucks some mysterious desert fruit from a brambly bush on the side of the road and pops it into her mouth. I eat one, too. It's some sort of wild plum that tastes sweet and tart and a little grassy, like a tomato. Another pleasant surprise.

The village of San Luis del Río is wedged into the mountainside in such a way that feels as though residents must cling to it for fear of falling off. The houses on one side look down onto the roofs of their neighbors across the street. Beyond that, the view is of craggy mountains. We stop into the home of Doña Josefina, Abel's mother. It's a traditional home with a brick oven just outside the kitchen door, where a fire is roaring away. The matriarch reaches into a big bowl of corn flour dough called *masa* and pulls out a small wad, slapping it into a flat tortilla shape. The fresh-pressed tortilla gets tossed onto a round steel plate that sits on top of the fire. In moments, it bubbles and fattens. She pulls it off as it quickly deflates and hands me the hot, slightly charred disk. It's probably the best tortilla I've ever had.

Doña Josefina then cracks a fist-sized egg directly onto the grill sheet over the fire: a turkey egg. (Chickens originally come from Asia, I'm told. Here, turkeys, native to North America, are raised instead.) Next, the woman tosses a few *nopales*—prickly pear cacti—that she's just finished paring the spines from onto the grill. Inside the darkened kitchen, a table is laden with platters of black beans and poblano peppers stuffed with queso fresco. Abel, his wife, his brothers, and a few children who belong to various siblings have gathered. Lunch at Doña Josefina's is integral to fueling the day's work. After the meal, we head to the palenque, where Abel shows me how he processes and cooks the maguey, then ferments and distills his mezcal. The process has changed little since the time of his father or his grandfather before that.

When they first discover mezcal, people always want to know: what's the difference between this and tequila? Considering that one spirit was born of the other, there are many distinctions, as it turns out. For one, tequila must be made from blue Weber but mezcal can be made from dozens of different species of agave. Tequila must be made in a well-defined territory that touches five states, but is focused in Jalisco. Mezcal is made across the country, each regional version of it distinct. Tequila is made in factories, in volumes large enough to meet a vast international demand. Mezcal is most often made for a local clientele in small, rustic facilities like Abel's palenque. Agaves for tequila are steamed in ovens and, increasingly, cooked using autoclaves or diffusers. The magueys used for mezcal are roasted in underground pits. Tequila is generally sold in the United States at 80 proof. Mezcal can be bottled at still proof—or whatever degree of alcohol the maker feels it tastes best at, be it 90 proof, 100, 110, or higher.

At least one large-scale mezcal company does exist in Oaxaca, manufacturing the spirit on a scale greater than even the biggest tequila companies. But most operations are intimate family affairs. The mezcalero harvests the agave himself, either from the hills he has cultivated outside his village or collected out in the wild, and transports it back to his palenque for cooking. Roasting begins with loading the agave into a conical pit oven dug into the ground. There, covered with spent maguey fibers, the piñas roast slowly over smoldering wood logs. The wood used—be it mesquite, eucalyptus, oak—has an effect on the resulting mezcal. Some mezcaleros use a tarp to cover the agave, while others opt for banana leaves. Even this variable can affect the final result. It takes at least four or five days for the agave heads to cook through—longer if it's too humid or cold out. It's this slow roasting in the fire pit that imparts the smoky flavor many people associate with mezcal.

The agaves are cooked until they're brown and caramelized, then pressed in a stone mill or mashed with a large club. This latter method is exceptionally demanding. As for the former, I met a few mezcaleros who talked about one day upgrading to a tractor to pull the heavy volcanic stone of the mill around the pit. But most prefer to use an animal for the job, if only because that's how their fathers and grandfathers did it. "Why change a good thing?" people will say. And who knows if the mule, with its musky scent and the flies it must constantly whip away with its tail, does something to enrich the flavor? Best not to mess with tradition.

As in the most artisanal of tequila distilleries, the agave juices and fibers are fermented together naturally in open wooden tanks. The wooden fermentation tanks can vary. Some are made of pine, others oak or some other local wood or even concrete. I tasted one mezcal that had been fermented in leather. It had the meaty whiff of animal skin and a distinctly salty edge. Fermentation can take a few days to several weeks, again depending on the weather.

Distillation follows, usually in small, copper pot stills, also with the fibers. "Small copper pot stills" in this case doesn't mean the same thing it does in tequila country. Tequila stills might have a capacity of anywhere from five hundred to ten thousand liters. In Oaxaca, you often find stills the size of grandma's favorite cauldron. They could fit on your kitchen countertop, yielding maybe 100 liters at a time. Certain mezcaleros distill in even smaller vessels made of clay.

Perhaps the most significant difference between the two spirits is the taste. Since it can only be made from one type of agave, tequila is rather limited in its range of flavors. Sure, tequilas from the highlands can differ from those made in the valley. Even within a given region, you'll find tequilas that vary in flavor thanks to terroir and different production methods. But variations from one tequila to the next are minimal compared to mezcal's breadth. Consider the differences you might notice between different chardonnays or pinot noirs. They surely can't compare to the differences between a chardonnay and a sauvignon blanc or a pinot noir and a cabernet.

What's more, as tequila companies switch to automated methods, the maker's hand in the recipe becomes less noticeable in the end product. Think of cooking with a microwave: it can't express a cook's skills or style the way slower cooking methods can. The variety of agave types, the hands-on production methods, and the range of terroirs in mezcal make for much more diversity in flavor. Diversity can even be found in two mezcales made by the same mezcalero. Aside from brands like Ocho, with its focus on terroir and vintage, tequilas tend to be consistent in their flavor profiles. One batch of Cuervo or Patrón will be identical to the next. And most big distillers buy agave from all over the appellation anyway, so the final product can't really have a link to a specific terroir. Mezcal, on the other hand, can vary significantly from batch to batch. Warmer temperatures or increased rainfall in a given season can impact flavor, as can the different micro-terroirs on a mezcalero's land. To taste tequila and mezcal side by side is to be struck by how wan tequila can be compared to the intensity and complexity of traditional mezcal.

While many tequila distilleries are equipped with nicely decorated tasting rooms to welcome visitors, most palenques don't have comfortable seating or even glassware for their tastings. Abel's palenque doesn't even have walls. We sip his spirit in the great outdoors under a cluster of tall trees next to the crystal clear creek Abel uses as his water source. The only sounds are those of the forest—chirping birds, rippling water, rustling leaves. Abel's horse takes a standing nap nearby and emits the occasional snort.

Before he pours it out for me to taste, Abel scoops up a bowlful of his mezcal in a *jícara*, a little cup made out of a halved and hollowed out gourd. I've seen other mezcaleros do this before. Using a long, hollow bamboo stick called a *venencia* as a sort of straw, he sucks up the mezcal. Only none touches his lips. Once the spirit reaches the top of the straw, he caps the top hole with his large, rough thumb, trapping the liquid inside. After a moment, he lets it out of the bottom and into the jícara. As it quickly fills the bowl, it froths and bubbles momentarily, then the bubbles pop and dissipate. "It's 51 percent alcohol," he announces. I raise an eyebrow and ask him how he knows. "I just do," he laughs, with a look more incredulous than my own. How could he *not* know? "My father taught me, my grandfather taught him. This is what we do."

Mezcaleros can tell the proof of their spirit using the venencia to within a degree or two of accuracy. They learn to read the bubbles or *perlas* (pearls): how fat and sparse they are or how small and foamy, how quickly they pop and dissipate, all point to the degree of alcohol in the spirit. Denser perlas mean a higher proof. And, as previously mentioned, a high proof is to be expected in mezcal. "Lower than 47 degrees [94 proof] and the flavor is no longer of maguey. It's water," I heard one mezcalero joke.

While there are dozens of agave varieties from which mezcal can be made, most of what is produced in Oaxaca is espadín. As an ancestor of blue agave, espadín looks and acts much like the tequila plant, except that it's bright green instead of bluish. Espadín takes on average eight to ten years to mature. Other varieties you're likely to come across in Oaxaca can take much longer. Wild-harvested madrecuixe can take up to twelve years to reach maturity. These long, baseball-bat-shaped piñas produce an aromatic, herbaceous spirit, often with a vegetal character. When it flowers, tepextate sprouts bright canary yellow flowers at the top of its quiote. These magueys can take an astonishing twenty-five years to reach maturity. This means that a mezcalero might spot one in the wild, but it won't be ready to harvest until he's passed his palenque on to his son. Mezcal made from this breed of agave is intensely perfumed, like strong cologne.

Tobalá, considered the king of the magueys, grows and ripens over fifteen years. Legend has it that tobalá is the original maguey. Aside from the lore attached to it, the reasons for its noble status are mostly biological. Firstly, it's small and therefore produces less mezcal, making it more precious than other varieties. On average, tobalá piñas won't grow much larger than a basketball. The mezcal produced from them has a distinct flavor, complex and rich, with fruity, floral, and savory notes. Finding the plants in the wild can be an athletic feat. They like to grow in high-altitude rocky soil, in the shade of other plants. Like other types of agave, tobalá reproduces sexually, but the plants do not produce hijuelos. The only chance tobalá has to propagate is to grow its quiote tall, past the trees and shrubs it likes to hide under, so that birds, moths, and bats will be able to locate and feast on its flowers.

Once the tobalá seed is spread, it has a much lower chance of survival than other types of maguey. Should it fall on solid rock, it will die. And any plant that grows from seed instead of an offshoot is less likely to make it to adulthood because it doesn't have a mother plant in whose shadow it can nourish itself. This also makes it more vulnerable to pests and predators. Once a mezcalero finds, waits for, and finally harvests his tobalá, you can bet he'll do everything in his power not to waste it. He'll cook it, ferment it, and distill it with the utmost care, and then peddle it proudly.

Not everyone agrees on how many varieties of agave are made into mezcal in Oaxaca. In a place where sixteen different ethnolinguistic groups are recognized and a third of the people speak an indigenous language wholly unrelated to Spanish, the notion of terroir can take on a whole new meaning. A particular species grown in one place is given a certain name, but the same genetic variety grown somewhere else might look, taste, and behave differently—and be called by a different name. Both geomorphic and ethnolinguistic variables are at play.

For example, under the genetic species of Karwinskii agave, you have madrecuixe. Only madrecuixe grown in, say, Chichicapam is called tobaziche. Because of these discrepancies, certain mezcal aficionados believe that agave varieties should be referred to by their Latin names instead of their colloquial ones. Most mezcaleros, however, are not all that concerned with these details. Traditional producers are known to make field blends using whatever types of agave happen to be harvested from a particular patch of land, much the way tequila was once made. For those making a spirit for their neighbors, specific varieties don't matter much, so long as the mezcal is delicious. Precise recipes and varietal data become more important when a mezcalero plans to bottle and export his product.

Most mezcal makes its way to the United States by way of a foreigner. Enchanted by the wild colors and flavors of Oaxaca, Americans and Europeans are known to come and stay. Or they come and decide to leave with a piece of the place to bring back to their own country. For many years, foreigners came to Oaxaca and left with its folk art, sometimes enough to start a lucrative art-dealing business back home. But recently the trend has been to come with the intent of finding a mezcal to build into a brand back home.

For an American looking to import the spirit, there are many maestro mezcaleros to choose from. The brand owner will build the company and its image, taking care of all the associated expenses and logistics from distribution to marketing, leaving the actual production of the mezcal to the craftsman in Oaxaca. The price the mezcalero gets for his product might be a fraction of what the brand owner will end up taking in back home. High-end mezcal can sell for a $100 a bottle or more in the United States. For both the mezcalero and the brand owner, mezcal is usually a labor of love. But few brands split their profits with their mezcalero, who is usually treated as a contractor.

Soon, the conversation at Abel's palenque turns to the business side of mezcal and I find myself fielding more questions than I'm asking. Flor and Abel are concerned with how the export of mezcal will affect their product and their culture. The story of tequila's so-called corruption is a cautionary tale among mezcaleros. No one wants to end up with a mass-produced, industrialized distillate. Yet everyone wants to make money, to share their handmade product with the world.

"We want to export, but we don't want to get too big, like tequila," says Flor, as the three of us sip Abel's mezcal under the trees. "We don't want to lose our culture."

"Already, most of the mezcal brands that export are owned by foreigners," Abel points out. "Some of them are good people, but . . . [it's a shame that it's the only way] for many of us to get our product into the United States."

"You've been to Jalisco," says Flor, turning to me. "What is it like there? Everything is industrialized? Big machines?"

"No, not everything," I answer, tentatively.

Neither she nor Abel have been to tequila country and both are curious. Like others in the mezcal industry, they have heard the horror stories of industrial production. They are surprised to learn that traditional producers do exist and are well respected among tequila enthusiasts. It seems to give them hope that financial success abroad and maintaining one's traditions at home might not be at the opposite ends of a spectrum of possibilities. Perhaps mezcal can find success beyond Mexico's borders without having to sacrifice its soul.

{7}

El Día del Magueyero

Gota gota gota gotita de mezcal
Dicen que tomando pierdes la cabeza y el dinero.
—LILA DOWNS, "MEZCALITO"

One of the first Americans to discover mezcal and bring it to the United States is a man by the name of Ron Cooper. Ron is slight and elfin, with a gentle curve to his upper spine that causes him to stoop ever so slightly. He wears his long black hair pulled back into a knot high on the top of his head, like a samurai. When I meet him in Oaxaca, he's dressed in jeans and a billowy white shirt. He likes to take credit for the growing popularity of mezcal in the United States, and rightfully so. Before he introduced good mezcal to Americans, they knew the spirit only as the foul stuff with the worm at the bottom of the bottle that was sold to tourists in Tijuana. Like a number of other Americans who are drawn to Oaxaca, he is an artist. He first came to this part of Mexico in 1970 on a lark.

"I grew up in Southern California and, as an artist, was one of the adventurous and crazy people who started the California light and space movement," Ron tells me as we make our way from the city of Oaxaca to Teotitlán del Valle, where his operation is based. "The movement was not particularly interested in images and telling stories, but about how we perceive things, what things feel like. Anyway, after a group show opening in L.A., a few of the artists involved sat down with the dealer, who was a tough Japanese poker player. She brought out the only good tequila in the US at the time, which was Herradura blanco."

The artists sat around drinking and talking, so the story goes. At one point, someone asked, "Does the Pan-American highway really exist?" Two weeks later, a few of the artists set off to find out. They drove south and in four months made it all the way to Panama. On the way, they had more than a few adventures, says Ron, including stopping in Oaxaca and discovering the place's many wonders. He and his friends were drawn to the village of Teotitlán del Valle, some fifteen miles outside Oaxaca. The village is known for its colorful handwoven rugs and tapestries, and the artists ended up collaborating with several of the local weavers on a series of works that were shown at galleries in the United States. But handicrafts weren't the only thing Ron would bring back to California. He returned to Oaxaca in 1990 to work on this art for three months. He also tasted good mezcal for the first time and fell in love.

Ron, whose work has been shown at the Whitney and the Guggenheim, used his time in Oaxaca to make art with the indigenous people there. One of the projects he intended to work on was a limited-edition blue glass bottle bearing the likeness of Ometochtli, the supreme god of intoxication and ecstasy, also known as the leader of the Centzon Totochtin, or four hundred rabbits. Ron hoped to fill the bottles with the best mezcal he could find. So, for three months, he stalked the dirt roads around Teotitlán, asking any native he came upon where to find the best mezcal. The answers he got would send him on daylong journeys into the mountains to remote ranchos and pueblos where farmers were making some of the finest mezcal he'd tasted.

"The flavors were incredible and so were the effects," Ron recalls. "It wasn't like anything I'd ever experienced. I realized I had to make this available to my friends back home."

Unlike tequila, mezcal must by law be bottled at origin. It cannot be exported in bulk and bottled elsewhere. The mezcal Ron was tasting in these remote mountain villages never left the area in anything other than used soda bottles or in jerry cans rinsed clean of fuel. So, the first few times Ron brought some of the spirit back to California with him, he transported it in one of these containers. On one trip, he was stopped at the border with a five-gallon jug of wedding mezcal given to him as a gift by a Zapotec weaver. When the border patrolman forced him to dump the precious liquid, made with care and time from plants that took more than a decade to grow, he decided right then and there to start a company that would bottle and label mezcal for legal export. He would call his venture Del Maguey.

"You don't find mezcal," he tells me, as we stand in his storage room surrounded by dozens of bottles. "Mezcal finds you." We are sipping a wild arroqueño, part of a line of varietal mezcales aptly called the Vino de Mezcal series, which he distributes in the United States. If you make the effort to go all the way to Oaxaca to visit Ron Cooper, he will probably at some point ask: "Do you want to have an adventure?" Twenty years after he started selling mezcal, he still makes regular trips out to remote villages to find great producers of the spirit so he can continue to expand his Del Maguey line. The villages might be hours away along rough roads, but the trip can be well worth it, he says. For now, he exports mezcales from eight different villages to the United States.

Instead of a mountain adventure, Ron and I head out to the village of Tlacolula de Matamoros, which attracts Oaxaqueños from around the region for its massive weekly markets where you can buy everything from live turkeys to fresh produce to artisanal goods, like ceramics and textiles. Today is not market day, though. It's El Día del Magueyero: maguey farmer's day, an annual event not unlike a county fair, with prize maguey competitions, practical farming resources, and plenty of networking and catching up between mezcaleros. Ron fills a plastic water bottle with some of his mezcal so he can dole out samples to anyone who might want a taste. "You're going to need one of these," he says, handing me a tiny terra-cotta copita. "I always keep one in my pocket so if ever I meet someone whose mezcal I want to try, I can just pull it out." This turns out to be excellent advice.

El Día del Magueyero is well attended this year, despite the overcast, softly spitting sky threatening a downpour. As soon as we arrive, Ron starts making the rounds, trading hellos with various mezcal producers and a few mezcal bar owners, whose city girlfriends in their high heels and dark eye makeup seem out of place in the dusty bucolic setting. The magueys entered into the competition are all lined up according to variety. The espadín are monstrous, like dinosaur eggs. The tobalá are smaller, but large for their breed, around the size of healthy Halloween pumpkins. Old, weathered men tote their jerry cans and soda bottles of mezcal. They pour out a capful for anyone interested in a taste, proud to share the fruits of their labor. A large tent covers several dozen tables, where a delicious lunch of tortillas, rice, beans, and a saucy, spicy chicken dish will be served. But before everyone is seated, a ceremony must take place.

On the dirt ground beyond the tent, a Zapotec priestess prepares to perform a ritual. Dressed in a long white tunic, she enters a circle drawn in the earth. The ritual involves tossing corn kernels around the circle as she speaks sacred words. Children in traditional white homespun cotton garb are called upon to gather the kernels. Once gathered, they collect agave plantlets that have been placed around the circle and present them to a few of the spectators. Those who receive the plants light up. "I will plant this and make the best mezcal from it!" one man says. The priestess begins wrapping up the ceremony. She blesses the day, the children, Oaxaca, Mexico, and Latin America. Then, she takes a bottle of good mezcal and empties half its contents on the ground as an offering to the gods and those who are no longer with us. She lowers herself to the earth, just barely touching her lips to it.

The sun beats down overhead. But in an instant, the skies open and the sandy ground turns muddy. Everyone takes cover under the tent. Several of the event's organizers begin circulating forms to fill out so they can keep track of who is in attendance. Soon after, boxes of chicken and rice are handed out. A few of the older men, with their rough farmer hands, grip the pencils they've been handed clumsily and look down at their sheets of paper with blank faces as the rest of us scribble our answers hastily and dig in. A helpful young woman moves briskly from table to table, reading the form questions out to those who cannot read Spanish and filling in the answers for them. Ron says that he too has often helped magueyeros with official paperwork, be it for business or just to see a doctor. He and I share a table with several other men, each of whom has plunked down a receptacle of his own spirit. Everyone begins trading samples, tasting each other's product and critiquing it rather openly. A man with a brown, weatherbeaten face, a few missing teeth, and fingers stained with dirt and the spicy red sauce from the chicken pronounces his mezcal better than Ron's. He's grinning impishly, but means what he says. I wonder what he would make of Ron's claim that he put mezcal on the map.

"When I started, there were only two mezcales in the United States and they were both diesel with a worm at the bottom," Ron says back at his warehouse. He points out the simple mattress on which he sleeps in the space above the storage room. There is no doubt he is passionate and committed to what he does: there are no fortunes to be made in small-batch mezcal. Not yet, at least. "Even in the city of Oaxaca, when I started, the only mezcales there—there were about four or five—were all adulterated with grain alcohol, food coloring, water, flavoring, and they all had worms in them. I changed the culture of Mexico. Because now, in Oaxaca, anyone under the age of thirty-five doesn't drink tequila. They drink mezcal. There are these incredible mezcal bars opening all over the place that are serving farmer-made mezcal. To give a gringo credit, when I started in 1995, there wasn't another organic, handmade, un-watered-down, unadulterated mezcal outside of these little villages."

It's a big claim, but Ron Cooper makes it: he changed the culture of Mexico. It may sound like an arrogant thing for an American to say, but he has a point. Before he began shining a light on traditional handmade mezcal, most people associated the spirit with the gimmicky bottles of harsh rotgut sold in border-town tourist traps. You still find the bottles with a worm swimming at the bottom in tacky bars and resorts. But it wasn't just Americans who were uninformed about mezcal. Even most Mexicans believed the lighter fuel that passed for mezcal was the real deal. The oldest mezcal bar in Oaxaca still sells firewater to drunken old men and rowdy tourists. But once the farmers of the region were given an opportunity to show off their true spirit and people outside the villages had the opportunity to taste it, better-made mezcales began gaining attention.

You once could tell how early Ron got into the mezcal game just by going to his website: for years the URL was www.mezcal.com. (He has since ceded the domain to the Mezcal Regulatory Council.) In addition to his single-village bottlings, Del Maguey sells the Vino de Mezcal series, which includes espadín, arroqueño, papalome, and wild tepextate mezcales. He also sells an azul mezcal, made from blue Weber. When tequila companies sent trucks to Oaxaca to illicitly buy espadín during the 2000 agave shortage, says Ron, they brought with them several blue agave pups to plant in case of a future shortage. The plants thrived in San Luis del Río. The mezcal made from the tequila variety is fruity and crisp.

Ron likes to call his product "pre-organic" because so much of it is made from wild agaves grown in places where plants have never been exposed to chemical herbicides or pesticides in the first place. Some of his mezcales are so small batch that their flavors and aromas vary from bottling to bottling. So you might buy the San Pedro Taviche one year and it will taste different from a bottle of the same village's spirit the next. The bottles are easy to recognize in their green glass and colorful hand-drawn labels (the artist was Ron's close friend, the late Ken Price). Depending on the variety, Del Maguey mezcal can sell for well over $100 per bottle in the United States. Ron does not disclose how much goes to the mezcaleros he works with. The amounts vary for each producer, he says, adding that each mezcalero can set his own price. But that price is fair, he asserts, reminding me that other brands are known to undercut their producers.

Mezcal is still a specialty product for a small, niche market. But even that is changing. Del Maguey sold ten thousand liters of mezcal in 2012. It's a drop in the bucket compared to tequila's numbers, which hovered around 250 million liters the same year. But it's impressive for a brand working with traditional mezcaleros who make only a couple hundred liters at a time.

"Unfortunately, everybody's jumping on the bandwagon," says Ron, who is able to get pretty riled up about his competition. He claims that a student once asked to spend time with him for research purposes and ended up stealing his concept and launching a copycat brand. Ron feels that a number of his competitors have appropriated his ideas, but are dishonest about what they're selling.

"Some of the bigger mezcal brands in the US are not farmer-produced," he claims. "They're made by some college graduate who throws in different yeast in each batch just to change the flavor. Then, there are these huge factories that have these things called diffusers. They're completely synthetic-production machines that are as big as a freight train. So, now you have mezcal that's being made like tequila."

He rails against one distillery, in particular, a giant facility bigger than any tequila factory, located on the road from Oaxaca to Tlacolula. The facility, called Casa Armando Guillermo Prieto, is owned by a corporation that bottles Coca-Cola and produces a brand called Zignum. The distillery was the first in Mexico to be certified green as well as kosher. What this state-of-the-art factory produces in a day using modern machinery a typical mezcalero would have trouble producing in a year. Ultra small-batch producers in the remotest mountain villages might take ten years to match a day's volume at Casa AGP.

In 2013, one of the largest spirits companies in the world bought the global distribution rights to Zignum. Bacardi, which long distributed Patrón and in 2018 bought the brand for $5 billion, was the first international spirits corporation to have a complete mezcal line in Mexico—if you can call what Casa AGP makes mezcal. The products are made using modern technology and end up tasting nothing like what's made at small palenques throughout the region. Sleek bottlings come in joven (the mezcal equivalent of tequila's blanco), reposado, and añejo. If you blind tasted the añejo, you might think it was tequila. It's sweet and caramelized; nothing suggests it's not blue Weber. The reason for the Bacardi deal was simple: mezcal is a fast-growing category in Mexico. It's booming in the United States as well, and Bacardi hoped to get a jump on international growth within the mezcal category.[1] Casa AGP's modern facility has the capacity to produce some 4.5 million liters of mezcal per year. Say you've heard about mezcal and it suddenly appears at your local bar. How are you supposed to know this spirit you've never tasted is an anomaly among mezcales, made more like tequila than traditional mezcal? Bacardi is counting on people's ignorance to get a foothold in the market.

On the subject of tequila, Ron is unsentimental. He hardly drinks it and can barely name a handful of brands he would recommend. He believes whopping marketing budgets and industrial production methods have corrupted the spirit, which he recognizes was once just another mezcal ("back when there was still good stuff being made"). He says the only people who benefit from the popularity of tequila are corporations and their shareholders.

"The culture in Mexico is that the wealthiest people have the ear of the government," he says. "So laws are put in place that favor corporate growth over the will of the people." He contends that the first tequila he had, Herradura, which led him to Oaxaca and to mezcal years ago, is nothing like what it used to be. The tequila changed as the company grew. Especially, he says, since the brand was acquired by the American firm Brown-Forman. The question is: can anything stop the same thing from happening to mezcal?

"We're trying," is Ron's answer. In 2017, Del Maguey was acquired by Pernod Ricard. "We're trying to establish foundations to protect the culture," Ron continues. "There are very few tequilas that taste like what tequila used to be. Del Maguey tastes like what tequila used to taste like two hundred years ago. For me, the flavor profile of tequila is very narrow. You have all these people battling to get into that very narrow area and they almost all taste the same. There are two kinds of tequila makers, those who make bottles and those who make tequila. So, there are just very few that taste like real tequila, that are rich. Tequila used to be an artisanal product, handmade by human beings. In the last fifty years, it has gone through this incredible change and is now completely industrialized. With mezcal, these guys are artists. They really are true artists. And, being an artist myself, I really am supporting these guys, supporting their art, and supporting their life and their magic."

Another mezcal is a brand called Pierde Almas, which translates as "lost souls." It, too, was started by an artist who was drawn to Oaxaca and, in the end, found himself unable to leave. Jonathan Barbieri is a painter from California who went to Oaxaca for inspiration. Actually, he was on his way to Spain, he says, when he detoured through Mexico. His intent was to stay for maybe six months. That turned into the rest of his life. The Pierde Almas headquarters is located in San Francisco Tutla, just outside Oaxaca. Jonathan lives and works there, occupying office space on the ground level and a sunny apartment upstairs. He is tall and chiseled, with a strong jaw, European nose, and salt-and-pepper hair and stubble. He has a way of emitting a sense of mild mania and utter insouciance at once. As soon as I arrive, I realize that our meeting won't be one-on-one. Two guys from an agave spirits appreciation website have just arrived from California. They are big fans of Pierde Almas and treat Jonathan like a minor celebrity, gushing and blushing as he tells us his story.

Before they arrive, Jonathan and I head up to his living space above the Pierde Almas offices to taste some mezcal. One corner of the kitchen is given over to a small studio where a work desk covered in paint splashes looks freshly used. Jonathan pours out several of his mezcales, but not in little tasting cups as Ron or any of the mezcaleros I've visited have done. He hands me a juice glass filled nearly to the brim as he tips his own back, drinking the fragrant liquid like wine. He fetches a smoked trout and smoked cheese from the fridge and we rip into them to stave off intoxication. It works—in more ways than one. The snack revives us, but is also a brilliant pairing. Smoky fish, smoky cheese, and smoky mezcal make for a great combination.

The agave website guys arrive and the four of us pile into a chauffeured van. The plan is to visit another brand's palenque, as well as the palenque where Jonathan's mezcal is made. We set out some two hours late. On the way, we stop for a meal in a typical roadside joint, complete with men in dirty jeans and well-worn cowboy hats who serenade us. Jonathan orders the house special: roasted quail, served with Oaxacan cheese, fresh tomatoes, avocados, salsa, and warm tortillas. As we tear tender quail meat off the bone and build makeshift tacos with the fixings, Jonathan requests a couple songs from the men with guitars and shares with them a nip of the mezcal he's brought in a plastic bottle. He sings along heartily with the men, getting misty eyed and red-faced at the melody. It's dark by the time we arrive in the town of Santa Catarina Minas.

At the palenque of Graciela Angeles Carreño, who runs the Real Minero brandwith her brother since their father passed away in 2016, we are welcomed with more mezcal. She shows us the eighty-liter (roughly twenty-gallon) clay stills her family still uses as she recounts how her great-grandfather, Francisco Angeles, started making mezcal back in 1889. Now, as fourth-generation mezcaleros, her family carries on the legacy. Her father and brother man production while her mother and sisters work on bottling. The family also produces *sal de gusano* or "worm salt," a delicious condiment that is rather ubiquitous in Oaxaca, made of ground rock salt, dried chilies, and maguey larvae. It's often served with mezcal alongside slices of fresh orange or pineapple. But, unlike tequila's salt-and-lime ritual, the sweet fruit and umami-rich sal de gusano are meant to complement the spirit—not eradicate it from the palate. You sip, you dip fruit pieces in the salt to nibble, you talk, you sip some more. Graciela is one of the few women in Oaxaca's mezcal community. At first, certain people were hesitant to accept her, she admits. Making mezcal is a physical job and has long been deemed one for men alone to do. But she has proven a deep understanding of the craft and brings her skills to the table as a marketer, too. Since joining her father, she has helped the family business grow.

We taste through her family's line of mezcales, which includes such varietal bottlings as cuishe, barril, tripón, and tobalá. Graciela's family also makes a *pechuga*, a traditional mezcal imbued with the flavors of heirloom apples, other fruits, nuts, and the flesh of an animal. Usually a chicken or turkey breast is used, suspended inside the still during the distillation of an already finished mezcal. Because the apples are wild mountain varieties, true pechuga can only be produced when they are in season, which is late fall. The result is a funky, sweet, and slightly meaty elixir that is prized by the locals. Christmas mezcal, Jonathan calls it.

By the time we set out to visit the palenque where Jonathan's mezcal is made, it's nighttime. We arrive in Chichicapam in utter darkness, and there is little light at the palenque. Alfonso Sánchez Altamirano is the maestro mezcalero behind Jonathan's mezcal now that his father Faustino has passed away. The process here is just as *(text continues on page 111)*

Jimadores on their way to work.

Harvesting agave in Amatitán.

A worker and his coa at Fortaleza's distillery.

Jimadores working the agave fields.

Jimadores enjoying *la merienda* between shifts.

Freshly harvested agave.

Horno, a traditional brick oven, filled with agave.

Agave juices fermenting with the fibers.

Fermentation tanks in a distillery.

A distillery worker loads a copper pot still with spent agave fibers.

Tequila as it comes off the still.

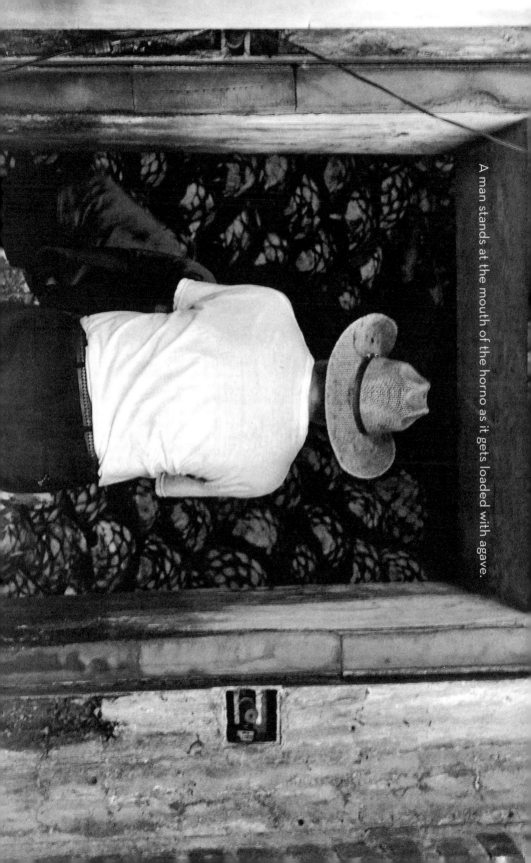

A man stands at the mouth of the horno as it gets loaded with agave.

Barrels filled with aging tequila.

The guest book at La Capilla in Tequila.

A man holds a cuernito of tequila.

A customer sips mezcal at Hecho en Dumbo in New York City.

A bartender shakes up a margarita.

The quiote of a wild tepextate agave.

A magueyero harvests espadín.

Agave roasting in a conical underground pit.

A mule pulls a tahona in Santiago Matatlán, Oaxaca.

A mezcalero listens to fermentation.

A clay pot used for distilling mezcal.

A mezcalero verifies the proof of his spirit using a venencia.

Prize agaves at El Día del Magueyero.

A Zapotec priestess pours out mezcal as part of a ceremonial blessing.

rustic as anywhere in the Sierra, except that fermentation takes place in tanks of concrete instead of wood. Pierde Almas mezcales can be characterized as artisanal more than traditional. "Gourmet," Jonathan calls them. He bottles several varietal mezcales, as well as two pechugas—one made with turkey breast and another with wild rabbit. He also produces a sort of agave-based gin called Pierde Almas +9 that infuses mezcal with nine botanicals normally found in gin, including juniper, coriander, star anise, and orange peel. Pierde Almas bottles are labeled with hand-printed paper made from the recycled fibers of magueys processed at the palenque. It doesn't get more artisanal than that.

In most circles, the words *artisanal* and *traditional* are used interchangeably. The Brooklyn butcher, baker, or pickle maker who considers himself an artisan prides himself on doing things the old-fashioned way. For true mezcal purists, however, the two terms can mean very different things. I learned this at a bar called Mezcaloteca, located on a narrow stone-paved road in Oaxaca's town center. The simple unmarked adobe façade is painted in cheerful Christmas colors. Per a tiny notice on the door, patrons require a reservation to be seated. Once inside, the atmosphere is staid, like a library. Imbibers sip thoughtfully and engage in conversation over the spirits before them. The room is lit by desk lamps. There is no music playing.

The bar insists that strict rules be followed. The rules pertain to the sorts of mezcales served and how these should be enjoyed. For example, no aged mezcal is offered. Owners Marco Ochoa Cortés and Silvia Philion believe that aging mezcal is a trend borrowed from the tequila industry, which itself was influenced by other spirits from around the world. The pair—he, a large gruff Oaxaqueño with a stern expression and black chin stubble; she a tall and elegant DF transplant with a cool, bohemian air—insist on traditional mezcal in their establishment. This means that even the word *artisanal* is taboo.

"To us, artisanal means that it has been modified for the American palate," says Silvia, leaning an elbow on her side of the bar. She has served me a wild papalome mezcal that was fermented in leather and is imbued with the meaty whiff of animal hide. I sip it from a little jícara that sits unevenly on the bar top. "We want traditional mezcal that hasn't been changed from how it was made for generations. It must taste historical."

The rules are written on a little postcard for patrons to take home as a sort of guide to help them identify true mezcales. One guideline on the postcard involves the proof at which a mezcal is bottled, which should be the same proof at which it came off the still—at least 45 percent alcohol by volume and usually higher. Watering down a spirit to proof is a liquor industry standard, says Silvia. Sure, antique navy-proof rums, pre-Prohibition-style whiskeys, and other overproof spirits have become en vogue in the United States. But for Marco and Silvia, it's not about the latest trend but a question of integrity. The spirits should remain undiluted, as they would be served in the villages where they are made. Another rule involves a mezcal's water source: it should be a natural spring. Palenques have traditionally been set up adjacent to natural water sources. But many modern mezcal brands tap a village's water supply, a local well, or even use purified water. Silvia says these mezcales are unable to have a "historical taste."

Despite the adherence to strict rules, Silvia admits that mezcal enthusiasts owe a debt of gratitude to so-called artisanal mezcal. She cites what she calls the Spanish conquest phenomenon, whereby Mexicans still embrace what is foreign in lieu of what is homegrown. "We still seek validation by outsiders," she explains, which may be why mezcal had to first find a following among foreigners before experiencing its true renaissance at home in Mexico. Although she considers Ron Cooper's mezcales artisanal rather than traditional—he makes a pechuga-style mezcal with Ibérico ham from Spain—she praises him for being a great ambassador for mezcal.

Marco, for his part, came to mezcal as a way to reconnect to his roots: his grandfather and great-grandfather were both maestro mezcaleros. He has become something of a mezcal activist, organizing tastings and discussion panels around Mexico and beyond. Many of the bottles Marco stocks come from mezcaleros in his family. The rest he has hunted down in the remote Mexican countryside or come across by happy chance. All are made to express the local terroir. Few of the mezcaleros he works with make more than two hundred liters per batch, maybe six times per year. On each bottle, labeled by Mezcaloteca (none of these producers has the means to commercially bottle their own product), the name of the producer and his village are printed along with the maguey variety and methods of cooking, mashing, fermenting, and distilling. The bottle also lists the proof and date of distillation. Bars like Mezcaloteca are the only places outside the villages themselves where mezcales like these can be experienced. Wine and whiskey bars around the world offer products that are bottled and sold in stores. But for traditional mezcal, bottling and distribution are often out of the question. Boutique mezcalerías are the gatekeepers of these spirits. Marco takes the role seriously.

"If we don't protect the maestro mezcaleros and the traditional ways, we will lose the culture of mezcal," he warns sternly. He then softens, showing me a trick: splash a little mezcal into the palms of your hands like a daub of perfume. Rub them together and the aroma of cooked agave should emerge.

Mezcaloteca is one of several mezcalerías in Oaxaca that are reintroducing people to traditional mezcal. But at La Casa del Mezcal, the eighty-year-old mezcal bar guidebooks send tourists to in the city center, the mezcal can be harsh and comes with a slice of fresh orange for relief. You might see gringos here knocking back shots of mezcal with lime and salt, like it was cheap tequila, as locals look on perplexed by the ritual. Or a drunken patron asleep at a corner table, the price of a copita worth the respite the dark, cool bar offers from the relentless Oaxacan sun. La Casa del Mezcal is a relic left over from a not-too-distant time when, even in this city, mezcal was the domain of alcoholics and misguided tourists.

Another local mezcal bar promoting small-batch traditional producers in Oaxaca is In Situ. Like Marco and Silvia, owners Ulises Torrentera and Sandra Ortiz Brena consider themselves more than just barkeeps. They're mezcal activists. In Situ stocks more than one hundred mezcales, but the atmosphere here is less studious. It feels more like someone's home bar than a business. Ulises is not only a peddler of mezcal, but also a scholar of the spirit, having published several books on the subject. With his bushy curls and round, owlish face, he peers over wire-rimmed spectacles to address his patrons like a professor addressing a class. To the mezcal geeks who come from far and wide to taste from his collection, he likes to dispense little nuggets of information about the spirit's history and cultural significance, all the while reminding them that mezcal was long considered a lowly drink. Only in recent years, he says, have Mexicans and Americans begun to seek it out as a sipping spirit, a cultural and intellectual pursuit.

People want authenticity, he tells me, his glasses reflecting a glare under the greenish glow from the back bar. They want to reconnect to the pre-Columbian past. He echoes the sentiments expressed by Ana Valenzuela, the ethnobotanist, who told me, "Tequila has become too much about looking out to the rest of the world. Mezcal is about looking into ourselves and back, to our past." The bottles lined up on the back bar at In Situ are mostly unlabeled or identified only by hand-scrawled sticker tags. The supply is in a constant state of flux, depending on what is available and from whom. This is business done the old-fashioned way: Ulises goes in search of fine mezcal and procures what he can carry back to sell to his customers.

"Is mezcal in danger of becoming industrialized and commercialized like tequila?" I ask him as we sip a tepextate, made from wild maguey that was harvested after the twenty-five years or so it took to reach maturity. The mezcal is ripe and pungent, like grandma's perfume.

"Yes," he allows, pointing to the giant distillery on the road out of town. "But true mezcal is regional. Production and consumption are small. You cannot make it in large volumes and have it be true mezcal."

A man named Francisco "Paco" García sits on a barstool next to me at the bar, nodding in agreement with everything Ulises says. That morning, Paco and I drove together to San Dionisio Ocotepec, a town of less than ten thousand people where the mezcal brand Wahaka is made. Paco, whose family made a name for itself in coffee farming, is one of its founders. He teamed up with a few friends from Mexico City who have known each other since boyhood to capitalize on the mezcal craze. They enlisted a mezcalero from San Dionisio and made him a partner. From the car, we saw the usual old men and women you see on country roads in Oaxaca, leading donkeys and mules loaded up with huge piles of food or materials on their backs. The animals carry everything from corn to bales of hay to leafy greens. When we came upon a donkey walking the long, dusty road into town alone, his back piled high with firewood, we both let out a chuckle. He had no human to lead him, but seemed to know exactly where he was going.

"Everyone wants to use wild magueys nowadays," Paco was saying as we pulled into the palenque of fourth-generation maestro mezcalero Alberto Morales Mendez, whom everyone calls Beto. Paco showed me the long club-shaped piñas of madrecuixe that had just been roasted. They were being crushed by the hand of a husky young man with a mallet. "They want to use wild magueys to be macho. But no one is taking care of reforestation."

Despite peddling a mezcal that is decidedly more artisanal than traditional—the brand sells a reposado—Paco sees himself as an activist, too. He has made the issue of reforestation his cause. His company has helped implement programs to reinforce species like tobalá, which is becoming rarer in the wild now that demand for mezcal made from it is rising. He also supports the reforestation of trees used for roasting the piñas. In many cases, the same trees are used for fuel to run the small copper pot stills. The Wahaka team uses gas instead of wood to run their stills. But perhaps most revolutionary about Wahaka is its Vino de Mezcal series showcasing extremely small-batch traditional producers from around Mexico. The 2014 lot included bottlings from Jalisco, Puebla, and Nuevo León, certainly the only such spirits available commercially in the United States at the time; the vast majority of mezcal sold is from Oaxaca. Most producers could only provide fifty bottles to be sold; for one mezcalero, the number was two.

In the United States and Europe, the number of mezcales on the market grows each year. Just a few years ago, there were only a handful of good mezcal brands exported from Mexico. Most brands available globally today are not owned by the mezcaleros who pass the craft on from generation to generation. Like tequila, global brands tend to be owned by global parties, be they Americans, Europeans, or wealthy Mexicans from the capital. Richard Betts, a sommelier turned mezcal importer, is well aware of the trend. He made the leap from wine to mezcal after becoming disillusioned with the booze business.

"In the wake of passing the Master Sommelier exam, I felt depressed. Because you put so much of yourself into this thing, then it's just over," he recalls over coffee and pastries in a Brooklyn café. "I really liked tequila and decided I wanted to try making it. So, I went to Tequila. But that was depressing, too. I was struck by how it was no longer made the way it once was. For me, a wine needs to reflect where it comes from. I thought tequila would be the same."

It wasn't until Richard went to Oaxaca that he was inspired by what he tasted. He was no stranger to mezcal. Raised in Arizona, he and his friends would skulk outside liquor stores trying to get older kids or less-than-reputable men to buy them bacanora.

"Only when I got to Oaxaca did it start to feel right," says Richard. "This is where I started to get a sense of place. The difference between land at five thousand feet near the airport and midway up into the Sierra at eight thousand feet, you can taste it in the mezcal. I would tell people that I was really excited to start a mezcal project and they'd say, 'Richard, mescaline is illegal. You're going to go to jail.' I'd say, 'No, not that! And, no, not the one with the worm in it, either.'"

He started Sombra Mezcal in 2009, importing a spirit made in San Juan del Río from espadín harvested at some eight thousand feet in elevation. The brand quickly became successful, but Richard never stopped thinking about his tequila disappointment. So, after four years, he went ahead and launched a tequila, after all. Astral is said to be made the way tequila was made one hundred years ago. The agaves are fermented and distilled on the fibers. (Richard likens making tequila without the solids to making red wine without the grape skins: it's where the flavor and character reside.) The spirit is bottled at 92 proof.

"In tequila, everyone bottles at 80 proof because that's the standard," says Richard. "It's not because it tastes good, but because they're trying to stretch a profit. When we were coming up with Astral, we tasted it at 100 proof, then at 95, 90, and 85. We were looking for the proof that carries the most information. And where it's the most delicious. No lime, no salt, no mixers needed."

While mezcal may be in danger of too much influence from the tequila industry, it's heartening to see that the tequila industry might just start taking a few cues from traditional mezcal producers. Even in adulthood, children can still learn from their parents.

{8}

Tequila Goes Top Shelf

I'm on Patrón, I just took some shots to tha dome
I'm gone, so gone, so yo, can I get a ride home?
—Paul Wall, "I'm on Patrón"

In a bar on New York's Lower East Side, a woman is extolling the virtues of tequila. According to her, it's the least caloric of all the spirits. It's also the only one that isn't a depressant. She has declared it her "drink of the summer." Before I can make my escape, someone announces it's time for shots and I freeze like a sober deer in headlights. It's a weeknight in the early aughts and I haven't had a shot of tequila since a fateful night I can barely remember in the nineties. I try to decline, opt for whiskey instead, but it's too late. Here they come, shot glasses filled with a clear pungent liquid, served with salt and lime. I instinctively hold my breath, waiting for that familiar stench of gasoline and dirty socks to penetrate my nostrils and tickle my gag reflex. But the smell is different. It's softer, herbal and citrusy. I take the shot in the customary way and, while the subtleties of it are lost on me, the lack of a burn down my esophagus is duly noted. I've just had my first Patrón.

I would taste Patrón again many times—eventually, sipped and not slammed, without the lime and salt—before moving on to richer, more complex tequilas and, after that, inevitably, mezcal. The iconic squat, domed bottle hit the East Coast with a vengeance a few years after its initial launch on the West Coast in 1989, where it quickly became the drink on everyone's lips. This was a world away from Cuervo Gold: a light, delicate spirit with sweet, bright flavors. Patrón was meant to be sipped over ice. Some people drank it with tonic. And it was expensive! Ordering it in the sorts of places that do bottle service behind a red velvet rope could set you back a couple hundred bucks. Even buying it at the liquor store was a luxury at just under fifty dollars a bottle. But the bottle was pretty and its contents much tastier than the tequila shots people had grown accustomed to. And while there was little truth to it having fewer calories than other drinks, the rumors that Patrón gave you a different kind of high than other spirits were not entirely unfounded. Anecdotal evidence suggested it didn't bring you down. Instead, it made you happy-drunk. I wasn't yet a spirits connoisseur—or much of a connoisseur of anything in my early twenties—but I liked this Patrón. I associated it with my friends who were less broke, more sophisticated. Some people didn't even seem to realize Patrón was tequila. It was in its own category.

It was around the late 1990s and early 2000s that another West Coast brand began infiltrating even the grittiest corners of New York City. Starbucks started as a Seattle phenomenon, then migrated to California and finally made its way to uptown Manhattan. By the time the first New York location—which had opened in 1994—closed in 2003 there were Starbuckses all over the island, even in Brooklyn. It wouldn't be long before the first Starbucks opened on the Lower East Side, where I lived, which at the time hadn't yet been overrun by glitzy bars and boutique hotels. In 2005, it was met with much protest and declarations of the neighborhood's descent into yuppiedom. But soon enough, the aging rockers and young hipsters of the area found themselves rubbing elbows over Frappuccinos. And everyone had to admit that the coffee at Starbucks was better than what they'd been drinking before. Most customers would end up sticking with their grande skinny mochas and pumpkin spice lattes for good. But some of them would start seeking out independent cafés that made serious coffee. And within a few years, New York would be overtaken by "third-wave" coffee bars, serving single-origin, craft-roasted beans. Starbucks, for many, was a gateway to better coffee. I like to think of Patrón as the Starbucks of tequila. For many, it's the destination, the object of a lifelong brand loyalty. For others, it's the first step on a path toward true agave spirits appreciation.

Patrón is the best-selling super-premium tequila brand in America. It's been imitated, rhapsodized about, even written into some two hundred songs (Several rappers, including Lil Jon, T-Pain, and The Game mention Patrón in several tracks. From Lil Jon's "Snap Yo Fingers": "Got Patrón in my cup/I pop, I drank/I'm on Patrón and purp, I can't thank"). What's more, it's credited with creating the super-premium tequila category. Without it, we might not have tequilas from the likes of Justin Timberlake, George Clooney, or P. Diddy today. Patrón was founded by two Southern Californians: entrepreneur Martin Crowley and John Paul Jones DeJoria, a businessman and philanthropist. The two had a rough childhood in common: both set out on their own at a young age. The son of immigrants from Italy and Greece, John Paul was sent to a foster home with his brother when his mother could no longer care for him. He spent part of his youth as a gang member in East L.A. Later he worked as a door-to-door salesman, sleeping in his car when times got tough. He was ambitious and determined. You might know him best as the bearded, perpetually ponytailed billionaire behind Paul Mitchell Hair Systems. He started that company with $700 and a ton of moxie, growing it into a multimillion-dollar business within years. By the time Martin approached him with the idea of a tequila company, John Paul could afford to bankroll the venture.

Martin discovered tequila in Mexico, where he sourced decorative items like handmade tiles for an import business. He would bring tequila back to California to share with John Paul and the two would while away hours, pondering what the best tequila in Mexico might be. Then, one day, Martin tasted it—or so he believed. He visited a distillery in the highlands of Jalisco that was small and quaint, working in the most traditional ways with a mule-drawn tahona. The tequila made there was complex and delicious. He brought some back to John Paul, who was also impressed. The two decided to ask the distiller to make them one thousand cases to be sold in the United States. John Paul figured, even if they didn't sell, he could give them away as gifts. Through his Mexican connections, Martin found a traditional glassblower who agreed to make beautiful handblown bottles for the product. Martin's girlfriend, a vivacious blonde from South Africa named Ilana Edelstein, added her own little design touches to the packaging, including tying little lime-green ribbons on each bottle.

John Paul needn't have worried about the tequila's acceptance in the United States. Patrón was a hit. It quickly became the drink of choice among many of his Hollywood friends, including Clint Eastwood and the chef Wolfgang Puck. Its fast rise to notoriety was thanks in no small part to a series of publicity stunts orchestrated by Martin and Ilana. These included hiring a buxom prostitute to work a spirits trade show, the first in a string of equally endowed young women who would come to be known nationwide as Patrón Girls.[1] The team also staged a blind taste test in Los Angeles, challenging the handful of other popular tequila brands. At a celebrity-studded party, Patrón was crowned the winner and began henceforth referring to itself officially as "the best tequila" on the market. By 2003, it was selling more than two hundred thousand cases per year. Just a decade later, the brand broke the two million cases per year mark.

"I went to my friend Wolfgang Puck's restaurant, Spago, and I said, 'Wolf, there's this new tequila that's higher end. It's not your seven-dollar-a-bottle tequila. It costs a lot to make it, but I think the world is ready for it,'" John Paul tells me over the phone from his Los Angeles office. "He agreed and turned a lot of his celebrity guests on to it, saying this is the new way of the world. It was fabulous. We went door-to-door at first. But once people [tasted it, they] liked how they felt drinking it—not just the taste, but how they felt afterwards."

From 1991 through 2002, Patrón was made at a small distillery in Atotonilco el Alto, where Martin Crowley first discovered it. The brand was sold exclusively in the United States. It eventually outgrew the distillery, Martin having wrought bad blood with the family that owned it. After eleven years, Patrón ended its relationship with them and set out to build its own distillery, also in Atotonilco, at the other end of town.

The project took several years to realize after at least one major false start. Patrón was distributed by the Seagram Company, the largest spirits company in the world at the time. Seagram's had offered to bankroll the new distillery, but was pressuring Patrón to change its production methods to be more cost-effective. The new distillery would be more automated, more efficient, less artisanal, but better equipped to meet the growing demand for Patrón. Martin wouldn't have it. The Patrón team ended up rejecting the plan and cutting their ties to Seagram's. It decided instead to handle distribution in-house. Martin died in 2003, but John Paul carried out his wishes to build a factory that could keep making the spirit the old-fashioned way—only on a scale far more vast.

How? The facility the Patrón team built is huge. From the outside, it looks like a billionaire's home. Entering the grounds feels like visiting Gatsby himself. Built as a true hacienda, complete with a church where employees can worship, the property is protected by a large, gated arch. The gates give way to a long drive, along the center of which is a long, narrow pool with a grand stone fountain at the end of it. A vast French colonial mansion is built from cantera stones carved from locally quarried volcanic rock. Inside the eighteenth-century-style building hangs an enormous wrought-iron chandelier, custom designed in Tlaquepaque, a suburb of Guadalajara known for its artisanal crafts. Behind closed doors, every aspect of production unfolds, from fermentation to distillation to bottling.

What sets operations here apart from other big distilleries is that Patrón's factory is built like a series of small distilleries, the tequila made in smaller batches. A tahona is still used for a portion of the distillate, which is blended with tequila made from machine-shredded agaves. The fermentation vats are open wooden tanks and the stills, lined up by the dozen, are small copper pots. Pulling out your camera to snap a photo will result in a quick reprimand. Yet visitors are invited to taste both the tahona-crushed and industrially milled distillates. The difference between the two is staggering. The first is round and rich, totally sippable even at still strength, around 110 proof. The latter is hot and harsh. You look around for a lime wedge or a beer for relief from the burn.

Also like small operations, the bottling line is almost completely manual, dozens of people applying the labels and numbering them by hand. The factory is built in such a way that, as the brand continues to grow, more small stills and wooden tanks and even tahonas will be added on, like Lego pieces. It has virtually limitless capacity.

"I built that hacienda so my people there could feel like they're someplace special," says John Paul. "We hired chefs to cook them lunch every day. Because I remember a time when I worked for people and I didn't even have enough money for lunch. And if you work the night shift, we have chefs cook you dinner.

"They're quite religious down there," he adds. "We built a chapel right in the middle of our hacienda so they can pray if they want to. It's a beautiful place to work in. We didn't skimp on anything. We wanted to make them feel good. We help the local community. We feel we have to share with our people. Here's the big difference: when people love you, when you're taking care of them, extra love goes into the product. People love to make it right."

Patrón employs more than sixteen hundred people at the distillery, many of whom are inhabitants of the fifty-thousand-person town of Atotonilco. Most of them have never and will never purchase a bottle of Patrón tequila. The brand is now sold in Mexico, but the cost of a bottle is prohibitively high, up to $60 in a country where the average household income is roughly $2,500 per quarter. Still, the company is proud to pay its employees more than the industry average. It's also proud of its sustainability efforts, especially in an industry that produces up to ten liters of wastewater for every liter of spirit distilled.[2] The nitrogen-rich sludge known as *vinazas* has been known to contaminate local streams and groundwater, killing aquatic life and wreaking havoc on the ecosystem at large. According to a press release issued by the Jalisco state government in 2010, only about 60 percent of vinazas were disposed of properly at the time. The rest of the industry was said to be working toward compliance with environmental standards. Patrón installed Mexico's first reverse osmosis plant to treat the byproduct of distillation in 2011. The system recycles 70 percent of the distillery's vinazas into clean water, and the remaining 30 percent is combined with used agave fibers for composting. The compost is used in the hacienda's gardens, which help provide food for staff meals, and given to farmers who grow agave for Patrón.

Of course, these green initiatives were only implemented after reports surfaced that the company had been cited by the state environmental regulator for dumping hazardous waste into local rivers.[3] You cannot make tequila without making waste, including bagasse (spent agave fibers). Patrón certainly wouldn't be the first company accused of dumping toxic stillage into Jalisco's spring water sources. Thankfully, more companies achieve compliance with environmental standards each year.

Ever the philanthropist, John Paul takes satisfaction in running companies that are involved in a great deal of corporate giving. Patrón has supported such charities as the St. Bernard Project, which helps rebuild homes destroyed by Hurricane Katrina, and the Waterkeeper Alliance, committed to preserving and protecting water sources from polluters. John Paul is also a member of the Giving Pledge, the exclusive club of billionaires led by Warren Buffett and Bill Gates that requires pledgers to give away half their fortunes to charity, either in their lifetimes or as part of their wills.

"I think that what we're doing and how we help the world out is just incredible," John Paul says. "It has nothing to do with tax write-offs or corporate image. It has to do with this: it's our obligation to help our community, our nation, and the world to become a better place to live. Because we are here and we're really blessed to have a good business."

On the other side of town, a much smaller company produces a tequila using a method similar to Patrón's. Siete Leguas has two factories: La Vencedora (the winner) and El Centenario (the centenary). They sit on a hill on the edge of town next to a spring water creek, one around the corner from the other. El Centenario is the oldest distillery in town. Located in a simple brick building, it houses a tahona pit, mounds of agave piled before it on the concrete floor. The walls are painted an antique-looking mustard yellow.

At seven o'clock and eleven thirty each morning except Sunday, two of Siete Leguas's half dozen mules get hitched to the tahona. The impressive beasts are as big and imposing as New York City police horses. Beautiful, long-legged animals with powerful flanks, one has a coat that is a deep chestnut brown with a white belly and muzzle, another is grey-speckled white. Together they pull the tahona around and around the large pit for about an hour and a half. The entire time, a pair of distillery workers makes sure all the agave is crushed, shoveling the leftover fibers here and there with a pitchfork. The two men are father and son. Many of the distillery's forty-odd employees have worked there since the company's inception.

Next to the tahona are three hornos. The ovens look like large rooms, and when they're at full capacity they hold between seventeen and twenty-five tons of piñas. Some 60 percent of the agaves are estate-grown, while the rest are purchased from growers with whom Siete Leguas has long-standing agreements. The plants are harvested at around ten years of age, or whenever they happen to reach peak ripeness. The agave bakes slowly in the ovens over thirty-six hours, then rests for a day before being crushed. Afterward, the juices and fibers are transferred to open tanks. It's one of the only distilleries that not only ferments the agave mash naturally with the fibers, but distills with the fibers as well. The practice imparts "that special Siete Leguas characteristic," says owner Juan Fernando González de Anda. It's more of a texture than a taste. "We cannot change it," he adds. "If we did, the tequila would change."

Founded in 1952 by Ignacio González Vargas, Fernando's father, Siete Leguas is named for Don Pancho Villa's horse. General Francisco Villa, who went by Don Pancho, was a revolutionary hero and remains an iconic figure in Mexico. His image, a prototype of machismo, is often referenced by tequila brands. Don Pancho, however, did not drink.[4] He was said to have christened his trusty steed in honor of the seven leagues (*siete leguas*) it once galloped in battle. Ignacio chose this symbol for his tequila brand because he admired the figure of Don Pancho and was an avid horseman. He bought the original factory from his uncle, who taught him how to make tequila. Not much has deviated from how it was made sixty years ago, other than a few modernizations, like switching to stainless steel tanks in the last two decades.

When her husband died in 1973, Ignacio's wife, Amparo, took over the company. Fernando was eight years old. The tequila industry, made up of barely a couple dozen distilleries at the time, was almost entirely male. Amparo stood out from the crowd. A few years later, one of her daughters took over the business, and soon after another daughter accepted the job. Fernando finished high school in 1982 and immediately dedicated himself to the family business. As the only one of seven children who still works at the distillery, he has run the company's day-to-day operations for the past twenty-five years. A brother and sister of his tend the agave fields. Their mother, in her nineties, still advises Fernando on important business decisions. He jokes that her regular copita of tequila helps keep her young.

At La Vencedora, the newer and larger of Siete Leguas's two facilities, a mechanical roller mill shreds the cooked piñas. The final product is a blend of stone- and machine-crushed agave from each facility. The brand produces a blanco, a resposado, an añejo, and an extra añejo. The blanco is rich and creamy, with fruit and earth notes and just a hint of pepper. The resposado is light in color, the original cooked agave flavors still coming through, but with an added essence of crème brûlée. The wood-spiced añejo is all butterscotch and pepper. The extra añejo spends at least five years in barrels and comes out tasting of caramel and licorice, but is rare to find north of the border.

If you haven't figured it out yet, Siete Leguas is the small distillery where Patrón was first made. The tequila produced here today is the one Martin Crowley discovered back in the 1980s, the one that sparked his dream of creating a top-shelf brand. When the Patrón team and the González family broke off their relationship, the split wasn't a cordial one. There was particular tension over the recipe, which Patrón adopted and Siete Leguas continues to use today. It still calls for a portion of the agave to be stone-crushed, which may sound similar to how Patrón makes its tequila, but Siete Leguas's process results in a richer, denser spirit than Patrón. Even the two brands' bottles are suspiciously similar.

With no comparable marketing budget or publicity vehicle to propel it to achieve a success on par with Patrón's, Siete Leguas has remained small by comparison. But the brand is far more popular among Mexicans—and more affordable to them, too.

Over time, Siete Leguas has slowly built brand recognition, both in Mexico and among tequila enthusiasts abroad. In the last ten years, the company has seen some 30 to 40 percent growth, says Fernando. It does not advertise, and so the growth has been entirely organic, driven by word of mouth. As a Mexican-owned company, it has a certain credibility in tequila-purist circles that Patrón could never achieve. Some Mexicans may be influenced by this as well. During my travels in Mexico, I often asked people what their favorite tequila was. The most popular answer was Cuervo, still the biggest and most prominent brand with its ubiquitous billboards and magazine ads. But Siete Leguas seemed to be increasingly popular in high-end restaurants, as well as among people working in the tequila industry or in hospitality. Meanwhile, in the United States, you're sure to find Siete Leguas at serious tequila bars, but it won't be sold as part of the bottle service at glitzy nightclubs the way Patrón is. Siete Leguas is the tequila lover's tequila. It's not an overly expensive or flashy brand—a bottle of blanco will run you around $48—but among purists it's a lauded product.

The two companies—Siete Leguas and Patrón—continue to coexist not only on liquor store shelves but at opposite ends of the small, sweet town of Atotonilco el Alto. They use the same water source and perhaps even some of the same agaves, although Patrón is so big it must source agave from across the appellation. But with its focus on smoothness, Patrón ends up tasting quite different than Siete Leguas, despite sharing a similar recipe. Where Siete Leguas is earthy and sweet, bursting with cooked agave flavors and hints of spice, Patrón is light and bright, showing citrus and herbal notes. It is, indeed, a good introduction to 100 percent agave tequila.

Fernando, for his part, continues to be approached by entrepreneurs looking for a distillery to manufacture their brand. But he consistently refuses, having learned his lesson. It's a lesson Fernando is grateful for, actually.

"I learned that I have a high-quality tequila that can compete globally. I think I needed for my product to be put on the global market to realize that I have a special spirit," he says. Yet, he's of two minds when it comes to the explosive growth of his industry and its increasingly foreign domination. "If I take a nationalist point of view, I'm saddened that so many small brands are bought out by large companies. However, tequila is where it is on the international stage because of these large companies. And me, being a small company with a high-quality product, as long as they open those international markets, I can begin knocking on doors and getting people to discover our product.

"I don't want to get too big," he continues, his manner reserved and earnest. "Siete Leguas cannot lose its essence. Our philosophy is to make our tequila by hand, to protect the old ways of doing it, and to adhere to the highest standard we can." John Paul Jones DeJoria, for his part, sold his 70 percent stake in Patrón to Bacardi (which already owned the other 30 percent) in 2018 for an astounding $5 billion.

The tequila industry is built on this business model of foreign entrepreneurs coming into Mexican distilleries to commission a spirit to be made under a new brand name, often to be sold exclusively beyond Mexico's borders. It's precisely how the industry has grown so impressively. Little more than 150 distilleries exist in tequila country (plus about 17,500 agave farmers), yet there are close to seventeen hundred tequila brands. (In 2018, there were 1,394 brands bottled in Mexico and 299 bottled abroad for a total 1,693.) How is this possible? A distillery might produce a dozen different brands. Perhaps it makes a house brand to sell domestically and several other brands for foreigners to sell abroad. To know for sure who makes your tequila requires a little detective work.

By law, each tequila brand must list its Norma Oficial Mexicana number on the bottle. That number is associated with a specific distillery. So, for example, the tequila brand Avión, which you might recognize from the HBO series *Entourage*, is listed under NOM 1416. Launched by a former private aviation executive named Ken Austin, Avión was able to capitalize on its founder's close friendship to Doug Ellin, a producer on the show. Taking a page—several, actually—out of Patrón's book, it aimed for maximum smoothness in the flavor profile. (Nowadays, the term *smooth* is overused in spirits. Products described as such tend to be innocuous or overly sweet, often designed to compete with super-premium vodkas, their flavor easily masked by a mixer. They are generally aimed at women, who represent up to 70 percent of alcohol purchasing decisions in American households.[5] Women certainly are a growing sector of the spirits market, but whether they actually prefer these tamer spirits is up for debate.)

Ken told me he wanted Avión to appeal to people like his wife who don't even like tequila. Indeed, Avión Silver is light and slightly sweet, with delicate hints of fresh herbs. Soon after he launched the product, Ken had a line of swag items made, including T-shirts and tanks, printed on good, soft cotton and featuring cool designs as opposed to the dry logos most promotional gear bears. His theory was that if people actually wanted to wear the shirts, he could promote his brand even better. He even struck a deal to have the shirts sold at the Gap. You had people buying the gear and watching the show who weren't even sure that Avión was a real product. All this only served to boost sales.

A couple of years after Avión launched, another tequila with a link to Hollywood surfaced. George Clooney and his partner Rande Gerber, who is married to supermodel Cindy Crawford, launched their tequila brand, Casamigos. With a saucy ad campaign that featured the leading man in bed with Gerber and Crawford, the tequila began popping up at hip parties and clubs in Los Angeles and New York. It soon became the fastest-growing brand in the category and, in 2017, sold to UK-based spirits giant Diageo for a jaw-dropping $1 billion. When he was first looking to create the brand, Clooney went knocking on the doors of several distilleries in Jalisco. The one that answered was Productos Finos de Agave, a.k.a. NOM 1416: the same distillery contracted to make Avión, as well as the Alacrán, Rancho Caliente, and a brand called El Cartel. It's one of tequila's more prolific distilleries.

That doesn't mean the two Hollywood tequilas are identical. Each brand owner has a say in the final flavor profile of the spirit and the distiller is able to make each one to taste. And don't discount the effect of different packaging on people's taste perception. But to believe the marketing spiel of any brand, which usually features an age-old tradition practiced by a multigenerational family, is to overlook the reality of the industry. Much of the tequila available in the United States is manufactured according to specs given by an outsider. It's a long way from a handmade product with a rich heritage.

This marketing spiel is the cornerstone of the spirits industry as a whole today. It wasn't always this way: alcohol was once marketed in a rather stale way. High-end brands, mostly imported whiskey and brandy, were advertised much like fancy cars: to mostly men at stodgy trade shows. Low-end brands, if they were advertised at all, were sold as little more than a means to an end—namely, inebriation. There was little focus on flavor and image. That all changed with pioneering brands like Patrón and Absolut Vodka, whose ad campaigns were stylish and clever. Suddenly, booze was no longer advertised solely to rich old men and young drunk ones. Spirits companies found themselves on the cutting edge of advertising and branding efforts. Today, each new brand that emerges, with its sleek, attractive packaging and sexy tagline, has the opportunity to be the next hot thing. New tequila brands targeting young, hip drinkers are cropping up at such a staggering rate that it's nearly impossible to keep track of them.

At La Cofradía, also known as NOM 1137, on the outskirts of the town of Tequila, about a dozen different brands are made, ranging from well tequilas—the ones you find in a bartender's speed rack next to the cheap vodka and gin—to super-premium labels. One of the premium brands is Casa Noble. The owners have invited me to stay at their sprawling estate. Relieved to check out of my budget hotel for one night, I accept. The boutique accommodations at La Cofradía, which receive only a couple hundred guests per year, are made up of four luxury adobe villas, each one decorated in a different theme, its name etched over the door. I stay in the Mayahuel suite. It houses a large, cream-colored stone bathroom with a walk-in shower. The white robes are luxuriously soft and weighty. The main room features a stone floor that manages to be warm to the touch of bare feet even when the temperature outside is chilly. The custom-made bed frame is done up like a piña, the headboard painted with the goddess's likeness. The duvet is thick and heavy. The sleep I fall into here is one of the deepest and quietest I've had in weeks. Unlike the forest, with all its whispering and crackling secrets, the desert can be as silent as the dead.

Surrounded by agave plants, the huts are removed from the bustle of the distillery. The property, with its 150-year-old mango trees and small chapel, is also home to an upscale restaurant and retail store selling dozens of different tequila products. A small pottery factory acts as a sort of working museum where visitors can see craftspeople shape and fire ceramics, painting the finished products by hand. Many of the bottles made here will hold the company's best tequilas, including Casa Noble.

I awake to thick silence, the sound of ducks swimming and chattering in a nearby pond dampened by the dry air and expansive space. It's a cloudless Tuesday. A young woman has a table of handicrafts set up in the courtyard that she mans with her young son. José Hermosillo, the brand's chairman and CEO, meets me for a hearty breakfast on a little patio behind the cellar. We sip the sweet, nutty café de olla and nibble fresh fruit with a side of Jalisco's famous birote bread, toasted and slathered with sweetened condensed milk. Pepe, as his friends call him, prefers his with just butter, sugar, and cinnamon. He is tall and broad and European-looking, yet another executive type whose appearance doesn't quite measure up to what most foreigners expect a Mexican to be. He wears a loose white linen shirt in the guayabera style that is so popular in Mexico, and a straw fedora on his closely shaven head. Pepe's family has made tequila since the 1700s, he says. They bought this property some fifty years ago. He took over the family business at just nineteen years old, when he was still in college, after his father passed away. Along with several partners not associated with La Cofradía, he launched Casa Noble in the 1990s. Pepe's goal has always been to grow the brand, but not too big.

"The thing about the big brands," he says over breakfast, echoing

Fernando at Siete Leguas, "is that they've done a lot for our industry. Patrón got people to pay fifty dollars for a bottle of tequila. That's great. But in terms of foreign ownership, as a Mexican, I think it's sad. But you can't stop things from evolving."

Casa Noble itself evolved in 2011 when it partnered with rocker Carlos Santana. He was a big fan of the tequila and, in turn, Pepe was a big fan of his. Pepe still blushes when talking about what it's like to work with the guitar legend. As part owner, Santana has joined a growing cadre of celebrities associated with a tequila brand.

The agaves for Casa Noble, which are certified organic, hail from Nayarit, one of the more remote parts of the tequila appellation, near the Jalisco border. It's far from the distillery, but the land there was cheap, says Pepe. As virgin land, it was rich in the nutrients agaves need to grow. The soil is volcanic and the climate is harsh in just the right way. Like winemakers, tequila producers talk about "stressing the plants." The idea is that the more unforgiving the land, the more grapes or, in this case, agave will struggle to grow. That struggle brings character to the final product.

After breakfast, we visit the distillery. It's an old brick and stone structure equipped with kilns for cooking the piñas and a mechanical mill for crushing the agave. The mill, featuring a large screw that spins as it presses, is certainly not a tahona, but it's not a shredder, either. The machine, rare in the tequila industry, produces a distillate that is sweeter and rounder than one made with shredded agave, avoiding the bitterness that comes with shredding the agave's tough fibers. Behind several stainless steel fermentation tanks are a few large pot stills, also made of stainless steel, but equipped with copper coils inside. Here Casa Noble gets distilled three times, once more than what is required by law. A small shrine to the Virgin of Guadalupe, an important symbol for Mexico, sits at the center of the distillery. The employees make a habit of bringing her flowers.

"We were the first to do the third distillation," says Pepe, immediately launching into an explanation of the process meant to satisfy skeptics. "It gives a fantastic purity to the tequila. After that third distillation, there's a light peppermint note and by doing it slowly, we're not extracting any of the aromas. And the third distillation gets us closer to the right alcohol volume that we like, so there's less added water."

Casa Noble is also the first brand to specialize in single-barrel tequila. It's an idea, like so many, borrowed from the whiskey world. Instead of multiple barrels of aged tequila being blended together to achieve a consistent, balanced flavor, a barrel of Casa Noble will be aged, tasted periodically, then when it's just right, bottled as is. Both reposado and añejo single barrels are made. Depending on the angel's share—more liquid evaporates from the longer-aged añejo—each barrel will yield about 300 to 360 bottles. That means each batch is different, at times dramatically so, which Pepe feels is part of the fun. That fun will set you back up to $125 per bottle.

The desert morning air is cool and clean, the sun slowly gaining strength as it rises higher and higher overhead. By the time I check out of my room, it's sweltering. I must pass through the security gate that guards the winding drive to La Cofradía. On the other side, the rough cobblestone road leads me past simple homes, some painted in cheerful colors, others left concrete gray. Several dogs roam the streets, and a few barnyard animals sit in the shade of a small pen. The outskirts of town aren't as manicured as the charming town center or the gated tequila estates. Soon the stones and dirt give way to asphalt. As we near downtown Tequila, there are roadside vendors selling agave plants and aguamiel, and even little white oak barrels. These are decorative, but the temptation for tourists is there: you could ostensibly start a tequila operation of your own.

{9}

Bottling Mexican Identity

What you call love was invented by guys like me . . . to sell nylons.
—DON DRAPER, *MAD MEN*

Sparkle Donkey, whose mascot El Burro Esparkalo is on the front of the bottle, was a product launched in 2012 by the team behind the equally tongue-in-cheek Bakon Vodka. It had no history or heritage associated with it, but the website told a different story, proclaiming that the burro itself was an ancient figure. It even featured a fake documentary telling the history of the brand and photographs of Aztec pottery painted with images of the Sparkle Donkey. It was meant to be facetious, not an actual lie. The joke is that every brand carves its image out of a story it feels will resonate with its target audience, a combination of some parts truth and a few parts fancy, if not outright fabrication. In the world of spirits, there is almost always mention of tradition and handcrafting, even when the product is made entirely by machines. But nowhere is the handcrafted heritage rhetoric more pervasive than in tequila. Sparkle Donkey's ridiculous—and culturally insensitive—spoof was all part of the initial marketing campaign. Press releases were circulated touting the brand's irreverent approach that poked fun at the tequila heritage cliche. But anyone stumbling upon the website without knowing the angle might be taken in by the ruse.

How Mexicans are viewed—either by themselves or by foreigners—has long influenced how tequila is marketed, both in the United

States and in Mexico. Luxury brands may focus on the sleek design of their bottles and the glamor associated with drinking their product, but few can resist mentioning the traditional Mexican family or village that makes the spirit. It's meant to communicate authenticity to the consumer. We are told that we are drinking "the spirit of Mexico." But just how did this spirit, from one small part of the country, come to represent the entire nation?

"It's crazy: fifteen years ago nobody in Mexico had tequila at a wedding. And now, it's a staple on every table at every baptism, every quinceañera, every wedding," says Marie Sarita Gaytán, a sociology professor at the University of Utah. She wrote her dissertation on the topic of tequila and Mexican identity and later turned it into a book. "Tequila became Mexico's spirit not simply because it tastes great. There are many other alcoholic beverages from Mexico—mezcal, sotol, pulque, bacanora—but it's tequila that wins. The reason, I believe, can be traced back to its close association with Jalisco and what it means to be an 'ideal Mexican.'"

This ideal Mexican, according to Gaytán, is a rather Spanish-influenced one. And Jalisco has always been a very Spanish-influenced place. Its capital, Guadalajara, was built by conquistadors and the economy that grew up around it thrived, at least in part, thanks to a lucrative nearby mine established by the Spanish. Tequila—or, generations ago, mezcal de Tequila—was mostly made on the haciendas of wealthy colonial land owners. The early industry relied on the labor of indigenous workers, but was run primarily by Spanish families. As Gaytán writes, while pulque was said to be associated with the "general confusion and disorder of rural life in the early colonial period," mezcal-producing haciendas came to represent a certain stability and way of life that maintained European standards.[1] The Spanish considered distilled spirits modern, a reflection of their bourgeois values.[2] Serving the prosperous city of Guadalajara allowed the tequila industry to grow, far outpacing mezcal production in more remote places throughout Mexico. Taxes paid on tequila helped the city blossom even more; a symbiotic relationship was formed.

But even with its early success as a taxable product, tequila did not become Mexico's national spirit overnight. In the late-nineteenth century, when it was first exported to the United States, the approval bestowed upon it by Americans boosted the spirit's notoriety back home. In the 1940s and '50s tequila was given a role in Mexican films starring rugged cowboy types—charros—who came to represent the Mexican ideal of machismo. Reinforced by its portrayal on the big screen, tequila now took on a nationalist flavor. It came to symbolize "national coherence in a period of post-revolutionary recovery . . . An emblem of *lo Mexicano*," writes Gaytán. Yet the image of rough men riding into rough towns and quenching their thirst with stiff pours at the local cantina was not admired by everyone. Affluent Mexicans often preferred imported products.

Meanwhile, north of the border, *Esquire* magazine named tequila its drink of the month in December 1953. In 1958, the Champs released their smash hit "Tequila," whose catchy refrain became permanently etched in the nation's collective consciousness. Twenty years later came Jimmy Buffett's "Margaritaville" and America's obsession with the cocktail it immortalized. Soon, the tequila boom would hit the United States. And only now that the second-wave boom is in full swing, with 100 percent agave spirits and their celebrity endorsements ubiquitous, is tequila heartily celebrated in Mexico at every echelon of society. So, what happens when a culture embraces a product that is technically their own only after its image has been filtered through the psyche of a different culture? Perhaps a better question would be, Is tequila truly Mexican?

"The way tequila was marketed in the US had a lot to do with how the United States treated Mexicans in the early part of the twentieth century, from the Prohibition era onward: as an uneducated and largely criminal population," says Gaytán. "This racialization got narrated through the language of tequila, so that tequila became closely associated with Mexican backwardness and criminality. But Mexicans themselves took up the crude stereotype and turned it into a symbol of strength. Tequila came to be associated with the image of the rebellious charro: this handsome, [tequila-drinking, cantina-hopping outlaw]. A Mexican cowboy . . . an icon of Mexicanness."

Tequila's image in the United States, first rooted in Mexican stereotypes, became shaped by its association with partying with reckless abandon. Later the focus of marketing campaigns would be the spirit's artisanality and heritage. This is the image the Sparkle Donkey brand lampooned. Today, the spirit is portrayed as a luxury, but also a cultural product. Tequila producers are characterized as respected families with long-held ties to their craft. The focus is less on their Spanish roots and more on their Mexican identity. The implication of many a premium brand's marketing campaign is that the consumer is sophisticated for having discovered this historical gem of a spirit from south of the border.

So, yes, tequila is a truly Mexican product. But it's also an American product—for better or worse. Made in Mexico, its image has long been shaped by American sensibilities. Yet somewhere along the way, part of the story gets lost in translation. What's missing from the narrative is how tequila went from being just another mezcal to the billion-dollar industry it is today. Other mezcales around the country are made by farmers—campesinos—and, if Gaytán's point about race is to be considered, by indigenous people. How tequila came to be dominated by Spanish-descended Mexicans and white foreigners is the part of the story that tends to be omitted.

Americans, for all their own country's diversity, rarely think of Mexico as a multicultural place. But the country is home to dozens—if not thousands, by some researchers' count—of indigenous tribes. It recognizes sixty-two official indigenous languages.[3] Some 15 percent of the country's population identifies with these groups, accounting for more than fifteen million people. The rest of the population descends largely from European ancestry or from mestizos. During the colonial period, indigenous and mestizo people were marginalized and have since struggled with higher levels of poverty and illiteracy. Today, Mexico's socioeconomic divisions still tend to run along color lines, much like they do in the United States. As researchers like Gaytán argue, these cultural divisions have been an ongoing factor in tequila's evolution.

The spirit has always relied on the labor of native Mexicans, but had strong ties to foreigners.

Today, tequila is widely consumed in major metropolitan centers throughout Mexico, as well as in the country's most popular tourist destinations, from Cancún to Cozumel. But in small villages around the country, and increasingly in Mexico City, mezcal is the tipple of choice. In DF, plenty of people still drink tequila, but the spirit is most popular among the working class. The city's artists, designers, scholars, and restaurateurs—the cultural elite—see the spirit as corrupted, not Mexican enough. They have turned instead to mezcal. The trend may have started with one or two hipster mezcal bars opened by idealistic types who, in the search for a truly artisanal spirit, discovered mezcal. But it has now spread to just about every new restaurant and upscale lounge that opens in Mexico City, as well as in the culinary capitals of Oaxaca and Puebla. A well-curated mezcal list these days is a must.

A growing number of spirits-savvy Americans are also beginning to feel disillusioned by how industrialized tequila has become, despite continuing to rely on the rhetoric of heritage and tradition in its marketing. But for now, the spirit is in no danger of losing its place at the American table. Tequila must be made in Mexico—*hecho en México*, as is printed on the bottle—but much of its image is crafted in the United States. That image continues to evolve as the American market—tequila's most significant market—itself evolves. From Mexican cowboy drink to terroir-driven sipping spirit, tequila's changing image is a reflection of changing American values.

And who better embodies American values than Oprah Winfrey? When asked about what she drinks at home, the television mogul did not name an expensive wine but rather a super-premium tequila. Casa Dragones bills itself as an artisanal tequila. It's priced at $275 a bottle. I meet the brand's CEO, Bertha González Nieves, not in a dusty agave field or remote distillery, but at a long, black, shiny conference table inside Rockefeller Plaza in midtown Manhattan. She sits on one side, flanked by underlings; I'm directly across, alone. The office is very modern: standing reception desk, projection screen for the presentation clicked through on a thin laptop. Bertha is the cofounder of the brand; her partner is MTV creator and media magnate Bob Pittman. They launched Casa Dragones in 2009.

Bertha has a wealth of experience in the tequila industry, having worked for a decade for the Beckmann family, who are the latest generation to run José Cuervo. A savvy entrepreneur, she was named one of Mexico's fifty most powerful women by *Forbes* and is the first woman to have been certified as a Maestra Tequilera by the CRT-approved Academia Mexicana de Catadores de Tequila (Academy of Mexican Tequila Tasters). Casa Dragones has won recognition not only for its suave flavor and high quality, but also for the design of its packaging. It's bottled in hand-etched crystal decanters tied with a black ribbon at the neck.

"We're a small-batch tequila producer and we believe in the power of focus," Bertha states at the top of our conversation. "We [started out] producing only one style of tequila, which is rare in the tequila industry: joven."

It's true. Most brands release a blanco, reposado, and añejo. Especially among 100 percent blue agave tequilas, joven is underrepresented. It was the company's only product until it released a blanco in 2014. As one of the five official classifications of tequila—blanco, joven, reposado, añejo, and extra añejo—joven is most often associated with less refined mixtos, like Cuervo Gold. Casa Dragones's is a blanco blended with a hint of extra añejo. Before bottling, the added color from the older tequila is filtered out using a proprietary filtration system so the spirit in the bottle appears crystal clear.

"We're quite obsessed with our clarity," says Bertha, sounding much like a diamond dealer. She's beautiful, with dark, cascading hair and the fine features of a tan Diane Lane. "We're using a quite modern filtration process that we imported from Germany. It enables us to deliver this particular clarity and also adds a shine to the liquid—we call it a platinum hue—that we're very proud of. If you look at the walls of your glass, you'll see the product also has long and pronounced legs that translate into a silky body. We believe this has a lot to do with the experience of taste. Casa Dragones is a sipping tequila. It's not a product that's meant to be mixed. It's meant to be savored straight. Now, let's move on to nosing the product."

I'm caught off-guard by the instruction. Bertha takes me through a technical tasting. She makes statements like, "We're not in the business of volume; we're in the business of taste." The tequila itself is soft and delicate. It has bright notes of citrus, but also vanilla and a hint of spice. The sweeter, rounder flavors are imparted by the extra añejo, which also gives the spirit a lush and creamy texture.

Casa Dragones does not own its own plantations. It has long-standing agreements with growers from the Tequila Valley. The agaves are harvested, on average, between eight and twelve years old. The company produces no more than five thousand bottles per batch, roughly five times per year.

"We believe it's all about the power of the fields and all about the care of the plants," Bertha continues. "We harvest our agaves when they're actually ripe and done. You can do that by measuring the Brix in the heart of the plant." Now she sounds like a winemaker, using the popular viticulture term for measuring sugar content. "Not only is it the characteristics of the soil, we talk a lot about altitude. The agave plant is actually a nocturnal plant that processes its photosynthesis at night. We're looking for an ideal nighttime temperature of five to fifteen degrees centigrade. As well, we're looking for the ideal inclination of the field. It's important to get the circulation of water under the soil, so the flatter the field is, the harder it is to work with. Rainfall plays an important role and we're looking for the ideal, which is right around six hundred to eight hundred millimeters."

All this talk of climate, soil, and topography smacks of terroir. Bertha sounds like she might have a background farming vineyards in Europe. Actually, she was bitten by the tequila bug as a student, when she was chosen to represent Mexico as a young ambassador to Japan. Trained to speak eloquently about her country's economy, politics, religion, and folklore, she also learned to speak about its industry and exports, and visited several tequila factories to prepare for it. The moment she visited her first agave field, she knew. She called her parents and told them what she wanted to do with her life. As soon as she finished her graduate studies, she applied for her first job in the tequila industry.

"We believe in extracting the juice from the heart of the plant in a different way," she continues. "Most companies use clay ovens or autoclaves. That's the most common way of cooking the heart of the plant and then extracting the juice. We believe in extracting the juice before cooking. So we cut the heart of the plant in small pieces and then extract the juice through steam and water, which allows us to bring some of those more floral and citrus notes that we wouldn't be able to bring otherwise. These are beautiful and really complement the product in a very special way."

Wait a minute. What Bertha is describing is a diffuser. Having seen these megalodon machines in action, it doesn't seem congruent with the artisanal image of the tequila. These are not machines that help agave communicate its terroir. The process she describes sounds gentle and precise, but what diffusers actually do is shred raw agave, then use a mixture of steam and chemicals—usually sulfuric acid—to extract the plant's sugars. Diffusers are able to extract up to 20 percent more fermentable material than other methods. What's more, Casa Dragones is column distilled, a method most often associated with vodka and mass-produced alcohol. The two technologies, especially when combined, make for a highly cost-effective production process. Not at all what you expect from a high-end small-batch tequila that takes such care to source its raw ingredients.[4]

It turns out that much of the artisanality in Casa Dragones has to do with the bottle. The crystal decanters are made using a semiautomatic process in Mexico, meaning that the artisan uses molds but takes the lead-free crystal out of the oven by hand. A limited-edition bottle priced at $2,000 is etched using the ancient art of *pepita* glass engraving. Using an aluminum oxide grinding stone, artisans from the Museo de Arte Popular in Mexico City, an institution that celebrates and preserves Mexican handicrafts, carve out patterns in decorative pepita, or pumpkin seed, shapes. No bottle ends up fully identical to another and each one is hand numbered. Benjamín García, Bertha's co-master distiller, shares her initials and both are charged with signing the bottles.

Casa Dragones is made in the town of Tequila, at the Leyros distillery (NOM 1489), which also makes Tarantula Tequila, a brand that blends tequila with bright pink strawberry or electric blue citrus-flavored liqueur. Casa Dragones built its own proprietary finishing facility within the building. This is where it filters the aged tequila back to colorless clarity. So, how does the company reconcile its artisanal image with such a tech-heavy approach to making tequila?

"We're all for using the 250 years of history of our category, but we are definitely a modern company," says Bertha. "There are a lot of different ways to get to the end product in tequila. We chose this particular way because we believe it enables us to deliver particular characteristics. Industrialization is not synonymous with something bad. The evolution of any product will require investment in new technologies and techniques."

Despite being made in Tequila, the brand's spiritual home is San Miguel de Allende, where Bob Pittman owns property. The tequila is named for the Dragones de San Miguel de Allende, a cavalry led by the revolutionary General Ignacio Allende. Being at the center of Mexico, San Miguel de Allende was once very important to the country's commerce and trade. The town is still very wealthy and is home to such luxury hotel chains as Oriental Express and Rosewood. It may not have a beach, but it attracts a more cultured traveler who seeks out high-end amenities, architecture, and art. Casa Dragones embodies this luxury status, from the packaging down to the liquid inside.

"We're using new American white oak barrels for our extra añejo," Bertha continues. "We invited some of the most recognized palates in tequila to help us write our tasting notes. From our DNA as a company, what we're trying to do is push the boundaries of what has been done before and truly expand the tequila repertoire. We want to make sure we're representing the industry in the best way possible. And also we're very serious about selling Mexican craftsmanship. We believe that many other cultures have been successful in selling their craftsmanship; the

French and the Italians and many European countries have been able to participate in that luxury platform. We believe that Mexico has everything it takes to participate there too."

As the tasting progresses, I do feel like I'm participating in an exclusive luxury experience. Casa Dragones even enlisted Michelin-starred chef Éric Ripert to design a pairing menu for it. Bertha assures me that her tequila pairs with more than just Mexican dishes. The chef found it to be a match for dark chocolate, as well as fluke carpaccio.

Stepping back out into the noise and traffic of midtown Manhattan on a typically cold, wet Thursday in February is something of a shock to the system after the cool, clean quiet of the Casa Dragones office. Or maybe it's the slight buzz from the tequila. My luxury tasting experience is over and I must ride the subway home like a plebeian. On the train, above the heads of passengers are ads for travel destinations, therapy sessions, English-as-a-second-language classes. What might lead a straphanger to pick up the phone and dial the number advertised is a mystery. But this is the goal for all marketers, to pinpoint the image or message that will insinuate itself into our brains and cause us, at some point, to make a purchase. On the hit TV show *Mad Men*, the part ads play in the process is depicted so romantically. A dashing creative genius awaits inspiration, then, like a monk on a hilltop, pronounces a magic formula: an image that not only tells a story, but taps into the very essence of our innermost desires.

In real life, there are focus groups to conduct, demographics to hit, and shareholders to placate. But those creative geniuses do exist. I'm more familiar with the other side of marketing, where the brand presents itself directly to the press, hoping to skip the advertising expense in favor of free coverage in a magazine article or blog post. I've become greatly disillusioned with my role in this process after years of receiving homogeneous press releases touting every shade of booze under the sun. My favorite approach publicists take is to tie the product they are pushing to any remotely relevant event or reference. Press releases pour into my inbox shouting: "Try this brand of vodka in your annual Groundhog Day cocktails!" or "Drink this whiskey, like that guy in that movie that just came out!" or "Go out and buy this bottle for the big game!"

One of the most popular events each year that publicists latch onto on behalf of their booze clients is Cinco de Mayo. Mexican beer companies and tequila marketers try to capitalize on the day's image as a drinking holiday. In recent years, Cinco de Mayo has become a warmer, more colorful St. Paddy's Day: an excuse for people to abandon their work stations and head for the nearest bar. Booze companies will be there waiting for you, eager to push their branded margaritas, shots, and beer on willing consumers. But ask most marketers—or most Americans, for that matter—what Cinco de Mayo is and you'll likely hear, Um, Mexican Independence Day? Wrong.

Mexican Independence Day, celebrated all over Mexico, is in September. The Fifth of May is a day recognized mostly in Puebla, marking a battle that took place there in 1862. A ragtag band of Mexican troops went up against Napoleon III's better-equipped French forces and, against all odds, defeated them. Historians believe that the outcome of this battle may have been a turning point in the American Civil War raging in the United States. The war could very well have been won by the South had the Confederates secured the French as an ally. The French Army, deemed the world's greatest military force at the time, had a significant interest in pushing forward into the United States. By helping the South defeat the North, it could have ended up with two less-threatening nations to contend with as opposed to an increasingly powerful United States. Luckily, Mexico staved off the French, which gave Union forces time to battle the Confederacy. It also helped cement the relationship between the two neighboring countries.[5]

In Puebla, Cinco de Mayo is celebrated with a lavish parade and a war reenactment. People take the day off work and school to participate in the festivities. In the rest of the country, the day goes by largely unnoticed. The United States saw its first Cinco de Mayo celebrations in small enclaves of Mexican immigrants, mostly in California, as early as the mid-nineteenth century. The day came to be celebrated by different groups from different parts of Mexico over the years. Eventually, beer marketers took note of the event and saw it as an opportunity to reach the Latino market. By the 1980s, beer brands were marketing directly to Mexicans in the days leading up to May 5, playing up the angle of cultural pride. Why Cinco de Mayo and not Mexico's actual Independence Day, which is far more widely celebrated in Mexico? Well, that day happens to be called *Dieciséis de Septiembre*. It doesn't exactly roll off the American tongue.[6]

What the beer marketers did not expect as a response to their efforts was for non-Latino Americans to get in on the Cinco de Mayo celebrations. Apparently, everyone likes a vaguely cultural excuse to get soused. Soon, tequila companies jumped on the bandwagon, offering branded margarita specials and shots in bars and restaurants across the country. Like St. Patrick's Day, Cinco de Mayo is now a day synonymous with excessive drinking and unabashed carousing. And you don't have to be Mexican to take part. "Kiss me: I'm Mexican (for the day)," the buttons should read, since Cinco de Mayo, like St. Paddy's, has been co-opted by booze peddlers and binge drinkers.

The next challenge for tequila marketers will be braving a potentially vast new market thanks to, of all things, a change in Chinese law. In the summer of 2013, Mexico sent its first shipment of premium tequila to China in six years, some four years after the two countries began negotiating a lift of the ban on 100 percent agave tequila in China. In 2008, China banned most imports of premium tequila. At issue was China's own rampant counterfeiting problem and the toxic levels of methanol fake tequila can contain. Only ten recognized brands were approved to be sold in the country, including José Cuervo and Pernod Ricard's Olmeca Altos. Other high-end brands were prohibited as part of an effort to crack down on knockoffs.

The ban was a black eye on the tequila industry. Mexico enlisted the support of both the United States and the European Union to push China to change the rules. In the spring of 2013, it demanded China give scientific justification for the ban. The pressure proved effective. The initial seventy thousand bottle load was said to be the first of some ten million liters Mexico plans to export to China in the next five years.[7]

The country is expected to become the second largest market for tequila after the United States. Now that China has become a major consumer of wines and spirits—its wealthiest citizens driving up the prices on rare and collectible bottles and making record purchases at auction—liquor producers around the world are doing everything they can to break into the Chinese market.

It's unclear how the message of Mexican craft and tradition will translate to Chinese consumers. Or if marketing the spirit to them will rely more heavily on themes of luxury and celebrity endorsements. But surely the message will move even further away from tequila's heritage. European winemakers often express frustration over trying to convey nuances of terroir when selling to the Chinese, who tend to care more about a brand's reputation and price tag. Certain wine producers have even been known to raise their prices to appeal to the Chinese market. On the other hand, you have Western winemakers talking about pairing their wines with "Asian flavors," with little understanding of China's complex and varied cuisine. In this global marketplace we now inhabit, it's impossible to control who buys your product or why. If the goal is to sell as much as possible, then the means must be shrewd and aggressive. It's what competing in a world economy demands. The tequila industry certainly appears to be up to the challenge.

{10}

The Agave Activists

Unless someone like you cares a whole awful lot,
Nothing is going to get better. It's not.
—Dr. Seuss, *The Lorax*

In 2008 and 2009, the US labor market shrank by 8.4 million jobs. Across the country, some 6 percent of all payroll employees lost their livelihoods. It was a tumultuous time. A small number of people, from idealistic first-time entrepreneurs to shrewd former Wall Street types, responded to the recession with a plan to develop their own liquor brands. They abandoned the shackles and drudgery of their former lives to launch new luxury vodkas and gins. Several of these souls decamped to Mexico to hunt for a tequila to repackage as their own. Since then, launching a premium tequila brand has become something of a trend among men and women of means. So just how does someone go about developing a tequila brand? Here is one way:

Brent Hocking made his fortune in finance. The son of a preacher from Compton, California, he is large and thickset, with a confident and forthright manner, and a face that could make him a convincing Andrew Dice Clay double. As he acquired his wealth, Brent cultivated a taste for the finer things. He is a self-proclaimed lover of fine wine, citing Château Margaux and Domaine de Romanée-Conti (expensive Bordeaux and Burgundy, respectively) as his favorites. He had long fantasized about owning his own vineyard in France. When this dream didn't pan out, Brent decided to invest in his other potable passion: tequila. He spent weeks combing tequila country sampling tequilas from small and midsize independent distilleries. After tasting about a hundred of them, he settled on a spirit he decided was perfect.

The small family operation that produced Reserva de Mexico was located in a village called Purísima del Rincón, in the state of Guanajuato. Literal translation: the purest of the corner. Brent fell in love with the tequila and loved that it came from a place named for purity. He could envision the entire marketing plan for such a product and made an offer to buy the rights to it right then and there. The family's patriarch, an elderly man of considerable means himself, flatly refused. He said he never wished to see the day his tequila was repackaged and sold outside of Mexico.

After multiple attempts to reason with the old man, Brent abandoned his pursuit of Reserva de Mexico. A few months later, back in Los Angeles, he ran into the guy who had deejayed at his wedding. The two got to talking about tequila and, when he realized Brent was such an aficionado, the young disc jockey told him that his family made tequila down in Mexico. You may be able to guess where the story is headed: the tequila his family made was called Reserva de Mexico. It was Brent's holy grail.

"I said, 'You're kidding, that's the stuff!'" Brent recalls. "'But your grandfather won't let anybody buy it.' And this kid goes, 'Yes, but he died nine days ago.'"

The young man's uncle was now in charge. Brent's heart skipped a beat.

"They still don't want any part of releasing it outside of Mexico," the young man said.

But Brent persuaded him to ask his uncle for a meeting. He didn't hear back from the DJ for several months. Then, one day, just as he had resigned himself to forgetting about his tequila dream, he got the call. The family agreed to hear him out. Over the next six months, Brent negotiated to acquire the distribution rights to their tequila. He would rebrand it for sale in the United States. It would no longer be called Reserva de Mexico. Instead, he settled on DeLeón, inspired by the nearby town of León, where the family was from. As he told his story, I had to ask: did he feel guilty about defying the final wishes of a dying man?

"I started to feel very close to the uncle and his brothers," Brent answers. "They said that their father had been approached many times by very big players. He didn't trust anybody and he felt that no one had anything in mind but to change his tequila. What everybody had wanted to do prior to my proposal was to take his tequila and turn it into something else—rebrand, repackage, everything. Now, granted, I did the same thing. But I paid tribute to the family. I think that was the difference-maker."

Or, perhaps the difference-maker was that the head of the company died and his sons decided to sell out against his wishes. Aside from the bottle and branding, Brent maintains that he stayed true to the family recipe, making only one change: aging the spirit in used Sauternes barrels. DeLeón is now one of the most expensive tequilas on the market. A bottle of the Diamante tequila (a joven) retails for $130. A bottle of the Extra Añejo comes with a suggested retail price of $320. The Leona Reserva, an añejo packaged in a black box accompanied by a python-skin flask, sells for $1,000. One can only wonder what the old man would say. Especially now that DeLeón has been bought by Diageo, the largest distributor of spirits in the world, which partnered with hip-hop mogul Sean Combs, a.k.a. P. Diddy, to take over DeLeón. And especially now that it's no longer made by the original family but produced in a completely different distillery in Arandas, Jalisco.

"You're seeing a lot of small or family-owned brands bought. I think it's definitely a problem," says Phil Ward, co-owner of Mayahuel, the tequila and mezcal bar in New York's East Village that was hailed as the most progressive agave spirits bar in the country until it closed in 2017. In a matter of years, Phil went from being a bar back to a mixologist in several of New York's best cocktail bars. He opened Mayahuel in 2009 with a mission to introduce his customers to true tequila and mezcal.

In the process, he's become something of an ambassador for the spirits of Mexico. An activist, too.

"Tequila is a victim of its own success right now. It's something that in the last couple of years is really hitting its stride," says Phil, sitting on the customer's side of the bar next to me. It's mid-afternoon and we're alone in the darkened boîte aside from members of the kitchen staff prepping the bar snacks for the night ahead. "There's an opportunity to take advantage of tequila, to market it. All that money from the billboards and ads you see usually comes out of the quality. There are a lot of brands that are changing in quality. It just breaks your heart when there's a brand of tequila that you really love that's been bought by another company and you find the flavor profile has changed."

Phil is tall and lanky, with facial hair that, since I first met him, has ranged from a full strawberry blond chinstrap beard to a cropped tuft contained just below his lips. He is soft-spoken and shuns the spotlight, unlike so many young, ambitious bartenders these days who strive for celebrity mixologist status. But being a generally quiet guy does not mean he isn't outspoken. For example, he does not hide his distaste for the corporate side of the booze industry, especially as it pertains to tequila. The Pittsburgh native becomes increasingly agitated as he talks about the industry, punctuating his words by pounding the beautifully tiled bar top with his fist. Tequila is what put Mexico on the map when it comes to global spirits consumption, he says, adding that he understands how important it is to the country's economy. But he laments how the spirit's popularity has come at the expense of its integrity.

"What we're trying to do at Mayahuel is save people from thinking tequila is a 51 percent mixto," Phil explains. "People come in here and are like, 'I hate tequila.' And they haven't even tasted it. Basically, the line in the sand is the palate of the population. We're trying to tell people that industrial tequila is not what tequila is supposed to taste like. A margarita is not supposed to taste like sour mix and it's not supposed to be a fourteen-ounce drink. Most of that isn't even booze. Palates and perception, that's what's hard to change. People see it on a billboard and think it must be good. I tell people all the time: there's almost nothing on a billboard you should buy when it comes to spirits."

"Is there any terroir left in tequila, then?" I ask.

"Honestly, I think there is," Phil answers. "I don't think it's drastic. I think even though it exists, the field of play that it can exist on is so much smaller. I always refer to mezcal as 'tequila with terroir,' because you have so many different areas, so many different types of plants, and so many makers who do things differently. The playing field is so much bigger in mezcal."

Most tequila bars around the country have amassed huge collections, boasting of lists of one hundred bottles or more. Phil says he never counted his tequilas, nor did he aim to have such a great number of them. He was always interested in selling only the best—and what he considers to be the best does not necessarily include the most expensive brands. He wants to showcase tequilas made with care and a respect for tradition. He also wants to use them in a way that has not been seen before, by making good craft cocktails beyond fruity margaritas and tequila sunrises.

When Mayahuel first opened, mezcal was still virtually unknown in cocktailing circles. Phil wanted to show how refined and delicious mezcal, too, could be—both on its own and as a cocktail ingredient. In the bar's early days, only a handful of good mezcales were available in the United States. So, while Phil never counted his tequila bottles, he did count his mezcales. He started with only about a dozen of them and now has more than fifty.

"I'm almost positive if I counted now, we have more mezcal than tequila," he said in 2013. "That number is going to dwindle even more. It's not totally hopeless. You have tequila brands that have come out in the States, like Tapatio, which is actually an older brand that is now available. They do a bottling that is overproof, which is encouraging because it's something we've needed tequila to do for a very long time. When you bring me a spirit that is 80 proof, it pretty much means you didn't think about it. There's no reason that you should take the status quo and make it 80 proof without tasting it at 81, 82, 83. [Or 90 or 100.]

It is insane how different something can taste between 83 and 84 proof. It's entirely different."

Like Phil, Bobby Heugel opened a bar that got billed as "game changing." He completed his master's degree in intercultural communication, with an emphasis on conflict resolution. As a student, he'd worked in bars to help pay for college and later decided to make bartending his career. But it wasn't until he discovered tequila and mezcal that he found a way to incorporate his education into his bar work. Now he's part of the movement the ethnobotanist Ana Valenzuela talked about: he's an agave activist.

Bobby opened the Pastry War, an agave spirits bar in Houston that serves no pastries at all, in 2013. It was named for a historical dispute between Mexico and France. In the years following its battle for independence in 1821, Mexico was not a stable nation. Civil disorder reigned and resulted in widespread bloodshed and damages to private property. One case involved a French pastry chef living near Mexico City whose bakery had been demolished. He appealed to his king in France for compensation, who in turn demanded that the Mexican government pay for the damages. These amounted to a staggering 600,000 pesos, a princely sum when you consider that Mexican workers earned less than a peso per day at the time.[1] The skirmish led Mexico to declare war on France. Trade between the countries was halted and Mexicans resorted to smuggling goods from the United States. But the brief war came to an end when Britain's ambassador intervened, smoothing things over diplomatically and negotiating payment of the debt.

Bobby found himself so taken with the story that he named his bar after it. The joint French and Mexican history inspired him to serve cognac as well as tequila and mezcal and to play both French and Mexican music. He says the bar is a reflection of his and his partner's passion for agave spirits. His partner, Alba Huerta, is from Monterrey. The bar, like Mayahuel, does not pride itself on a lengthy tequila and mezcal list, but rather on a well-curated one. Bobby is so adamant about what he will and will not serve that he had the latter printed on the chalkboard wall of the bar when it first opened. In block letters, it stated: WE ARE

PROUD TO NOT SERVE THE FOLLOWING: FLAVORED OR FLAVORLESS AGAVE SPIRITS, DON JULIO TEQUILA, ZIGNUM MEZCAL, SAUZA TEQUILA, JOSE CUERVO TEQUILA, TEQUILAS WITH OFFICIAL CELEBRITY ENDORSEMENTS, THAT SHIT THAT MADE YOU SICK THAT ONE TIME, PATRON TEQUILA, 1800 TEQUILA, JUAREZ TEQUILA, SPIRITS WITH WORMS, SCORPIONS & OTHER INSECTS, CAZADORES TEQUILA, BRANDS THAT ADVOCATED NOM 186. (More on NOM 186 later.)

It's a bold statement that many bartenders might agree with privately but few would scrawl on the walls of their establishment. Bobby didn't care what liquor companies made of it, especially those he called out in the disclaimer. He just wanted his customers to read it and start asking questions. And they did. The message on the wall was eventually replaced with happy hour specials. But a year later Bobby had another controversial message posted on his chalkboard. It described how diffuser technology works, and listed various distilleries that use diffusers, calling out their NOM and the brands they produce.

"I saw the impact that the tequila and mezcal industries were having on local communities and the exploitation of local cultures for profits for global spirit conglomerates," he explains. "I don't think the situation is unique to Mexico. But what makes tequila and mezcal special is that we're talking about an agricultural product that's finite. It's particularly vulnerable to the pressures of a global spirits economy."

The Pastry War organized its spirits list by agave variety, so all the tequilas are listed under Tequilana Weber. When it opened it also served vintage tequilas, such as Herradura and El Tesoro, so that patrons could taste what these spirits were like when they were still independently owned. The bar prides itself on an excellent and reasonably priced margarita—just $9—which comes shaken or frozen and features two types of lime, key and Persian.

In addition to sparking debates within the walls of his bar, Bobby is known to start rather controversial conversations on the wall of his Facebook page with his thousands of friends. Many of these are liquor industry folk, including people who work for some of the big brands he openly criticizes. In this era of social media influence, he's able to initiate transnational conversations on the impact of big spirits companies.

Misty Kalkofen is another bartender who has achieved star status within the cocktail community and is using that influence to shine a light on agave spirits. After years of being behind the stick, she left the nocturnal life of bartending and took a gig as a brand ambassador. She's lucky to be able to represent a brand she firmly believes in, one she would promote even if it weren't paying her: Del Maguey. It's a dream job, she says, for a mezcal lover such as herself.

"I was an appreciator of tequila, but my love for agave distillates really started when I met Ron Cooper [founder of Del Maguey]," says Misty. "When I first tasted mezcal, well, I had never before tasted anything in the world quite like it. It opened my eyes to a category of spirits from Mexico—including raicilla, bacanora, and sotol—that are much truer to tradition than tequila is."

With her jet-black hair and sleeve tattoo, Misty looks like the archetypal bartender. But she first learned about classic cocktails while tending bar by night as she earned her master's in theological studies from Harvard Divinity School by day. She ended up ditching her plan to pursue a PhD and sticking to bartending. That was twenty years ago. In her new role she still gets to do what she loves—pour drinks, talk and learn about spirits, even come up with new cocktail recipes—but she gets to do it while traveling the world. When she's not helping sell Del Maguey, she is speaking out about the issues facing the tequila industry.

"A lot of people, when they hear me talk about tequila, they think I don't like it. But it's absolutely the opposite of that," she says. "It's out of my concern for tequila and the fact that I really want it to be around for many generations to come that I raise questions about sustainability and industrialization. It's important for me to say that to people, especially in Mexico. They can get really angry that some gringa comes down and is asking questions about chemical inputs in the soil and how workers are treated. But it's because I care about tequila that I'm asking those questions."

She recounts visiting Macario Partida Ramos's plantations, in Zapotitlán near the Colima volcano, whose rustic wooden still we saw in the second chapter. Misty asked him to show her the blue agave plants he'd planted a few years previous. When he pointed them out, she saw how puny and diseased they were. His other plants were so much healthier, with piñas that could grow to be well over one hundred pounds. "What have you done differently with them?" she wanted to know about the blue agave. He answered, "Absolutely nothing. Even the ants will kill these plants."

His main problem is the *picudo del agave* or agave snout weevil, a small, shiny, hard-backed black bug with a long, curved snout. Macario says the weevil came when he planted the blue agave and poses a threat to his other healthy plants. He doesn't know how to stop it.

"In Mexico, the people who are making tequila tend to have their heads in the sand about practices of horticulture and cultivation," says Misty. "In Jalisco, you have tequila producers coming to small mezcal producers and asking them to eradicate all the other types of agave on their land, which could be ten or twelve different types, and only to plant the agave tequilana Weber. And when they do plant it—even if they only try with two or three plants, just to see what happens—they treat those plants exactly how they treat the other plants on their land, with no chemicals or fertilizers. The blue agave can't hold up.

"[And why should they plant blue agave instead of other heirloom varieties?] These are people who have been surviving by making agave distillates in their villages for hundreds of years. Because the tequila industry doesn't want to lose even the smallest share of the market to customers who might become interested in the other agave distillates of Mexico? That's not fair."

The mezcal category is growing, but remains small compared to tequila and other spirits. Global exports jumped nearly 50 percent from 2007 to 2011, according to the Mexican government. Production has tripled since then. Revised regulations introduced in 2017 ban the use of diffusers and encourage traditional production methods. While the tequila industry has about 150 factories and more than sixteen hundred brands, for mezcal it's the opposite. Thousands of producers exist but only a few hundred brands.

David Suro-Piñera is another agave spirits activist. But unlike those we've met so far, he also happens to be a tequila producer. To the ire of many of his colleagues and competitors, he has no interest in keeping quiet about the environmental, social, and economic problems that plague the industry. In addition to owning a tequila brand, David owns the restaurant Los Catrines Tequilas, in Philadelphia, known affectionately by the natives simply as Tequilas.

Not long ago, David's restaurant was the only place in the city to get 100 percent agave tequila. Born and raised in Guadalajara, he's the picture of a healthy gourmand: plump and cheerful, with an easy smile framed by a neatly cropped salt-and-pepper mustache. We meet in his restaurant in Rittenhouse Square shortly before it opens. He's a little hungover from an impromptu party in the bar area the night before, but you can barely tell. He's as spry as ever.

David was inducted into the restaurant world some thirty years ago, back in Mexico, and moved to the United States in 1985 with the intention of starting his own place. He opened Tequilas with his now ex-wife a year later. The restaurant moved to its current location in 2001. Despite his decades-long experience in the business, David considers himself more of a tequila guy than a restaurant guy. He's been researching the industry for nearly thirty years and got serious about it some fifteen years ago when he first considered starting his own brand. The idea he had was not only to make his own tequila, but to use some of the profits from the venture to invest back into tequila research and education. It took at least a decade to build the project out. Siembra Azul Tequila was launched in 2007. The name of the brand translates as "blue harvest." David recognizes that the spirit has come a long way; he has seen the evolution of tequila consumption in the United States firsthand.

"When we opened the restaurant, we had five tequilas in our bar," he says, in his clipped accent. "That was all we had because that was all I considered drinkable. During those years, I preferred to drink scotch rather than tequila because there really wasn't much available. Now, the restaurant has many more tequilas. It's completely mixto- and diffuser-tequila free."

He recalls people having one of two reactions to the word tequila back in his restaurant's early days: either a cowering fear of it or an expectation that it would lead to getting wasted and rowdy. Nowadays, he says, the perception of tequila has drastically changed. A big part of that change is the embrace of the spirit by the craft cocktail community: high-end bars like Phil Ward's Mayahuel, where drinks were treated like so much more than just a viaduct by which alcohol can enter the body. Another driver of change has been academia. It used to be rare to find scholars focusing their research on the tequila industry. Today, there's a cadre of academics from a variety of fields studying agave spirits.

"I used to be the little guy throwing stones at the big guys, trying to get their attention and bringing up topics that they should take into consideration," David recalls. "It was very frustrating that no one was acknowledging important issues, like the sustainability of agave plantations or how the industry was affecting the lives of the workers in tequila. So, I decided to invite the most influential bartenders in the United States and the most influential professors in Mexico and put them together."

The result was the Tequila Interchange Project (TIP), his nonprofit consumer advocacy group for tequila that acts as a sort of watchdog for the industry. Since its inception in 2010, it has been involved in research projects ranging from tracing the migratory patterns of jimadores to studying the dangers to blue agave's genetic health. It also hosts regular trips to Mexico, inviting groups of bartenders and scholars in order to show them what industrialization has done to the craft of tequila. On the academic side, ethnobotanists like Patricia Colunga and Ana Valenzuela have participated in TIP trips. Phil Ward, Bobby Heugel, and Misty Kalkofen are all founding members. Those invited not only learn about tequila, but also get to visit distillers working outside the industry: maestro mezcaleros making ultra-traditional agave spirits in the foothills of the Colima volcanoes, for example.

In late 2011, TIP was given a true raison d'être when new legislation was put forth that could have hurt the interests of small, artisanal producers of tequila and mezcal. Representatives from the appellations of origin for tequila, mezcal, and bacanora were behind the drafting of the proposed legislation known as NOM 186. It quickly became a cause célèbre throughout the agave spirits world, with small producers and the purists who enjoy their products speaking out against it. On the surface, it appeared to call for a tightening of regulations and a clarification in labeling on tequila and mezcal bottles: a move in the right direction. Reading further into it, however, revealed that NOM 186 was designed to improve sales for the biggest tequila and mezcal corporations, especially in the United States, the largest market for the spirits already.

NOM 186 called for further limiting what can be called mezcal. Within the mezcal appellation of origin, producers in only nine states are officially recognized. But mezcal is made in nearly all of Mexico's thirty-one states, as it has been for centuries. That leaves thousands of mezcaleros around the country working outside the boundaries of the appellation of origin. They already cannot officially commercialize or export their product as mezcal. NOM 186 took it even further, stating that mezcaleros outside the appellation would be forced to label their product *aguardiente*, a generic term that translates literally as "firewater." In addition, they would be forbidden to use the phrase "100 percent agave" on their labels, forced to limit the proof of their spirits so as not to compete with sanctioned mezcales, and barred from using unauthorized—albeit heirloom—agave varieties.

The proposed law would have been a tragedy for mezcal producers all over Mexico who have made traditional agave spirits for generations. Critics denounced it as violating Mexican laws that are meant to protect workers and entrepreneurs, as well as national statutes that ensure the preservation of Mexican culture. The Tequila Interchange Project and its TIPsters, as its hipster bartender contingent has been nicknamed, took up the cause of fighting this proposed legislation. In early 2012, it enlisted its academic members to draft a petition outlining changes to be made to the proposed legislation and in less than a week gathered sixteen hundred signatures in support. Thanks in large part to TIP's efforts, the Mexican government rejected NOM 186.

"When we found out about the Machiavellian intentions of these groups pushing NOM 186, we had only about a week to react," says David. "I still pinch myself to believe what we did. For the big transnationals to stop and to rethink what they were doing and the government to decide to throw out this initiative, that's huge. It's very, very huge."

I miss David by a couple of days in Arandas, in the highlands of Jalisco. I show up at the distillery where Siembra Azul is made on a sunny Thursday, just days after he came to check on his latest batch of tequila. He travels frequently from Philadelphia to Mexico during the winter months, which is the best time to produce tequila. (Cooler temperatures slow everything down, he explains, which can mean a lengthier cooking time and richer fermentation.)

At Feliciano Vivanco y Asociados, the family-owned facility where Siembra Azul is made, David is known as the pickiest of clients. It's a compliment, actually. The staff there appreciate the way he insists on the best organic agaves and shows up for as much of the process as possible. The owner's grandson, Sergio, shows me around the property, which is small and simple. There is no visitors' center or events space: it's a working distillery. Beyond the fence that contains the hornos, fermentation, and distillation areas, you can see the Vivancos' own agave plantations. Sergio says his grandfather, now in his nineties, practiced organic farming before it even had a name. The Vivancos are also pretty progressive with their distillation methods: the process unfolds to the sounds of classical music, which they believe results in a smoother, more harmonious product. My visit coincides with the fermentation stage; the only sounds are the fizzing and frothing of agave juices in large steel tanks. The warehouse that houses the tanks is warm and clammy, an ideal environment for yeasts to flourish. Aromas of baking bread, overripe fruit, and cider filled the space. A few workers are busy filling the kilns with the freshly harvested agave piñas that just days ago David saw come in from the fields.

He prefers to use agave from the highlands, citing it as the best terroir to grow the plants. However, he laments the fact that so many plantations are treated with herbicides and pesticides. As a result, he says, the agaves aren't as vibrant as they should be. David also calls out the large tequila companies developing what he calls "Frankenstein agaves," designed to have shorter life cycles or modified to resist the pests running rampant in the fields. The problem with this sort of genetic tinkering, he claims, is that you may stave off "one fungus, one virus, one insect, but you develop ten other points of vulnerability."

Instead, he says, "What about introducing other agaves? The other agaves that used to be used in tequila, they are still available in Jalisco. I have seen them. We found plantations that have a dozen different varieties right next to each other. They are healthy, beautiful agaves. It's doable. Right now, we allow mixtos. But why don't we allow sugars from other agaves in the mixto? The majority of tequila production comes from corn and cane sugars from God-knows-where. Probably Cuba, Venezuela, Veracruz . . . and we call it tequila, that stuff? If we are so proud of our appellation of origin, then we should not allow outside materials in our tequila. Explain to me why we can't allow 51 percent of blue agave and 49 percent of other agaves. It would be delicious."

David also rails against the sale of bulk tequila for bottling abroad. On January 17, 2006, the Office of the United States Trade Representative issued a press release announcing that the US and Mexico had signed "an historic agreement on cross-border trade in tequila." The event was said to be "the culmination of two years and ten rounds of negotiations between the United States and Mexico." In 2003, a proposal was put forth to require all tequila to be bottled at source, creating a de facto ban on bulk exports. This would have "threatened the huge investments US companies have made to build bottling plants and develop brands in the United States." But bottling abroad not only threatens jobs within Mexico; it puts the tequila at risk.

"Humans are the most interesting part of the culture of this spirit," says David, bemoaning the industry's treatment of workers, small producers, and farmers. "We have this romantic idea of the jimador, for instance. You'll see them pouring tequila beside donkeys at the big distilleries. These aren't jimadores, they're actors. In tequila, you no longer have small farmers, real jimadores. During the crisis of 2000, with the shortage of agave, we had the highest prices of agave ever. The price per ton that was paid to a jimador was the same then as it is today. There's no incentive for them to stay, to teach their kids. It's a breed that's disappearing."

The place many have disappeared to is the United States. There was a time when jimadores would opt to cross the border—often illegally—when agave fieldwork was slow. According to Princeton sociologist Doug Massey, one of TIP's academic members, the migration pattern once showed them going back and forth, depending on the season. New, tougher sanctions on illegal border crossings make it more difficult for farmers to come back, so they either stay in the United States for longer periods of time or for good. And, while Mexican wages have actually increased relative to the United States' in recent years, thanks to rising education levels and employment opportunities leading illegal immigration to slow to a trickle, farming in Mexico is in decline. Instead of taking up the family business, young people from rural areas are opting to work in cities. The agricultural workforce throughout the country is collapsing, and the face of the jimador is changing.

As the farming of agave is taken over by large agribusinesses, the tequila industry at large has come to be dominated by multinational and foreign-owned corporations. Agave activists denounce this trend as a threat to tequila's—and Mexico's—heritage.

"I understand that, for a lot of people, when you hear so many tequila companies are being bought by British or American conglomerates, it's a concern," says Rubén Aceves, the brand ambassador for Tequila Herradura. "People think that we are losing part of our identity. Something so Mexican, so iconic for Mexico. I understand that. Now, it's in the hands of someone else. But legally, tequila has to be produced in Mexico, so we're not losing anything. We're keeping the distilleries, we're keeping our terroir. It's still a very Mexican product."

We're taking lunch out in the sprawling gardens behind the Herradura distillery located in Amatitán. The air smells of flowering mango and lime trees. On the menu are huge lobsters, imported from Maine. I long for the simple tortilla soup and fresh soft tacos I had here on another visit years ago. Still, the setting is rather idyllic.

Rubén is tall, broad, and dashing, with the fair complexion and strong, angular profile of someone with Northern European ancestry. He could be a leading man in one of Mexico's ever-popular telenovelas. According to his company bio, he is a "proud native of Guadalajara." Herradura, a nearly 150-year-old brand, was acquired by the American corporation Brown-Forman back in 2007, which also has Jack Daniel's and Finlandia Vodka in its portfolio. (Herradura's reposado and añejo tequilas are aged in used Jack Daniel's barrels.) The way he tells it, family-owned tequila brands can greatly benefit from a corporate—even foreign—buyout.

"I can tell you that Herradura has never been better now that we are in the hands of Brown-Forman," he asserts. "If every tequila company sold to an American conglomerate has the same success story like the one we have so far, I think it's great. Brown-Forman has been very respectful of the tradition and ways of producing tequila. Nothing has changed. I would even say we learned things about the production process, the administration, and ways of thinking about marketing. If a family wants to see their brand and heritage all over the world, the only way to get started is to be part of a large conglomerate."

Herradura was officially founded in 1870 by Félix López, who christened his hacienda San José del Refugio. The tequila didn't acquire its modern-day name until some fifty years later. Herradura translates as "horseshoe" in Spanish, a tribute to a lucky horseshoe found on the property. According to Aceves, Herradura has only ever been made with 100 percent blue agave—even during the many shortages that forced other brands to lower their agave content or buy under-the-table espadín from Oaxaca. For several decades during the mid-twentieth century, just about every tequila brought into the United States was mixto. It was none other than crooner Bing Crosby who brought an end to that. He and his close friend, bandleader Phil Harris, discovered good tequila while traveling in Mexico and resolved to import it to the United States. The brand the pair fell for was Herradura.

When Bing Crosby discovered Herradura, it was still made in an old factory on the hacienda, complete with traditional hornos and tahona. Once he brought it to the United States, it remained the only pure tequila readily available north of the border for some thirty years. Soon after its introduction to the US market, the old factory was turned into a museum and production was modernized. (Notably, it was Herradura that put forth the application for tequila's appellation of origin in 1973. In most other appellation of origin cases, it's a group of producers who puts forth the initial proposal, not a single company.)

The brand claims it hasn't changed. But, of course, it has. And why not? The oldest corporations around the world must adapt and progress to keep apace with growth and shifting market conditions. Yet, when it comes to a culturally significant product such as tequila, change is a delicate subject. Several years ago, rumors began to circulate that the company had implemented diffusers, those mammoth machines that use steam and chemicals to process agaves in record time instead of cooking them slowly. Connoisseurs say they can taste the difference between modern Herradura and older bottlings; there are even several online discussion forums dedicated to the topic. When I ask Rubén about this, he assures me that these people, be they self-proclaimed connoisseurs or activists, are misinformed.

"Tequila has changed a whole lot because people have come up with new ways of producing it," he explains. "In the end, the recipe has stayed the same. But people have been looking for shortcuts, new ways of cooking or fermenting or distilling the agave. Tequila, for us, has not changed. We keep on producing it the same way we did in the old days. We harvest fully mature agave, we still use the old-fashioned brick ovens, we enjoy natural fermentation, we distill twice in pot stills, and we age in white American oak. If you sense some change in flavor—let's say, you have a Herradura reposado from 1974 and one from 2014 side by side—it's because the climate has changed, the soil is very stressed, the water is different—it's due to Mother Nature. Not because we have changed anything."

Rubén also cites changes in style. He has a 96 proof blanco in his office from the mid-1950s, before the 80 proof standard was adopted. The higher-proofed spirit would surely taste different than today's Herradura. But he doesn't believe that older versions of Herradura taste different because they were made in smaller batches or in a more rustic facility. When I tell him that I've come across at least one bar selling "vintage Herradura" explicitly to showcase how the product has changed over the years, he is surprised. He admits that he does field occasional calls from people who are disappointed in the more modern flavor profile. But he maintains that the process, at its heart, has remained the same.

As for those diffusers gossiped about on online message boards, they are not just a rumor. But Rubén clarifies that these are not used to process Herradura's agave—not exactly.

"The diffuser has a very bad reputation," he says. "It can be used in two different ways. You can use a diffuser instead of an old-fashioned process, which means it does the milling before the agave gets cooked, then hydrolyzes or 'cooks' the juice. That's what has the connoisseurs and the mixologists pretty upset. But you can also cook your agave in brick ovens, mill it, then send the fibers through the diffuser to get some extra juice out of it. You do that, that's OK."

The company can extract an extra 3 percent of juice from the milled agave fibers using a diffuser. It admits to using this practice only for its secondary brands, including El Jimador and Antiguo—not for its flagship Herradura brand. The company also makes Pepe Lopez, a mixto gold tequila similar to Cuervo Especial. For this brand, diffusers are used for the entire process.

Visitors to Herradura's distillery are invited to see the original production facility where the old tahona still sits. It's now a museum that you can reach via the Tequila Express, the train that takes tourists from Guadalajara to Casa Herradura. It's one of the last big brands to maintain a fully functioning hacienda, including a small housing community of cheerfully painted adobe homes provided to accommodate longtime distillery workers. Those who qualify to live there get to do so rent-free as a perk for being loyal employees.

During a tour of the old distillery on my first visit to Herradura, a guide told a charming story about an old man who worked at the distillery and drank tequila every day. He lived to be one hundred, goes the tale, which he attributed to his daily nip. Enchanted by the story, I asked who he was. The guide looked perplexed, then frowned at me as the rest of the group patiently awaited the answer. "It's just a story," we were told. "There was no old man."

The visitor experience at Herradura continues like this, as guests are shown a jimador dressed in a folky white costume and bright red sash as he prepares an agave head using a coa. An adorable little donkey named Cuco follows the group around, carrying a small barrel of tequila on its back, recalling the days when a beast of burden was used in the distillery. Guests are welcome to tap the barrel or pet the donkey at any time. Several of them pose for photos with Cuco. The experience feels unnecessarily Disneyfied. Imagine you visited a winery in Napa and the workers were dressed as peasants, stomping grapes with their bare feet just for show, while the real work was done behind closed doors. Sure, it's entertaining. But why assume people don't want a more realistic, informational experience, complete with explanations about modern diffuser technology and evolving production practices?

Critics of the agave advocacy movement argue that its proponents have a tendency to fetishize traditional production methods. It's a valid point, especially in this era of artisanality standing in for authenticity. But there is also validity in demanding transparency within the industry. Agave activists say that, more than anything, they want the truth about tequila to be told.

America's Favorite Cocktail

There's booze in the blender
And soon it will render
That frozen concoction that helps me hang on.
—JIMMY BUFFETT, "MARGARITAVILLE"

Growing up in Montreal, I used to go to a bar downtown called Carlos & Pepe's. It could have existed anywhere in North America. The highlight of the happy hour menu was the huge five-dollar frozen margarita that came in flavors like strawberry and mango, the fishbowl-like glasses garnished with a salt rim and big chunks of fruit. Slurped through a wide straw, the margaritas would invariably lead to brain freeze and, after a couple rounds, brain fuzziness. These tequila and triple sec Slurpees would wash down big plates of nachos and fifty-cent wings, hard-shell tacos, and cheesy quesadillas. The food was as cheap as the drinks: an excellent deal for the many underaged drinkers the bar inadvertently served. The inexpensive fare reinforced young, resilient bellies when the rounds inevitably progressed to shots, with the requisite salt and lime.

More than a decade later, I started going to a different tequila bar. Mayahuel, in New York City, promised to show patrons a different side of tequila and Mexican food. There were no fifty-cent wings or mega-cheap drink specials. The margaritas were not huge, but they probably had more booze in them than the fishbowls at Carlos & Pepe's. In addition to margaritas, it served other cocktails made with tequila, many of them created by co-owner Phil Ward, whom we've met. Several of his recipes paired the spirit with Spanish sherry, which it turns out marries with tequila about as gloriously as gin does with dry vermouth. Other drinks incorporated bitter Italian amari, obscure liqueurs, or small-batch bitters in exotic flavors ranging from chocolate mole to jalapeño. The bar, with its imported Mexican tiles and red-lit upstairs lounge presided over by a large stained-glass spider-shaped chandelier, was not like your average tequila bar. It resembled the breed of upscale cocktail lounge that had been cropping up in the city where bartenders are called mixologists, mustachioed men and period-dressed women preside over an inventory of top-shelf booze, and drinks are treated like a culinary experience.

The bar bites were conceived of by a chef whose menu did not include nachos but did feature oh-so-trendy pork belly. Patrons did get drunk here—make no mistake—especially after two or three cocktails, each made with several ounces of top-shelf alcohol. But getting drunk didn't seem to be the point. You noticed people swapping sips of their drinks with friends, everyone excited to have as comprehensive a tasting as possible. Perhaps even more exciting than the cocktails and the ambiance were the strange and smoky elixirs the bar served, many of which were rare to find elsewhere in the city. Mezcal still felt brand new in 2009.

Soon enough, word of Mayahuel spread beyond those who refer to themselves as the "cocktail community." Customers came demanding shots with salt and lime, Patrón, Corona, even vodka sodas. The staff remained patient, offering alternatives. Phil, who could often be found behind the bar, did as many of his fellow barkeeps: without sanctimony or condescension, he gently guided customers into new and exciting directions. You only drink Patrón? Then, you might like this small-batch tequila from the distillery where Patrón was first made. You hate tequila and only drink vodka? You might like this light and refreshing cocktail that uses tequila and fresh-pressed fruit juice. Eventually, Mayahuel settled into catering to a steady stream of booze geeks, as well as its more mainstream customers who ordered beer and looked surprised when the tequila shots were served in something resembling a wine glass. The bar also made a mean margarita, which appealed to tequila novices and experts alike. It could hardly call itself a tequila bar if it didn't.

The demand for margaritas is at an all-time high: by industry calculations, it's the most popular cocktail in America. According to Restaurant Sciences, a firm based in Newton, Massachusetts, that tracks and analyzes restaurant food sales, of fifty million cocktails ordered at major restaurants and food-service outlets in 2013, more than 20 percent of those were margaritas, the greatest market share for any one drink. Brown-Forman, the Louisville-based spirits company, puts the number even higher, claiming that Americans drink 185,000 margaritas every hour.[1] How this raging popularity came to be is part cultural inevitability, part dumb luck.

In the nineteenth century, American bartenders were experimenting with drinks made with a variety of ingredients. These fell into different categories, such as the cocktail: a specific recipe consisting of spirit, sugar, water, and bitters (the water would come to be replaced with ice in the latter part of the century with the advent of refrigeration). Other types of drinks included sours (spirit, lemon juice, sugar, sometimes an egg white), fizzes (essentially a sour with seltzer), and cobblers (muddled fruit, sugar, and wine—sherry, champagne, or claret, say).[2]

The Golden Age of cocktailing lasted until Prohibition. Bartenders of the day were proud craftsmen, their customers the hipsters and trendsetters of that era. Once Prohibition ended in 1933, the craft of bartending in the United States never fully recovered. The 1930s saw the Great Depression, during which time few had the funds or wherewithal to splurge on fancy drinks. Then came the Second World War, when cocktailing was impacted by strict restrictions on whiskey production due to concerns about grain shortages.[3] By the 1950s, the prosperous had moved out of urban areas and were doing their cocktailing at home. Men were greeted at the door at the end of their workdays by manicured wives holding chilled martinis. Suburban couples threw cocktail parties. By the 1960s and '70s, Americans were discovering wine. The 1980s gave us the movie *Cocktail* and all the Tom Cruisery we could handle. Drinks were now made with prepackaged mixes, canned juices, and soda out of a gun. Then came the '90s, when Slippery Nipple and Kamikaze shots reigned. The cocktail was officially dead. But this was also the decade during which a few rogue bartenders started researching how drinks were once made. By the mid-aughts, these bartenders, renamed mixologists, were introducing their patrons to long-forgotten recipes, like the sazerac and the old-fashioned. And a sweet-tart drink called the daisy.

Daisies, like sours, fizzes, and cobblers, are a type of drink. Comprised of spirit, citrus, and orange liqueur, the most popular version a century ago was the brandy daisy; gin daisies were also common. But no one had ever made the drink with tequila until, according to the spirits historian David Wondrich, a bartender in Tijuana was asked to make a brandy daisy and reached for tequila instead. The result was so tasty that the customer requested another and christened the happy mistake a tequila daisy.[4] As you may have gathered, daisy in Spanish translates as "margarita." And that may very well be how the margarita was born.

Other accounts of the birth of the margarita include a Mexican bartender creating the drink for a famous Ziegfeld girl in 1938, a Texan originally from Mexico inventing the drink at a bar in El Paso in 1942, and a Dallas socialite coming up with the drink at a Christmas party in Acapulco in 1948. We may never know which story is the right one, or even if there is one true history. As another cocktail historian (who knew there were so many), Greg Boehm, likes to say, every cocktail has two histories: that of the recipe and that of its name. Greg, who runs the online barware shop Cocktail Kingdom and publishing firm Mud Puddle Books, known for its high-quality reprints of vintage cocktail books, points to a copy of a 1937 volume titled *Café Royal*, published in London. It includes the recipe for a picador, made with fresh lime juice, Cointreau, and tequila. Sound familiar? It would appear that people have been drinking the ingredients that amount to a margarita for some eighty years.

Whichever origin story you choose to believe, the margarita is an American phenomenon, rather than a Mexican one. In Mexico, tequila is taken in a shot glass at room temperature, though most often sipped instead of slammed. And, in lieu of salt and lime, designed to staunch the heat and harshness of bad alcohol, Mexicans prefer to take their copita by itself, or with a sangrita chaser. Sangrita, which translates as "little blood," is a nonalcoholic drink made with the juice of tomatoes, oranges, lime, and other fruits like pomegranate, papaya, or jicama, and a dose of chili powder. It's meant to complement the acidity and pepperiness of tequila.

Here in the United States, the cocktail is experiencing a renaissance. No serious restaurant opens nowadays without a signature cocktail list. And working behind the bar is more like working in a kitchen. The days of prepackaged mixes and canned juices are coming to a close. In progressive bars, staff press fresh juices for mixing into cocktails, chop fresh herbs. The status of bartender has been elevated to craftsman once again. Tequila could not have evolved to exotic cocktail ingredient without the influence of certain well-known American bartenders. The margarita, which began as a happy accident and evolved to ubiquity, has also been influenced by certain industry figures.

In 1971, Dallas restaurateur Mariano Martinez dreamt up a machine that would dispense frozen margaritas. People had been freezing their margaritas for several decades by using a blender with ice. But ordering one at a bar could put undue pressure on the bartender, especially if it was a busy night. Martinez had seen the problem firsthand at his eponymous Tex-Mex restaurant. One day, at a local 7-Eleven, he caught himself staring at the Slurpee machine and realized he had an idea. He ended up buying a soft-serve ice cream machine and making a few modifications to it so that it would dispense the restaurant's most popular drink. After taste-testing several versions of his father's margarita recipe in it, he put it to work. This would be the first frozen margarita machine. The restaurant continued to use it well after manufacturers began mass-producing frozen margarita machines for bars and restaurants around the world. In 2005, the original contraption was inducted into the Smithsonian's National Museum of American History.[5]

In bars across the United States, frozen margarita machines and bartenders who hand-press their limes manage to coexist. Prepackaged mixes certainly haven't disappeared altogether. In particular they account for a huge chunk of at-home cocktailing. One of the most popular brands of margarita mix was started by a Real Housewife of New York, who ended up selling it to Beam, Inc. in a multimillion-dollar deal. Skinnygirl margarita and cocktail mixes reported close to 400 percent growth in the first year after the buyout.[6] Since then, sales have dipped. Whether this points to a shift away from mixes and back to fresh ingredients isn't clear.

Those who do make their margaritas with fresh ingredients saw the drink come under threat in 2014. This was the year of the great lime shortage, when prices jumped nearly 500 percent. It hit tequila bars especially hard—both the kind that serve shots with lime and salt and those that press juice from two breeds of lime. Bad weather and disease in several lime-growing states in Mexico were to blame. The vast majority of all limes consumed in the United States come from our neighbor to the south. The situation was made worse when drug cartels got in on the action, muscling lime farmers and driving up prices even further.[7] For the most part, it was depicted as a quirky news item in the United States. But for Mexican lime farmers, it was a terrifying and trying time.

In tequila's hometown, where margaritas are served mostly to tourists, a different cocktail has made a name for itself. Here the ever-smiling Javier Delgado Corona presides over La Capilla, the oldest cantina in Tequila. "The chapel," in English, is a humble saloon that has stood in the town center since the 1930s. Javier claims he's well into his nineties, but it's hard to believe judging by the youthful sparkle in his eye and the rosy hue to his plump, brown cheeks. Some half a century ago, he created a cocktail that would go on to become legendary in his town. It may not be as famous as the margarita, but the batanga has its following.

Tequila and cocktail geeks come from great distances to sit at Javier's bar and have him prepare his signature drink. Which is surprising, considering it's nothing more than tequila, Coca-Cola, lime juice, a spare salt rim, and "lots of ice," according to Javier. Named for a long-gone regular at the bar—batanga is slang for someone who's "thick in the middle"—he says the secret lies in the knife he uses to stir each drink, which is also used to cut avocados for guacamole, and tomatoes and onions for fresh salsas. No doubt it adds an extra dimension to the drink. But the batanga is not the main reason you come to La Capilla. It's the ambiance, the magic of the place that makes it special.

The first time I walked into La Capilla, I was with several friends and colleagues. We'd spent the afternoon visiting distilleries and exploring Tequila's charming town center. Named a UNESCO world heritage site, Tequila is also one of Mexico's *Pueblos Mágicos*, a list of specially selected "magical villages" that embody the country's natural beauty, cultural riches, or an important piece of history. It was dark out by the time we entered the simple cantina. The inside was brightly lit, exposing drab checkered floors. The walls were adorned with photographs of Javier with various patrons, framed articles about the bar, and soccer trophies. The place attracted both tourists and locals, who joked with the barkeep and slammed shots before stumbling out into the darkened cobbled roads of the town center. My group, inevitably, got rowdy. We missed the cue that the bar was set to close. So Javier just kept on pouring. Finally, he took his leave, bidding us a good night and disappearing behind the swinging saloon doors beyond which no customers dare stray. We finally got the hint: it was closing time. Javier needed his rest.

Upon my return a few years later, I try to get a local tequila producer to come with me. But he claims that the town is crawling with drug cartel and that he rarely goes out walking or drinking at night without armed protection for fear of being kidnapped and held for ransom. Difficult to argue with that. So I end up going on my own instead. It's a Monday evening, early, and only a handful of customers are here. I sidle up to the bar and ask Javier for a batanga. He obliges with a grin. I ask him if he remembers me and the group of American journalists I came with years ago. He obliges again, saying he does remember, despite the fact that groups of American journalists are ferried here regularly. Even so, I believe him. A green leather-bound guest book embossed with his name and the bar's moniker sits on the bar. I page through it and there, among the drunken proclamations of tourists from around the world, is my signature from a few years back.

Most of the tequilas Javier serves I've never heard of and few of them you would call premium. They are brands known in Mexico, but with little or no distribution abroad. To my surprise, he has a bottle of mezcal on the bar. It was a gift, he says. He seems as curious about it as I am, so the two of us sample it together. It brings a smile of recognition to his face.

"It reminds me of how tequila used to taste many years ago!" he exclaims.

The Nightcap

Tequila. Straight. There's a real polite drink. You keep drinking
until you finally take one more and it just won't go down.
Then you know you've reached your limit.
—LEE MARVIN

In Guadalajara, I like to stay downtown at the Hotel Morales. A colonial building with a stone facade dotted with delicate-looking wrought-iron balconies, it was built as a private home in 1888 before being converted into a guest house, then a luxury hotel. The structure sat abandoned for three decades until a group of Spaniards renovated and reopened the hotel in 2004. Today, it still breathes an air of grandeur despite visible wear and tear. The rooms, which can be suffocatingly musty for all their updated decor, are laid out over four floors overlooking an atrium. At its center is a stone fountain, around which a number of tables and comfortable chairs are scattered. A waiter materializes to offer guests a drink and a bowl of salted peanuts. It's easy to kill an afternoon putting away tart margaritas and crisp Mexican lagers here.

After doing just that, venturing out only for something more sustaining than peanuts at a local birriería (the specialty, birria, is a hearty goat stew), I set out to find Pedro Jiménez Gurría at his bar nearby. Pedro is a filmmaker who opened Guadalajara's first mezcal bar in 2009. Not only was it the first, but it's one of the best places to taste mezcal in

Mexico—no small accomplishment given that it's smack in the center of tequila country. Pedro left his native Mexico City in 2005 because it was getting "too hectic," and headed for the country's second-largest city: Guadalajara. Besides, he says, there was a woman. They had seen each other casually, then less so, over the years when she would visit Mexico City and when he came to screen his experimental films in Guadalajara. Soon after relocating, they moved in together and, eventually, married. He loved his new city. The one thing missing were the handful of mezcal bars that had cropped up in DF. He started to hunt down mezcales to build his own collection. He was known to bring bottles to parties to share with friends. It turned out he wasn't the only one who wished there were a mezcalería in town.

When it opened, Pare de Sufrir (translation: "stop suffering"—as in, "stop suffering: drink mezcal") brought the mezcal craze that was already in full swing in DF to Guadalajara. The rough-and-tumble space, with its hand-painted murals covering the walls and a DJ spinning, is the kind of place where you get a bowl of skin-on peanuts with your drink and no one judges you for drinking beer instead of the house spirit. It attracts local students, bohemian types, and the bearded-and-tattooed set, as well as several of the academics who study the tequila industry. Pedro has hosted tastings and discussions here, but a regular night at the bar is completely without pretense.

Even though I am looking for him, Pedro and I meet only by chance. As I sit alone at the bar, completely absorbed in a seven-maguey blend from Jalisco, he just happens to plunk down on the stool next to me. We've never met so it takes a moment to realize who the other is. We get to talking and the conversation soon turns to NOM 186. Pedro considered it a violation of the rights of families who have made a living making mezcal for generations. But he's no fan of the current regulations governing mezcal either. The problem, he says, is that the appellation of origin for mezcal was drawn up using tequila's appellation of origin as a blueprint. Not only is it burdened with the same issues tequila's appellation has, including protecting commercial interests over the local culture and terroir, but it also fails to take into account the very nature of the spirit. Each regional mezcal is unique, so having a single appellation for all of them makes little sense.

"NOM 186 was defeated, but the ideas are still on the table," Pedro warns. "They are always trying to do different kinds of laws, to make similar restrictions but with another approach." The "they" he refers to includes the biggest tequila and mezcal companies.

"We have to be paying attention all the time. Because they make this or that legislation, burying it within larger bills where no one can see. So, we have to be searching all the time to see what they are trying to do," he says. "For example, they are still trying to regulate the use of the word 'agave.' The argument is that [tequila] put the word agave on the worldwide stage and the word has prestige now because of the tequila industry, so they should own it."

Yes, Pedro is another agave activist. He is not against regulation altogether. There have to be rules about how the spirit should be produced and tested. But he feels that the focus of these rules should be to protect the traditions of mezcaleros and the fragile environments in which they work. To that end, the smallest producers should be consulted. As it is, they have no power, he says. Biologists, anthropologists, and other researchers should also advise on policy, he believes.

In 2014, the president of the Mezcal Regulatory Council was pushing for reform to mezcal's appellation of origin regulations. After research trips to Cognac, Champagne, and Scotland, Hipócrates Nolasco drafted a proposal for a modified mezcal NOM that calls for greater emphasis on terroir and tradition—ostensibly veering away from the old tequila-influenced framework. The new regulations, which went into effect in 2017, recognize artisanal and ancestral mezcal as separate and distinct from the greater mezcal category, with stricter qualification criteria. They do away with mixto, which was previously permitted in mezcal, though the ratio differed from tequila—80/20 compared to 51/49 percent agave to other sugars. Most surprising, new rules ban diffusers altogether—a crippling blow to industrial producers.

"In the best case scenario, we should rebuild the appellation of origin for mezcal from scratch, so that it could include all the traditional producers and all the states that have been producing mezcal for hundreds of years," Pedro muses. "In fact, there should be geographic indicators for each regional type of mezcal, like wine, instead of one for all of them. It doesn't make sense to have one denomination of origin for mezcal: there is no place called mezcal."

Puebla was the most recent state to be inducted into the mezcal appellation, in 2015. The state of Mexico could be next. On the one hand, if it succeeds it will get to legally commercialize and export mezcal. For now, the vast majority of mezcal available north of the border is from Oaxaca. Within the other states included in the appellation—Guerrero, Zacatecas, Guanajuato, Tamaulipas, San Luis Potosí, Durango, and, Michoacán—negotiating the obstacles involved with achieving certification for export can be beyond the realm of possibility for most mezcaleros. In addition to bureaucratic hoops to jump through, certification for export can cost some 40,000 pesos or $3,000—an inconceivable sum for many.[1] But even if more states were included in the appellation and certification were not so out of reach, Pedro points out, it only further builds on a faulty legal construct. Mezcal is vast, like wine. It shouldn't be an appellation of origin like tequila; it should be a category with multiple appellations. Tequila should be just one of them.

After an hour or so at Pare de Sufrir, Pedro, who is slight and handsome, which is less obvious when he's fully bearded, suggests we check out his other establishment. To help spread the word on farmer mezcal, especially little-known distillates from Jalisco, he founded a nonprofit organization and tasting room called Mezonte. We walk his bike the few blocks from the bar to the tasting room, which is closed. It opens only for specific events, and you have to be a member to attend. The inside looks and feels like a secret lodge with plenty of rough wood surfaces and hand-labelled bottles lined up on shelves behind the bar.

"I only have a little bit left of this one," he says, uncapping a small bottle of raicilla, a regional mezcal from the mountains overlooking Puerto Vallarta. He pours several different spirits, each in a palmable jícara. Every bottle lists the name of the mezcalero, the variety of agave, and other details about the mezcal, like cooking method, distillation vessel, and distillation date. He has mezcales from about eighteen producers, mostly maestro mezcaleros from around Jalisco and Michoacán, but also beyond. Several, like the raicilla, are not protected by mezcal's appellation of origin. Pedro has one mezcal made only from the quiote of the agave, not the piña. Another is a pechuga, infused with turkey breast, cow neck, and iguana.

"Very eccentric," is how he describes it. Yet another mezcal is made of just the heads of distillation, so it's high in volatile alcohols, which is dangerous, but also delicious. "You have to be careful with that one," he grins.

Each spirit is distinct, some sweet and fruity, others herbal and spiced. The raicilla has funky notes of cheese and sauerkraut. As we sit and talk, some of the mezcal seeps into the jícara, curing it for future use. Pedro likes the thought of this. He produces a few more of the little cups and fills those, too. He collects his elixirs by hunting them down himself, buying directly from the makers. He features several of his favorite mezcaleros in the documentary film he made called *Viva Mezcal*. In the film, he also interviews several academics, who bemoan the plagues that have befallen tequila's blue agave and extoll the virtues of Mexico's diverse mezcal heritage. If this heritage is not protected and cherished, they warn, it will disappear.

It's getting late; a fat rust-colored cockroach scuttles across the rustic floor. Pedro fills another jícara, this one not with mezcal but with roasted grasshoppers: *chapulines*. They spent their lives feasting on apples before being roasted in lime, chili powder, and salt. Indeed, they smell of apples and taste like spice-roasted nuts. The texture of these little red insects, their legs and wings folded neatly against their bodies, is crispy and airy at once. I forcibly put the roach out of my mind as I pop another grasshopper into my mouth.

That a tiny bastion of mezcal appreciation could flourish in tequila's capital city is a wonder. The effects of establishments like these and people like Pedro spreading the word about the tradition of mezcal can already be seen on either side of the border. Sure, we can all lament the overbearing influence of the biggest tequila corporations on the rest of the agave spirits industry. But the smallest mezcal producers, too, are exercising influence. Now that their spirits can be accessed in mezcalerías in Mexico City, Oaxaca, and Guadalajara, as well as bars in major cities north of the border, tequila brands are looking to emulate them. Hoping to capitalize on the cachet of mezcal's authenticity, several tequila companies have released overproof bottlings. At least one tequila producer I spoke to planned to push the boundaries of the appellation of origin's regulations by experimenting with an all-quiote tequila, made from the long stem of the plant's sexual organ instead of the piña. And none other than Patrón came out with a line of 100 percent tahona-milled tequilas. The Roca Patrón bottlings, more robust than the original, are priced between seventy and ninety dollars and bottled between 84 and 90 proof.

But maybe there's more to the story than one spirits category trying to stay on-trend by borrowing from a smaller, more modish one. (A marketer I spoke to referred to mezcal as the Williamsburg of the spirits industry, then corrected himself, citing an even trendier Brooklyn neighborhood: "Actually, it's the Bushwick of the spirits industry.") At the heart of the ongoing saga of agave spirits is how people relate to the goods they consume. How a product is made and by whom is important to people nowadays. The life cycle of the goods we consume matters.

Tequila is unlike other spirits. It's a product rooted in a country's history and ecology, its main ingredient inextricably tied to a people's culture and myth. But over the centuries it has changed. It evolved from a simple mezcal to a mass-market product, and evolved again to become a luxury good. It no longer belongs solely to Jalisco or even to Mexico. The gringos appropriated it. Tequila now belongs to the world.

Acknowledgments

A great many people helped bring this book to fruition. My agents, Becky Vinter and Stephany Evans, who patiently guided me through the book-birthing process; my friends, Sheri and Carolyn, whose booze acumen came in handy when they offered their insights into the earliest drafts; my husband, Rich, who was also writing a book (or two) at the same time I was and shared his expertise and keen eye; and my parents, Brenda and Claude, a constant source of love and support.

On both sides of the border, there were people who sat down to talk and/or drink tequila and mezcal with me. These included Pedro Jiménez Gurría at Pare de Sufrir and Mezonte; Marco Ochoa Cortés and Silvia Philion at Mezcaloteca; Danny Mena at Hecho en Dumbo; Phil Ward at Mayahuel; Bobby Heugel at the Pastry War; Don Javier Delgado Corona at La Capilla; the Wine Geek Steve Olson; Ron Cooper at Del Maguey; Flor de Maria Velázquez Mijangos at Yuu Baal; Abel Nolasco Velasco; Graciela Angeles Carreño at Real Minero; Paco García and Raza Zaidi at Wahaka; Jonathan Barbieri at Pierde Almas; Carlos Camarena at Tapatio; Juan Fernando González de Anda at Siete Leguas; David Suro-Piñera at Siembra Azul; Guillermo Erickson Sauza at Fortaleza; José "Pepe" Hermosillo at Casa Noble; Rubén Aceves at Herradura; Bertha González Nieves at Casa Dragones; Richard Betts at Sombra and Astral; Paola Alejandra García Butrón, Yésica Paola Castillo Hinojoza, David Aguilar Hernández, and Martín Muñoz Sánchez at the Tequila Regulatory Council; Ana G. Valenzuela-Zapata; Patricia Colunga; Rodolfo Fernández; and Marie Sarita Gaytán.

Notes

Preface: In the Beginning, There Were Body Shots

1. Ernest Small, *Top 100 Food Plants* (Ottawa, Canada: NRC Research Press, 2009), 526.
2. Manuel Aguilar-Moreno, *Handbook to Life in the Aztec World* (New York: Oxford University Press, 2007), 288.
3. Sarah Bowen, *Geographical Indications: Promoting Local Products in a Global Market* (PhD diss., University of Wisconsin–Madison, 2008), 133.
4. James Lockhart, ed., *Nahuatl as Written: Lessons in Older Written Nahuatl, with Copious Examples and Texts* (Stanford, CA: Stanford University Press, 2001), 241.

Chapter 1: Before Tequila Came Pulque

1. Marina Warner and Felipe Fernández-Armesto, eds., *Worlds of Myths: Volume Two* (Austin: University of Texas Press, 2004), 273.
2. Carolyn Y. Johnson, "What's really up on Beacon Hill," *Boston Globe*, July 11, 2006.
3. D. L. Hawksworth and Alan T. Bull, eds., *Plant Conservation and Biodiversity* (New York: Springer Science & Business Media, 2007), 80.
4. Sara V. Good-Avila, et al., *Timing and rate of speciation in Agave* (Washington, DC: The National Academy of Sciences of the USA, 2006).
5. Amy Stewart, *The Drunken Botanist: The Plants that Create the World's Great Spirits* (Chapel Hill, NC: Algonquin Books, 2013), 2–4.

6. Keith H. Steinkraus, ed., *Industrialization of Indigenous Fermented Foods, Revised and Expanded* (Boca Raton, FL: CRC Press, 2004), 568.

7. Y. H. Hui and E. Özgül Evranuz, eds., *Handbook of Plant-Based Fermented Food and Beverage Technology* (Boca Raton, FL: CRC Press, 2012), 703.

8. Maria Áurea Toxqui Garay, "El Recreo de Los Amigos: Mexico City's Pulquerías During the Liberal Republic (1856–1911)" (PhD diss., University of Arizona, 2011), 171.

9. David M. Fahey and Jon S. Miller, eds., *Alcohol and Drugs in North America: A Historical Encyclopedia* (Santa Barbara, CA: ABC-CLIO, 2013), 439.

10. Herman W. Konrad, *A Jesuit Hacienda in Colonial Mexico: Santa Lucía, 1576–1767* (Stanford, CA: Stanford University Press, 1980), 203.

11. Gretchen Pierce and Áurea Toxqui, *Alcohol in Latin America: A Social and Cultural History* (Tucson: University of Arizona Press, 2014), 195.

12. Gretchen Kristine Pierce, "Sobering the Revolution: Mexico's Anti-Alcohol Campaigns and the Process of State-Building, 1910–1940" (PhD diss., University of Arizona, 2008), 137.

13. Gretchen Pierce and Áurea Toxqui, *Alcohol in Latin America: A Social and Cultural History* (Tucson: University of Arizona Press, 2014), 195.

Chapter 2: The Mysteries of Distillation

1. Dana Cimilluca, Paul Sonne, and Simon Zekaria, "Diageo Ends Its Attempt to Buy Jose Cuervo Tequila," *Wall Street Journal*, December 11, 2012.

2. Bill Owens and Alan Dikty, eds., *The Art of Distilling Whiskey and Other Spirits: An Enthusiast's Guide to the Artisan Distilling of Potent Potables* (Beverly, MA: Quarry Books, 2011), 13.

3. Stephen G. Haw, *Marco Polo's China: A Venetian in the Realm of Khubilai Khan* (New York: Routledge, 2006), 147.

4. Daniel Zizumbo-Villarreal and Patricia Colunga García Marín, "Early coconut distillation and the origins of mezcal and tequila spirits in west-central Mexico," *Genetic Resources and Crop Evolution* 55 (2008), 493–510.

5. Duane S. Nickell, *Guidebook for the Scientific Traveler: Visiting Physics and Chemistry Sites Across America* (New Brunswick, NJ: Rutgers University Press, 2010), 197.

6. Lucinda Hutson, *Viva Tequila!: Cocktails, Cooking, and Other Agave Adventures* (Austin: University of Texas Press, 2013), 58.

7. Adam Rogers, *Proof: The Science of Booze* (New York: Houghton Mifflin Harcourt, 2014), 178–186.

Chapter 3: The Long, Hard Life of Agave

1. Sara Oldfield, comp., *Cactus and Succulent Plants: Status Survey and Conservation Action Plan* (Cambridge, UK: IUCN, 1997), 5.

2. Hector T. Arita and Don E. Wilson, "Long-Nosed Bats and Agaves: The Tequila Connection," *BATS* Magazine 5 (1987).

3. Ana G. Valenzuela-Zapata and Gary Paul Nabhan, *Tequila: A Natural and Cultural History* (Tucson: University of Arizona Press, 2004), XXIV–XXV.

4. Ana G. Valenzuela-Zapata and Gary Paul Nabhan, *Tequila: A Natural and Cultural History* (Tucson: University of Arizona Press, 2004), 55–57.

5. Lloyd Mexico Economic Report, (Mexico City: Lloyd SA de CV, 2000).

6. Jorge A. Pérez Alfonso, "En riesgo de extinción el agave en Oaxaca, por saqueo desmedido," *La Jornada*, January 19, 2014, 25.

7. Jorge A. Pérez Alfonso, "Tiran 200 litros de mezcal en protesta por cosecha desmedida en Oaxaca," *La Jornada*, September 4, 2014.

8. Jorge Mario Martínez-Piva, ed., *Knowledge Generation and Protection: Intellectual Property, Innovation and Economic Development* (New York: Springer, 2009), 44.

9. D. L. Hawksworth and Alan T. Bull, eds., *Plant Conservation and Biodiversity* (New York: Springer Science & Business Media, 2007), 88.

10. Melanie Haiken, "New Sweetener from the Tequila Plant May Aid Diabetes, Weight Loss," *Forbes*, March 17, 2014.

11. Associated Press, "Still hungry? It could be that fructose in your drink," *USA Today*, January 1, 2013.

12. Damian Carrington, "Tequila gives new biofuel crops a shot," *Guardian*, July 27, 2011.

13. Javier Morales, Luis Miguel Apátiga, and Víctor Manuel Castaño, *Growth of Diamond Films from Tequila* (Mexico City: National Autonomous University of Mexico, 2008).

Chapter 4: Putting Tequila on the Map

1. Ana G. Valenzuela-Zapata and Gary Paul Nabhan, *Tequila: A Natural and Cultural History* (Tucson: University of Arizona Press, 2004), 18.

2. Sarah Bowen and Ana Valenzuela-Zapata, "Geographical indications, terroir, and socioeconomic and ecological sustainability: The case of tequila," *Journal of Rural Studies* 25 (2009), 117.

3. Nuria Ackermann, *Adding value to traditional products of regional origin: A guide to creating an origin consortium* (Vienna: United Nations Industrial Development Organization, 2010), 24.

4. Patricia Romo, "Tequila, producto más protegido en el mundo," *El Economista*, May 22, 2013.

5. Sarah Bowen, "Geographical Indications: Promoting Local Products in a Global Market" (PhD diss., University of Wisconsin-Madison, 2008), 90–96.

6. Bob Emmons, *The Book of Tequila: A Complete Guide* (Chicago: Open Court: 2003), 136–137.

7. Marie Sarita Gaytán, "Fermented Struggles and Distilled Identities: How Tequila Became Mexico's Spirit" (paper presented at the annual meeting of the American Sociological Association, New York, August 11, 2007), 5.

8. Anthony Dias Blue, *The Complete Book of Spirits: A Guide to Their History, Production, and Enjoyment* (New York: HarperCollins, 2004), 112–113.

9. Hubert Howe Bancroft, *History of Mexico*, Volume XIV (San Francisco: The History Company, 1888), 571–572.

10. Marie Sarita Gaytán, "Drinking the Nation and Making Masculinity," in *Toward a Sociology of the Trace*, ed. Herman Gray and Macarena Gómez-Barris (Minneapolis: University of Minnesota Press, 2010), 207–229.

11. Jack S. Blocker, David M. Fahey, and Ian R. Tyrrell, eds., *Alcohol and Temperance in Modern History: An International Encyclopedia*, Volume 1 (Santa Barbara, CA: ABC-CLIO, 2003), 618.

12. Daniele Giovannucci, et al., *Guide to Geographical Indications: Linking Products and Their Origins* (Geneva: International Trade Center, 2009), 9.

13. United Press International, "U.S. Sets Standard for Bourbon," *Pittsburgh Press*, May 31, 1974, 16.

14. Marsha A. Echols, *Geographical Indications for Food Products: International Legal and Regulatory Perspectives* (Alphen aan den Rijn, Netherlands: Kluwer Law International, 2008), 84–85.

15. Sarah Bowen, *Geographical Indications: Promoting Local Products in a Global Market* (PhD diss., University of Wisconsin–Madison, 2008).

16. Sarah Bowen, *Case Study: Tequila* (Raleigh: North Carolina State University, 2008), 22.

17. Jennifer Barnette, "Geographic Indications as a Tool to Promote Sustainability? Café de Colombia and Tequila Compared," *Ecology Law Quarterly*, October 2012.

18. Sarah Bowen and Marie Sarita Gaytán, "The Paradox of Protection: National Identity, Global Commodity Chains, and the Tequila Industry," *Social Problems* 59 (2012), 85.

Chapter 5: The Terroir of Tequila

1. Jorge Mejía Prieto, *Asi Habla El Mexicano: diccionario básico de mexicanismos* (Mexico City: Panorama Editorial, 1984), 131.

2. James E. Wilson, *Terroir: The Role of Geology, Climate, and Culture in the Making of French Wines* (Berkeley: University of California Press, 1999), 55.

Chapter 7: El Día del Magueyero

1. Gustavo de la Rosa, "Mezcal, la nueva estrategia de Bacardí," CNNExpansión, November 7, 2013.

Chapter 8: Tequila Goes Top Shelf

1. Ilana Edelstein, *The Patrón Way: From Fantasy to Fortune—Lessons on Taking Any Business from Idea to Iconic Brand* (New York: McGraw-Hill, 2013), 9–21.
2. Emilio Godoy, "Tequila Leaves Environmental Hangover," *Tierramérica*, August 7, 2009.
3. M. A. Morales, *Vinazas: The Corpse of the Spirit of Mexico*, self-published, 2013.
4. Marie Sarita Gaytán, "Fermented Struggles and Distilled Identities: Tequila and the Making of a National Spirit" (PhD diss., University of California Santa Cruz, 2008), 113.
5. Emily Bryson York and Robert Channick, "Skinnygirl Margarita deal shows women's buying power," *Los Angeles Times*, March 30, 2011.

Chapter 9: Bottling Mexican Identity

1. William B. Taylor, *Drinking, Homicide, and Rebellion in Colonial Mexican Villages* (Stanford: Stanford University Press, 1979), 72.
2. Marie Sarita Gaytán, "Fermented Struggles and Distilled Identities: Tequila and the Making of a National Spirit" (PhD diss., University of California, Santa Cruz, 2008), 82.
3. Richard B. Baldauf and Robert B. Kaplan, *Language Planning and Policy in Latin America*, Volume 1 (Tonawanda, NY: Multilingual Matters, 2007), 115.
4. Lucinda Hutson, *Viva Tequila!: Cocktails, Cooking, and Other Agave Adventures* (Austin: University of Texas Press, 2013) 69.
5. David E. Hayes-Bautista, *El Cinco de Mayo: An American Tradition* (Berkeley: University of California Press, 2012).
6. Oscar Carares, "Holiday of Cinco de Mayo is minor event in Mexico," *Houston Chronicle*, May 5, 2010.

7. "Mexico exports 100% blue agave tequila to China," BBC, August 30, 2013.

Chapter 10: The Agave Activists

1. David Marley, *Wars of the Americas: A Chronology of Armed Conflict in the New World, 1492 to the Present* (Santa Barbara, CA: ABC-CLIO, 1998), 486.
2. Richard J. Salvucci, "Mexican National Income In the Era of Independence, 1800–40," in *How Latin America Fell Behind: Essays on the Economic Histories of Brazil and Mexico, 1800–1914*, ed. Stephen Haber (Stanford, CA: Stanford University Press, 1997), 222–225.

Chapter 11: America's Favorite Cocktail

1. Matthew Huisman, "Frozen margarita machine, invented in Dallas 40 years ago, shook up Tex-Mex history," *Dallas News*, May 10, 2011.
2. David Wondrich, *Imbibe!: From Absinthe Cocktail to Whiskey Smash, a Salute in Stories and Drinks to "Professor" Jerry Thomas, Pioneer of the American Bar* (New York: Penguin, 2007), 98–127.
3. Jack S. Blocker, David M. Fahey, and Ian R. Tyrrell, eds., *Alcohol and Temperance in Modern History: An International Encyclopedia*, Volume 1 (Santa Barbara, CA: ABC-CLIO, 2003), 527.
4. David Wondrich, "Behind the Drink: The Margarita," Liquor.com, May 5, 2010.
5. Gustavo Arellano, *Taco USA: How Mexican Food Conquered America* (New York: Simon & Shuster, 2012), 237–244.
6. Tiffany Hsu, "Bethenny Frankel's Skinnygirl leads spirits growth with 388% boom," *Los Angeles Times*, April 9, 2012.
7. Neil Irwin, "Why Everyone's Talking About the Great Lime Shortage," *New York Times*, April 25, 2014.

Epilogue: The Nightcap

1. Bobby Heugel, "Chasing Mezcal in One of Mexico's Most Dangerous Regions," *Punch*, June 26, 2014.

Bibliography

Ackermann, Nuria. *Adding value to traditional products of regional origin: A guide to creating an origin consortium.* Vienna: United Nations Industrial Development Organization, 2010.

Aguilar-Moreno, Manuel. *Handbook to Life in the Aztec World.* New York: Oxford University Press, 2007.

Arellano, Gustavo. *Taco USA: How Mexican Food Conquered America.* New York: Simon & Shuster, 2012.

Arita, Hector T., and Don E. Wilson. "Long-Nosed Bats and Agaves: The Tequila Connection." *BATS Magazine* 5 (1987).

Associated Press. "Still hungry? It could be that fructose in your drink." *USA Today*, January 1, 2013.

Áurea Toxqui Garay, Maria. *El Recreo de Los Amigos: Mexico City's Pulquerías During the Liberal Republic (1856–1911).* PhD diss., University of Arizona, 2011.

Baldauf, Richard B., and Robert B. Kaplan. *Language Planning and Policy in Latin America, Volume 1.* Tonawanda, NY: Multilingual Matters, 2007.

Bancroft, Hubert Howe. *History of Mexico, Volume XIV.* San Francisco: The History Company, 1888.

Barnette, Jennifer. "Geographic Indications as a Tool to Promote Sustainability? Café de Colombia and Tequila Compared." *Ecology Law Quarterly*, October 2012.

BBC. "Mexico exports 100% blue agave tequila to China." August 30, 2013.

Blocker, Jack S., David M. Fahey, and Ian R. Tyrrell, eds. *Alcohol and Temperance in Modern History: An International Encyclopedia, Volume 1*. Santa Barbara, CA: ABC-CLIO, 2003.

Blue, Anthony Dias. *The Complete Book of Spirits: A Guide to Their History, Production, and Enjoyment*. New York: HarperCollins, 2004.

Bowen, Sarah. *Case Study: Tequila*. Raleigh: North Carolina State University, 2008.

Bowen, Sarah. *Geographical Indications: Promoting Local Products in a Global Market*. PhD diss., University of Wisconsin–Madison, 2008.

Bowen, Sarah, and Ana Valenzuela-Zapata. "Geographical indications, terroir, and socioeconomic and ecological sustainability: The case of tequila." *Journal of Rural Studies* 25 (2009).

Bowen, Sarah, and Marie Sarita Gaytán. "The Paradox of Protection: National Identity, Global Commodity Chains, and the Tequila Industry." *Social Problems* 59 (2012).

Bryson York, Emily, and Robert Channick. "Skinnygirl Margarita deal shows women's buying power." *The Los Angeles Times*, March 30, 2011.

Carares, Oscar. "Holiday of Cinco de Mayo is minor event in Mexico." *Houston Chronicle,* May 5, 2010.

Carrington, Damian. "Tequila gives new biofuel crops a shot." *Guardian*, July 27, 2011.

Cimilluca, Dana, Paul Sonne, and Simon Zekaria. "Diageo Ends Its Attempt to Buy Jose Cuervo Tequila." *Wall Street Journal,* December 11, 2012.

de la Rosa, Gustavo. "Mezcal, la nueva estrategia de Bacardí." *CNNExpansión*, November 7, 2013.

Echols, Marsha A. *Geographical Indications for Food Products: International Legal and Regulatory Perspectives*. Alphen aan den Rijn, Netherlands: Kluwer Law International, 2008.

Edelstein, Ilana. *The Patron Way: From Fantasy to Fortune: Lessons on Taking Any Business From Idea to Iconic Brand*. New York: McGraw-Hill, 2013.

Emmons, Bob. *The Book of Tequila: A Complete Guide.* Chicago: Open Court, 2003.

Fahey, David M., and Jon S. Miller, eds. *Alcohol and Drugs in North America: A Historical Encyclopedia.* Santa Barbara, CA: ABC-CLIO, 2013.

Gaytán, Marie Sarita. "Drinking the Nation and Making Masculinity." In *Toward a Sociology of the Trace,* edited by Herman Gray and Macarena Gómez-Barris, 207–229. Minneapolis: University of Minnesota Press, 2010.

Gaytán, Marie Sarita. "Fermented Struggles and Distilled Identities: How Tequila became Mexico's Spirit." Paper presented at the annual meeting of the American Sociological Association, New York, August 11, 2007.

Giovannucci, Daniele, Tim Josling, William Kerr, Bernard O'Connor, and May T. Yeung. *Guide to Geographical Indications: Linking Products and Their Origins.* Geneva: International Trade Center, 2009.

Godoy, Emilio. "Tequila Leaves Environmental Hangover." *Tierramérica*, August 7, 2009.

Good-Avila, Sara V., Valeria Souza, Brandon S. Gaut, and Luis E. Eguiarte. *Timing and rate of speciation in Agave.* Washington, DC: National Academy of Sciences of the USA, 2006.

Haiken, Melanie. "New Sweetener from the Tequila Plant May Aid Diabetes, Weight Loss." *Forbes*, March 17, 2014.

Haw, Stephen G. *Marco Polo's China: A Venetian in the Realm of Khubilai Khan.* New York: Routledge, 2006.

Hawksworth, D. L., and Alan T. Bull, eds. *Plant Conservation and Biodiversity.* New York: Springer Science & Business Media, 2007.

Hayes-Bautista, David E. *El Cinco de Mayo: An American Tradition.* Berkeley: University of California Press, 2012.

Heugel, Bobby. "Chasing Mezcal in One of Mexico's Most Dangerous Regions." *Punch*, June 26, 2014.

Hsu, Tiffany. "Bethenny Frankel's Skinnygirl leads spirits growth with 388% boom." *Los Angeles Times*, April 9, 2012.

Hui, Y. H., and E. Özgül Evranuz, eds. *Handbook of Plant-Based Fermented Food and Beverage Technology.* Boca Raton, FL: CRC Press, 2012.

Huisman, Matthew. "Frozen margarita machine, invented in Dallas 40 years ago, shook up Tex-Mex history." *Dallas News*, May 10, 2011.

Hutson, Lucinda. *Viva Tequila!: Cocktails, Cooking, and Other Agave Adventures.* Austin: University of Texas Press, 2013.

Irwin, Neil. "Why Everyone's Talking About the Great Lime Shortage." *New York Times*, April 25, 2014.

Johnson, Carolyn Y. "What's really up on Beacon Hill." *Boston Globe*, July 11, 2006.

Konrad, Herman W. *A Jesuit Hacienda in Colonial Mexico: Santa Lucía, 1576–1767.* Stanford, CA: Stanford University Press, 1980.

Lloyd Mexico Economic Report. Mexico City: Lloyd SA de CV, 2000.

Lockhart, James, ed. *Nahuatl as Written: Lessons in Older Written Nahuatl, with Copious Examples and Texts.* Stanford, CA: Stanford University Press, 2001.

Marley, David. *Wars of the Americas: A Chronology of Armed Conflict in the New World, 1492 to the Present.* Santa Barbara, CA: ABC-CLIO, 1998.

Martínez-Piva, Jorge Mario, ed. *Knowledge Generation and Protection: Intellectual Property, Innovation and Economic Development.* New York: Springer, 2009.

Mejía Prieto, Jorge. *Asi Habla El Mexicano: diccionario básico de mexicanismos.* Mexico City: Panorama Editorial, 1984.

Morales, Javier, Luis Miguel Apátiga, and Víctor Manuel Castaño. *Growth of Diamond Films from Tequila.* Mexico City: National Autonomous University of Mexico, 2008.

Morales, M. A. *Vinazas: The Corpse of the Spirit of Mexico*, self-published, 2013.

Nickell, Duane S. *Guidebook for the Scientific Traveler: Visiting Physics and Chemistry Sites Across America.* New Brunswick, NJ: Rutgers University Press, 2010.

Oldfield, Sara, comp. *Cactus and Succulent Plants: Status Survey and Conservation Action Plan.* Cambridge, UK: IUCN, 1997.

Owens, Bill, and Alan Dikty, eds. *The Art of Distilling Whiskey and Other Spirits: An Enthusiast's Guide to the Artisan Distilling of Potent Potables.* Beverly, MA: Quarry Books, 2011.

Pérez Alfonso, Jorge A. "En riesgo de extinción el agave en Oaxaca, por saqueo desmedido." *La Jornada*, January 19, 2014, 25.

Pérez Alfonso, Jorge A. "Tiran 200 litros de mezcal en protesta por cosecha desmedida en Oaxaca." *La Jornada*, September 4, 2014.

Pierce, Gretchen, and Áurea Toxqui. *Alcohol in Latin America: A Social and Cultural History.* Tucson: University of Arizona Press, 2014.

Pierce, Gretchen Kristine. *Sobering the Revolution: Mexico's Anti-Alcohol Campaigns and the Process of State-Building, 1910–1940.* PhD diss., University of Arizona, 2008.

Rogers, Adam. *Proof: The Science of Booze.* New York: Houghton Mifflin Harcourt, 2014.

Romo, Patricia. "Tequila, producto más protegido en el mundo." *El Economista*, May 22, 2013.

Salvucci, Richard J. "Mexican National Income in the Era of Independence, 1800–40." In *How Latin America Fell Behind: Essays on the Economic Histories of Brazil and Mexico, 1800–1914*, edited by Stephen Haber. Stanford, CA: Stanford University Press, 1997.

Small, Ernest. *Top 100 Food Plants.* Ottawa, Canada: NRC Research Press, 2009.

Steinkraus, Keith H., ed. *Industrialization of Indigenous Fermented Foods, Revised and Expanded.* Boca Raton, FL: CRC Press, 2004.

Stewart, Amy. *The Drunken Botanist: The Plants that Create the World's Great Spirits.* Chapel Hill, NC: Algonquin Books, 2013.

Taylor, William B. *Drinking, Homicide, and Rebellion in Colonial Mexican Villages.* Stanford: Stanford University Press, 1979.

United Press International. "U.S. Sets Standard for Bourbon." *Pittsburgh Press*, May 31, 1974.

Valenzuela-Zapata, Ana G., and Gary Paul Nabhan. *Tequila: A Natural and Cultural History.* Tucson: University of Arizona Press, 2004.

Warner, Marina, and Felipe Fernández-Armesto, eds. *Worlds of Myths: Volume Two.* Austin: University of Texas Press, 2004.

Wilson, James E. *Terroir: The Role of Geology, Climate, and Culture in the Making of French Wines.* Berkeley: University of California Press, 1999.

Wondrich, David. "Behind the Drink: The Margarita." *Liquor.com*, May 5, 2010.

Wondrich, David. *Imbibe!: From Absinthe Cocktail to Whiskey Smash, a Salute in Stories and Drinks to "Professor" Jerry Thomas, Pioneer of the American Bar.* New York: Penguin, 2007.

Zizumbo-Villarreal, Daniel, and Patricia Colunga García Marín. "Early coconut distillation and the origins of mezcal and tequila spirits in west-central Mexico." *Genetic Resources and Crop Evolution* 55 (2008).

Index

A Montreal native based in New York, Chantal Martineau writes about wine, spirits, food, travel, and culture. Her work has appeared in *Vogue*, *Food and Wine*, *Departures*, *Saveur*, and the *Atlantic*.